ENCYCLOPEDIA OF

Medieval Church
Art

Contents

Preface

IT WAS IN 1949 that I first visited a great church with Edward G (Ted) Tasker. I was newly returned to civilian life, professionally qualified and looking for wider interests. Happily I fell in with Ted who, some ten years my senior, had a considerable collection of photographs of church funishings, examples of which are to be found in the present volume. Thus began for me some forty years during which I learned from Ted some of the background to medieval church art which was his lifelong interest. He disliked driving and his wife was indefatigable in conveying him on his journeys to churches large and small throughout the length and breadth of England. On some of these trips I was privileged to accompany him, and to observe the depth of his great learning. This book might have seen the light of day earlier had Ted not been such a perfectionist, but there was always one more example to record for the sake of completeness. Ted was a sincere Christian who saw the art he recorded as a visual aid to the understanding of the faith by the unlettered of the Middle Ages and as an important part of our Christian heritage.

All the photographs that appear in this volume, and the content of the text, were prepared by Ted Tasker. The choice of illustrations was also his, and in some respects it is a personal choice. Where representations are numerous, then the choice has commonly been a particularly clear or an aesthetically pleasing example; in many cases the representations are unique. The selection must also reflect the pattern of Ted Tasker's travels, but these were so comprehensive that they have imposed little limitation on the availability of subjects from which the choice has been made. More important has been the feasibility of obtaining good photographic images, as record photography in the darker recesses of a parish church, perhaps on an overcast day, is far from easy. As an Associate of the Royal Photographic Society, Ted was always concerned to provide images of the highest quality that could be obtained.

In arranging the work for publication it has been necessary to impose some order upon the material, and to make some minor revisions to the text. However, beyond the order of the contents, such changes are limited and, I hope, in the spirit of Ted's conception. Any errors of fact or judgment which have been inadvertently introduced are, of course, entirely my responsibility.

Since 1969 the Redundant Churches Fund has saved over 250 churches: Torbryan and York, Holy Trinity Goodramgate being two to which reference is made in these pages. The vesting of churches in the Fund is a continuing process, and no attempt has therefore been made to indicate those affected; the more so as the Fund essentially rescues churches in danger.

All but two of the places mentioned in the text are in England, and these two are in Wales. Scotland is entirely absent from the Encyclopedia. While there are further examples of medieval church art to be found in the Principality and north of the border (and Wales possesses its own very rich Christian traditions from before the establishment of Christianity in England), the distribution in this volume accurately reflects the distribution of surviving representations in Britain and, indeed, the fact that it was the relative wealth of England during the medieval period which provided the patronage for the art illustrated here. Where places are mentioned in the text, the placename but not the county is given, except where any ambiguity might result. The counties in which the relevant places are situated are, however, given in the index at the end of the book.

Over the years, the restoration of panels of glass to their original places has resulted, in some cases, in placements which differ from those illustrated, but the panels themselves remain unchanged.

I would like to acknowledge the assistance of Mrs Maureen Rogers in preparing an electronic version of the text; and also the warm support and co-operation provided by Mr Anthony Seward, Ms Tracey Beresford and the staff of BT Batsford Ltd. Most of all I must record my appreciation of the great assistance of my wife, who has helped enormously in the scrutiny of the text and particularly in the checking of the many illustrations. My son also has been a source of encouragement and help throughout.

I consider it a great privilege to be associated with the production of this work, which I feel sure will be a valuable source of information to many.

John Beaumont
Southwell, Notts
1992

Acknowledgement

MY HUSBAND, Edward George Tasker MBE, JP, ARPS, died suddenly on 3 July 1989. I should like to express my sincere thanks to the late Mrs Louie Nicholson, retired headmistress, for all the encouragement she gave, many years ago, when the work was first being compiled. My special thanks go to my dear friends John and Margaret Beaumont, and their son Dr J Graham Beaumont, who have all given invaluable assistance and worked untiringly in preparing the text for publication.

Mary Tasker
Barnsley, Yorks
1992

1
Old Testament

ISOLATED PANELS OF glass which have survived indicate that the lives of the Old Testament patriarchs were recorded by the medieval glass painters. The stone work in the chapter house of Salisbury Cathedral has proved to be more enduring. Here, in a continuous frieze are depicted the events of Creation and episodes from the lives of the patriarchs recorded in the Book of Genesis.

The choice of some Old Testament subjects and the neglect of others is puzzling until it is realised that the selection was based on the belief that Old Testament events prefigured those of the New Testament. The choice was governed by typographical teaching. Old Testament events were seen as types of, and were paralleled with, events recorded in the Gospels. This scheme was fully developed in the *Biblia Pauperum*, where each New Testament subject is flanked by an Old Testament subject on either side. The choice of some prefiguring types is obvious but in other cases the choice is obscure and the association would not be expected without reference to the *Biblia Pauperum*. This approach to the Old Testament influenced the medieval artist in his choice and positioning of subjects. This is demonstrated in Canterbury Cathedral, where the pages of the *Biblia Pauperum* have been translated into pages of glass.

ABRAHAM AND ISAAC
Representations of the events surrounding the life of the patriarch Abraham were more than a record of Old Testament history, for allegory and symbolism related them to the events of the New Testament and current theology.

REPRESENTATIONS
1 **Single figures of Abraham** These occur in glass as in New College Chapel, Oxford.
2 **The sacrifice of Isaac** Two misericords in Worcester Cathedral tell this dramatic story. On the first [1.1] Abraham, carrying a sword and torch, with Isaac bearing the faggots in the form of a cross, is on his way to the place of sacrifice. On the second misericord [1.2] Isaac kneels on a draped altar in front of which, a ram by his side, stands Abraham raising a sword which has been seized by a hand emerging from the clouds above. There is a similar misericord in Gloucester Cathedral [1.3].

1.1 *Abraham and Isaac* Worcester Cathedral

1.2 *The sacrifice of Isaac*
Worcester Cathedral

1.3 *The sacrifice of Isaac*   Gloucester Cathedral

1.4 *The Covenant and the incredulity of Sarah*   Malvern Priory

1.5 *The circumcision of Isaac* Worcester Cathedral

1.6 *Abraham meeting the three angels* Salisbury Cathedral

1.7 *Abraham entertaining the three angels* Salisbury Cathedral

The episode is recorded in glass in three stages in Malvern Priory.

(a) Abraham receiving from an angel the command to sacrifice Isaac.

(b) Abraham, holding a lighted torch, on the way to the place of sacrifice.

(c) Abraham, with a sword, standing before the blind-folded Isaac.

On five bosses in the nave of Norwich Cathedral are depicted the events.

(a) Isaac kneels in front of a pile of wood.

(b) Isaac sits on an altar.

(c) The servant of Abraham holds an ass.

(d) An angel points out the ram.

(e) A ram is caught in the thicket.

3 The Covenant and the incredulity of Sarah This is depicted in glass in Malvern Priory [1.4]. God appears out of a cloud and speaks to Abraham; Sarah stands before him in an attitude of questioning.

4 The circumcision of Isaac On a misericord in Worcester Cathedral [1.5] Abraham, knife in hand, and Sarah flank a stone altar on which Isaac is standing.

In glass in Malvern Priory Abraham is seen circumcising Isaac who is held by his mother on an altar.

5 The visit of the angels On the frieze in the chapter house of Salisbury Cathedral [1.6, 1.7] Abraham is meeting the three angels and entertaining them as they sit at a draped table.

In the nave of Norwich Cathedral are three bosses, on each an angel is seated at a covered table.

On a tomb at Framlingham, Abraham and Sarah face three angels in front of a stone-built doorway.

6 The meeting of Abraham and Melchizedek In one of the panels in the east window of York Minster is recorded the meeting of Abraham and Melchizedek. Abraham is still arrayed in battle armour.

7 Fetching a wife for Isaac EM Goulburn and E Hailstone in *The Ancient Sculptures in the Roof of Norwich Cathedral* suggest that a boss, depicting a man leading two camels, represents Abraham's servant fetching a wife for Isaac.

8 The marriage of Isaac and Rebecca A panel of glass in Malvern Priory is much disarrayed and interpretation of the subject is difficult. G McN Rushforth (*Medieval Christian Imagery*) gives good reason to think that it represents the marriage of Isaac and Rebecca.

1.8 The creation of Eve Malvern Priory

1.9 The Sabbath Rest Salisbury Cathedral

9 Abraham holding the souls of the just in his bosom
This is depicted on a boss in Durham Cathedral where he holds a napkin in which are three small figures. (*Roof Bosses*, CJP Cave, fig 82)

ADAM AND EVE
The many representations of Adam and Eve are due to their being the central figures of the Creation Cycle and the constant parallelism that was drawn between the old and the new dispensations.

REPRESENTATIONS
1 **The creation of Adam** On the Romanesque font at East Meon, Adam stands before God. A later representation is in a quatrefoil on the west front of Wells Cathedral.

In the east window of York Minster, Adam appears

1.10 *God points to a tree bearing fruit*
Malvern Priory

to be descending from Heaven; in Malvern Priory God
bending over the nude figure of Adam lifts His right arm.
At Hengrave Hall Adam is created from the dust. Beyond
trees are stags and a bear is seen in the foreground. In the
sky is a flight of swans. (*Hengrave Glass*, C Woodforde)

In the nave of Norwich Cathedral is a rare representation
on a boss.

2 The creation of Eve In glass at Malvern Priory [1.8]
and Hengrave Hall, Eve rises from the left side of sleeping
Adam at the command of God.

In the nave of Norwich Cathedral on a boss Eve rises
naked before God. (*Roof Bosses*, CJP Cave, fig 146)

3 The Sabbath Rest In the chapter house of Salisbury
Cathedral [1.9], on the sculptured frieze after the creation
of Adam, is depicted the Sabbath Rest. God, with hand
raised in blessing, is seated in an aureole.

1.11 *God talks to Adam and Eve in the Garden of Eden* Salisbury
Cathedral

1.12 *Adam and Eve flanking the tree* Worcester Cathedral

1.13 *Tree bearing fruit – The Temptation* Ely Cathedral

1.14 *The Temptation* Salisbury Cathedral

1.15 *Adam and Eve hiding from the face of God* Salisbury Cathedral

4 The Garden of Eden In glass at Malvern Priory [1.10], in a walled garden God points to a tree bearing golden apples. On the frieze at Salisbury Cathedral [1.11] God, standing by a tree bearing fruit, talks to Adam and Eve.

5 The Temptation This is the commonest episode in the Adam and Eve series of representations. It is depicted on

misericords as at Worcester Cathedral [1.12] where Adam and Eve, naked, flank a tree above which appears the human head of the serpent. Adam is eating his apple; Eve holds one in her right hand and takes one with her left from the serpent's mouth. At Ely Cathedral [1.13] the tree is bearing fruit and the serpent is a pleasant-looking creature.

1.16 *Serpent crawls away in the form of a dragon*
Malvern Priory

1.17 *The Expulsion* Worcester Cathedral

1.18 *The Expulsion by an angel with a sword* Ely Cathedral

Adam and Eve are already showing signs of disquiet.

The Temptation is included in the frieze in Salisbury Cathedral [1.14].

In glass in Malvern Priory the Worcester pattern is followed. It is found on bosses at Ely Cathedral, Beverley St Mary, and elsewhere. In glass in St Neot ('Creation' [1.26]) the serpent has a human head. At Fairford, in glass, Eve stands before a fruit-bearing tree, identified with the tree of knowledge of good and evil. Around the trunk of the tree is coiled the serpent with paws and a human head. With a fruit in its paw it tempts Eve. The practice of representing the serpent with a human head may have originated with the idea that originally it possessed human speech which it lost at the Fall. The practice would be furthered by stage personification.

6 After the Temptation On the frieze at Salisbury Cathedral [1.15] Adam and Eve in the garden are shown hiding from the face of God. In glass in Malvern Priory [1.16] God is seen facing Adam and Eve as the serpent crawls away.

On a boss in Ripon Cathedral God is speaking to Eve.

7 The Expulsion On a misericord in Worcester Cathedral [1.17] Adam and Eve, hiding their nakedness, are being driven from the garden by an angel.

In Ely Cathedral [1.18] they shrink away from an angel with a sword. In the scene in the spandrels of the wall arcading in Worcester Cathedral [1.19] they are being driven from a walled city. The Expulsion is included in the series in glass in Malvern Priory [1.20], and in the stone frieze at Salisbury Cathedral [1.21].

1.19 *Adam and Eve expelled from the walled city* Worcester Cathedral

1.21 *The Expulsion* Salisbury Cathedral

1.20 *The Expulsion* Malvern Priory

1.22 *Adam digging and Eve spinning* Worcester Cathedral

1.23 *Adam tills the ground and Eve suckles a child* Salisbury Cathedral

1.24 *The murder of Abel and God chastising Cain* Salisbury Cathedral

1.25 *The murder of Abel* Bradninch

8 **After the Expulsion** On a misericord in Worcester Cathedral **[1.22]** Adam has his spade and Eve her distaff and spindle. In glass at Hengrave Hall, Adam digs and Eve suckles Abel whilst Cain plays at her feet. At Malvern Priory Adam digs and Eve, seated with a child on her knee, holds a spindle in her right hand and a distaff and thread in her left. On the frieze at Salisbury Cathedral **[1.23]** Adam tills the ground and Eve suckles a child. On a boss in Winchester Cathedral Adam and Eve are clothed in skins. (*Roof Bosses*, CJP Cave, fig 259)

9 **The death of Adam** This is recorded in glass at St Neot. 'A legend was told that on his deathbed he sent his son Seth to fetch three pips of the fruit of the Tree of Life from the Garden of Eden. Seth put them under Adam's tongue and they grew up into three trees from which the Cross was made.' (*Imagery of British Churches*, MD Anderson)

BALAAM

Balaam is rarely represented but he is found in glass in Canterbury Cathedral where his journey is seen as an antetype of the journey of the Magi. This is emphasised by the association of the two subjects and the positioning of the representations of the subjects so that Balaam, riding on his ass, and the Magi, journeying on their horses, point to the star.

1.26 *The Creation – Window 1* St Neot

CAIN AND ABEL

The sacrifice of Abel typified the sacrifice on the Cross, and his murder, the Crucifixion.

REPRESENTATIONS

1 **The sacrifice of Abel** This is recorded on the frieze in the chapter house of Salisbury Cathedral, on a tomb at Framlingham and in glass at St Neot.

2 **The murder of Abel** This is the subsequent episode depicted at Salisbury [1.24], and on the tomb at Framlingham.

A painting on the screen at Bradninch [1.25] of a man with an uplifted jaw bone of an ass towering over a man whose head he holds by the hair, may depict the murder of Abel although CE Keyser (*Archaeologia*, vol 56) suggests that it refers to Samson.

3 **God chastising Cain** This episode follows the previous two at Salisbury [1.24], and is the subject of a wall painting at Kingsdown.

4 **The death of Cain** According to an old Jewish legend: 'when Lamech grew old and blind he took his young son

Tubalcain with him to direct his footsteps and the aim of his bow. Seeing movement in the bushes, the lad told Lamech to shoot, but when the fugitive Cain fell mortally wounded, Lamech, in horror at his own act, slew Tubalcain. This scene is shown in one of the quatrefoils on the facade of Wells Cathedral, on a boss in the nave of Norwich Cathedral and in the Creation window at St Neot.' (*Imagery of British Churches*, MD Anderson; illustrated in *Roof Bosses*, CJP Cave, fig 148)

THE CREATION

The Days of Creation are recorded in glass and in stone. They all follow a similar pattern suggesting a manuscript influence. The first three panels of the Creation window at St Neot [1.26] show:

(a) The creation of the world and of light.
   God stands looking to the sky in which is the sun and the moon.
(b) The dividing of the water and the dry land.
   God stands on the land and directs a flowing river.
(c) God, with raised hand, creates the fishes, birds and animals.
   A similar series of panels occurs in the east window of York Minster and in Malvern Priory [1.27] where is seen:
(a) The creation of Heaven and Earth.
   God the Father, holding a large pair of compasses, confronts a large circle which represents either the sun or the earth.
(b) The creation of the heavenly bodies.
   God, with raised hands, faces a sky in which are the sun, moon and stars.
(c) The creation of fishes and birds.
   God stands beside a stream full of fishes. In one hand He holds a fish and birds fly away from the other hand.
(d) The creation of animals.
   God stands surrounded by the animals He has created.

On the stone frieze in the chapter house of Salisbury Cathedral [1.28, 1.29, 1.30] a similar sequence of events is recorded.

In the nave of Norwich Cathedral are a number of bosses on which the day by day events of the creation are recorded.

It is interesting to note that sometimes, as at Norwich and York, God is holding a pair of compasses. This is a reference to *Isaiah* 40 v 12.

DANIEL

Daniel is frequently found represented, especially in glass, as an Old Testament character. The only incident from his life which is recorded with any frequency is his encounter with the lions in the den, and this dramatic story does not occur as often as would be expected. A Romanesque relief built into the west front of Lincoln Cathedral shows Daniel in the den surrounded by lions. (*English Medieval Sculpture*, A Gardner, fig 156)

1.27 *The Creation* Malvern Priory

1.28 *The creation of trees* Salisbury Cathedral

1.29 *The creation of the sun and moon* Salisbury Cathedral

1.30 *The creation of the birds and fishes* Salisbury Cathedral

1.31 *David presents Goliath's head in the Temple* Norwich Cathedral

DAVID

A figure of David, holding a harp, is often found but representations of scenes from his eventful and dramatic life are less often seen.

REPRESENTATIONS

1 **David holding a harp**   Single figures of David, holding his attribute, the harp, are most often found in glass. He so appears on a painted screen panel at Southwold. In a spandrel of the choir arcading of Lincoln Cathedral is a figure of him, crowned, aged and holding a harp.

2 **Strangling the lion**   Because of Samson's similar conflict with a lion it is almost impossible to say when David or Samson is intended, but at Sherborne a misericord, the supporter of which is a youth strangling a lion, may be intended for David. (See 'Children at Play' [8.15])

On a boss in the cloisters of Norwich Cathedral the combatant wears a crown, this again suggests that David was intended.

3 **David and Goliath**   On one boss in the nave of Norwich Cathedral is depicted Goliath, in armour and brandishing a huge stone. He has been hit on the forehead by a stone from David's sling. On a second boss David has grasped Goliath's beard and is lifting his sword to cut off the giant's head. On a misericord in Westminster Abbey the encounter is depicted. In the centre David stands beside the body of Goliath. One supporter shows the conflict, and the other Goliath reaching over the wall of a castle.

On a boss in the cloisters of Norwich Cathedral [1.31] is depicted David presenting Goliath's head in the Temple. David carries aloft the head on a spear.

1.32 *David holding a sceptre sits on a throne*   Fairford   **1.33** *David and the Amalekite*   Fairford

4 The coronation of David   On a nave boss in Norwich Cathedral, David, holding a harp and sitting on a throne, is flanked by two figures who place a crown on his head.

5 David and the Amalekite   This is seen in three lights at Fairford [**1.32, 1.33**].

(a) David holding a sceptre sits on a throne.

(b) A young man holds the head of the Amalekite by the hair. The headless body lies on the ground and armoured soldiers look on.

(c) David's soldiers crowd in to witness the scene.

6 David and Achish   In glass in Lincoln Cathedral is depicted David feigning madness by walking on his hands before the throne of the King of Gath.

7 The death of David   On two bosses in the nave of Norwich Cathedral the king lies on his bed. On one the youthful Solomon kneels by the bed to hear his father's charge, on the other a woman appears to be making a request.

8 The death of Absalom   On a panel of glass in the east window of York Minster is depicted the death of Absalom. David is looking at the body of his son which has been pierced by arrows.

9 David and Nathan   In glass in Wells Cathedral is depicted Nathan chastising David for his treatment of Uriah and for taking his wife.

ELIJAH

The ascension of Elijah is depicted in a medallion of glass in Canterbury Cathedral. The prophet ascends in a chariot and his cloak is wafted towards Elisha.

1.34 *The fall of Sodom and Gomorrah* Salisbury Cathedral

1.35 *Lot leaves his wife who has turned into a pillar of salt* Salisbury Cathedral

1.36 *Gideon* Fairford

1.37 *The Grapes of Eschol* Ripon Cathedral

THE FALL OF SODOM AND GOMORRAH

The story of the fall of Sodom and Gomorrah and the fate of Lot's wife is recorded in glass at Hengrave Hall. It is depicted on a tomb at Framlingham and is included in the Old Testament history recorded on the frieze in the chapter house of Salisbury Cathedral [1.34, 1.35]. Here are seen the buildings of the tower toppling down and Lot and his daughters turning their back on his wife who has been turned into a pillar of salt.

GIDEON

The story of the manifestation to Gideon of the dew falling only on the fleece and not on the ground, typified the Incarnation as being out of the normal course of nature. It is well depicted in glass at Fairford [1.36], where Gideon in armour, his helmet by his side, is kneeling in prayer. In front of him is the fleece. An angel, holding a staff, descends. Also in the picture is a stream on which can be seen a man in a small boat.

1.38 *The Grapes of Eschol* Milverton   **1.39** *Isaac blessing Jacob* Salisbury Cathedral

THE GRAPES OF ESCHOL

Two of the spies sent by Moses to Canaan are depicted returning with the bunch of grapes which they cut by the Brook of Eschol. The grapes are suspended on a long pole carried on their shoulders. A eucharistic symbolism is obvious but medieval writers also saw a more involved symbolism. The subject is found on misericords in Beverley Minster and Ripon Cathedral [1.37]. A late example is found on a bench end at Milverton [1.38]. It is depicted in glass in Canterbury Cathedral and in French glass at Twycross.

ISAIAH

The sign on the sundial of Ahaz is depicted in glass in Canterbury Cathedral. Isaiah stands by a bed in which lies the sick Hezekiah wearing his crown. Above is the sun and a sundial.

JACOB AND ESAU

Few incidents from the life of Jacob and Esau have been recorded apart from two long series of illustrations. The first series is eight episodes shown in small scenes with a minimum of detail on the stone frieze in the chapter house of Salisbury Cathedral. Secondly on a number of bosses in the nave of Norwich Cathedral is depicted a series of incidents. (*Norwich Roof Sculptures*, EM Goulburn and E Hailstone)

The story told in Genesis chapters 27 to 33 can be summarised as follows:

(a) The aged Isaac sends his son, Esau, for venison.
On a boss Esau is hunting. He has pierced the side of a deer with an arrow.

(b) Rebecca sends Jacob for two kids and makes savoury meat.

1.40 *Rebecca seeing Jacob off* Salisbury Cathedral

On a boss a kid is laid out on a table in front of a house.

(c) Rebecca disguises Jacob and tricks Isaac.
At Salisbury [1.39] Isaac is blessing Jacob who stands by his bed. At Norwich on one boss Jacob kneels before his mother who is applying a skin to his neck. On another boss Isaac, who is lying in bed, feels the hand of Jacob. A third figure, with bow and arrow, is probably Esau.

(d) Isaac blesses Esau who vows to kill Jacob.
In the second scene of the series at Salisbury [1.39], Esau has taken the place of his brother at the bedside. On one boss in the nave of Norwich Cathedral Esau with his bow in his hand and a deer over his shoulder

1.41 *Jacob meets Rachel and she takes him to meet Laban*   Salisbury Cathedral

1.42 *Jacob wrestles with an angel and two angels ascend a ladder*   Salisbury Cathedral

is returning to Isaac. On a second, Isaac, from his bed, holds the hand of Esau who is still holding his bow.

(e) Rebecca sends Jacob to Padan-Aram.
   At Salisbury [**1.40**] Rebecca is seeing him off from the house. On a boss at Norwich, Jacob is making the journey with his staff in his hand.

(f) Jacob's vision of the ladder and the anointing of the stone at Bethel.
   The telling of this episode is spread over four bosses. Jacob, his staff by his side, is lying asleep. Two angels are climbing a ladder which reaches from the ground into the clouds. Jacob is wrestling with an angel and lastly he is pouring oil on a square stone which resembles an altar.

(g) Jacob meets Rachel and Laban.
   At Salisbury [**1.41**], first Jacob meets Rachel who is surrounded by her sheep and then she takes him to meet Laban in front of a house. On a boss at Norwich he is moving the stone from the well with his staff.

(h) Jacob marries Leah and then Rachel.
   The two unions are recorded on two similar bosses. On the first, a priest joins the hands of Jacob and Leah. On the second, her place is taken by Rachel.

(i) The division of the flocks.
   Jacob peeling a rod is depicted on a boss in the nave of Norwich Cathedral. (*Roof Bosses*, CJP Cave, fig 153)

(j) Jacob and his family flee from Padan-Aram.
   On another boss Jacob is leading a camel and carrying a box, and on another Leah and Rachel, each with a swaddled child, are seated on a horse.

(k) Jacob wrestles with an angel at Peniel.
   At Salisbury [**1.42**] Jacob is wrestling with an angel and adjacent to this two angels ascend a ladder. This

1.43 *An angel touching the thigh of Jacob*   Salisbury Cathedral

seems more applicable to the angelic encounter at Bethel. If so, it is out of sequence. In the next spandrel an angel is touching the hollow of Jacob's thigh [**1.43**]. 'The angel touches Jacob's thigh with a wand, like that with which Christ is shown performing miracles in the Catacomb paintings.' (*Imagery of British Churches*, MD Anderson)

(l) Jacob and Esau are reconciled.
   On a boss at Norwich Jacob and Esau are embracing. A group of sheep, part of the present to Esau, are nearby. At Salisbury the brothers are not alone when they meet.

At Malvern Priory the story was told in glass but only one panel depicting Isaac sending Esau for venison is intact. Esau, with his bow, stands before his father who is seated on a chair. In the doorway stands Rebecca.

1.44 *Jonah and the whale*   Ripon Cathedral

1.46 *Joseph with sheaves and relating his dream* Salisbury Cathedral

1.45 *The whale casting forth Jonah* Ripon Cathedral

1.47 *Joseph cast into a pit*   Salisbury Cathedral

JONAH

Single figures of Jonah are found along with other Old Testament prophets as in glass in the chapel of New College, Oxford. The story of Jonah and the whale was seen as an antetype of the Resurrection.

Jonah's encounter with the whale is shown on two misericords in Ripon Cathedral **[1.44, 1.45]**. On the first, three men are casting him overboard to a waiting whale. On the second, the whale is casting forth Jonah who is clinging to a rock.

JOSEPH

The story of Joseph and his brothers is told on the stone frieze in the chapter house of Salisbury Cathedral and on a series of bosses in the nave of Norwich Cathedral. (*Norwich Roof Sculptures*, EM Goulburn and E Hailstone)

There was recorded a similar series of incidents in glass in Malvern Priory but most of this has perished.

The story as told in Genesis can be summarised as follows:
(a) Joseph dreams and tells his dream.
    At Salisbury **[1.46]**, in one spandrel Joseph's brothers' sheaves are making obeisance to his sheaf. In the adjacent spandrel Joseph surrounded by his family is telling his dream.
(b) Joseph visits his brothers.

This episode is recorded on three bosses at Norwich. On one the seated Jacob appears to be blessing Joseph or directing him prior to his journey. On a second boss Joseph is making the journey in the manner of a pilgrim and on the third, two of his brothers watch his approach.
(c) Joseph is stripped of his coat and cast into a pit.
    At Norwich on one boss his coat has been pulled over his head by his brothers and on a second he is being lowered into a pit which resembles a well. (*Roof Bosses*, CJP Cave, fig 154.) A similar pit occurs at Salisbury **[1.47]** and at Malvern Priory **[1.48]**.
(d) Joseph is sold to the Ishmaelites.
    The brothers are seen on one boss eating in the open and on another the Ishmaelite is leading Joseph from amongst his brothers. A man riding a camel, on a third boss, may be part of this incident. At Salisbury Joseph goes off behind a rider on horseback, leaving two brothers, one of whom is holding his coat and the other a bag (containing the twenty pieces of silver).

1.48 *Joseph being lowered into a pit*
Malvern Priory

In a medieval account of the history of Joseph he was sold to the Seneschal of Egypt. In Queen Mary's Psalter and in the Salisbury carving he takes the place of the Ishmaelite merchant. 'In both the Psalter and the carvings the Seneschal sells Joseph direct to Pharaoh, whose own wife, not that of Potiphar, plays the temptress, and both show the dreams of Joseph's two fellow-prisoners being fulfilled in one illustration.' (*Imagery of British Churches*, MD Anderson)

(e)   The brothers return with the coat dipped in blood.

Three incidents are recorded on bosses. As a kid is being killed its blood is being collected in a pan, the coat is being dipped into the pan and Jacob is being shown the blood-stained coat. At Salisbury **[1.49]**, Jacob, seated, receives the coat from his sons.

(f)   Joseph is brought to Pharaoh.

At Salisbury **[1.50]**, Joseph is kneeling before the king.

(g)   Joseph is tempted and accused.

At Salisbury the wife of Pharaoh has clutched hold of Joseph's garment as he turns to leave her and in the adjacent spandrel she is accusing him.

(h)   Joseph is cast into prison.

1.49 *Jacob receives the coat of Joseph* Salisbury Cathedral

1.50 *Pharoah receives Joseph* Salisbury Cathedral

Joseph's imprisonment is recorded at Salisbury and on a boss at Norwich where he has been placed in the stocks and his keeper can be recognised by the keys he is holding.

(i) The dreams of Pharoah's butler and baker.

At Salisbury the fulfilment of the dreams is shown. The butler is again offering the cup to Pharoah but the baker is hanging from a tree.

(j) Pharoah's dream and Joseph's interpretation.

The dream, the ensuing anxiety and the interpretation each are treated as an incident in the Salisbury frieze.

(k) Joseph is overlord in Egypt.

On one boss Joseph kneels before Pharoah who holds a sceptre which he is handing to him. On another Joseph is surrounded by sacks of corn.

In the Salisbury representation is included a man throwing sheaves into the Nile; this is a reference to the legend that corn was carried to Palestine and Jacob so learned of plenty in Egypt.

(l) The brothers' two journeys to Egypt and their encounter with Joseph.

At Norwich on two similar bosses are depicted two of the brothers with empty sacks. On a third, one of them (Judah) is kneeling before Joseph (interceding for Benjamin).

In glass in Canterbury Cathedral is seen Joseph, sitting on a throne, on his right hand are his brothers and on his left a group of Egyptians, two of whom hold bowls of coins.

In the Salisbury frieze is included the hiding and finding of the cup in Benjamin's sack and the confrontation between Joseph and his brothers.

(m) Jacob's journey to Egypt and his reception by Joseph and Pharoah.

On the Salisbury frieze is seen Jacob journeying to Egypt and the final reconciliation of Joseph and his brothers. In glass at Malvern Priory, Pharoah extends his hand to receive Jacob who is accompanied by his eleven sons.

JUDITH AND HOLOFERNES

A misericord in Lincoln Cathedral depicting a woman with raised sword about to strike off the head of a man which she is holding by the beard has been interpreted as an illustration of the Apocryphal account of how Judith saved the besieged Israelites from the Assyrians by a clever ruse. She penetrated the enemy camp where she attracted the amorous attention of Holofernes, leader of the Assyrian army. After a banquet she cut off his head whilst he was in a drunken stupor.

MOSES AND AARON

Owing to a mistaken translation, instead of being represented with light shining from the skin of his face, Moses is usually shown with horns on his head. This is a more easily recognised and more easily depicted characteristic.

Incidents from the life of Moses are recorded on bosses in the nave of Norwich Cathedral, on the frieze in the chapter house of Salisbury Cathedral and in glass in six panels of the east window of York Minster.

REPRESENTATIONS

1 **Moses with the Tablets of the Law** There is a fine figure of Moses, horned and holding the tablets, in the Yorkshire Museum at York [1.51]. A similar figure is on the

1.54 *The golden calf*   Worcester Cathedral

1.51 *Moses*   Yorkshire Museum   **1.53** *The burning bush*   Fairford

1.52 *The finding of Moses and the Manna*   Malvern Priory

1.55 *The golden calf* (left) *and the doom of the idolators* Malvern Priory

font at Southrop. In glass at North Tuddenham rays of light are issuing from his ears.

2 **Moses in the bulrushes** This is the subject of a boss at Norwich. Moses is swaddled and his mother puts him in a rocker basket. (*Roof Bosses*, CJP Cave, fig 151)

3 **The finding of Moses** In glass at Malvern Priory [1.52] the daughter of Pharaoh, with two of her ladies-in-waiting, receives Moses from his sister. On the ground is a wicker basket and in the distance is a city. This incident is in one of the panels at York.

4 **Moses minding Jethro's sheep** On a boss at Norwich is seen Moses, with a shepherd's crook, seated amongst the sheep. On another boss are Miriam and women with timbrels.

5 **The burning bush** This is depicted on two bosses at Norwich. On the first is Moses and the burning bush from which an angel rises. On the second Moses has taken off his shoes. At York, God appears in the burning bush. In glass at Fairford [1.53] Moses reclines before the bush. The episode is recorded at Salisbury and in glass in Canterbury Cathedral.

6 **The manna** In glass in Malvern Priory [1.52], this rarely depicted subject is seen. Moses, his rod in his hand, watches two men collecting manna into baskets. The manna is shown as white disks resembling sacramental wafers.

7 **The golden calf** On a misericord in Worcester Cathedral [1.54], Moses and Aaron flank a pillar on which stands the golden calf with body and legs of a bird. In glass in Malvern Priory [1.55], Moses is seen pointing to the calf supported on a pillar.

8 **The doom of the idolators** A scene in glass in Malvern Priory [1.55] relates to the Jewish legend that when Moses powdered the golden calf and made the Children of Israel drink it, the beards of those who were guilty of idolatory turned yellow. A group of men, several of whom have yellow beards, face Moses; they are drinking out of golden cups. One man with a yellow beard kneels in front of an executioner with a large sword.

9 **Moses striking the rock** This incident is seen in glass in Canterbury Cathedral where Moses strikes the rock with his rod and two men catch the water in bowls.

It is seen also at Salisbury and in glass at Stamford, St Martin.

10 **The crossing of the Red Sea** In glass in Canterbury Cathedral Pharaoh on a throne, crowned and holding a

1.56 *The Salisbury Ark and Noah and the Ark afloat* Salisbury Cathedral

1.57 *The Ark depicted as a barque with three turrets* Ely Cathedral

sceptre, dismisses Moses and the Israelites with a wave of his hand. Moses, with his rod, points to the Red Sea. In the left-hand corner is the Pillar of Fire. The drowning of the Egyptians is included in the York window and on a boss at Norwich Pharaoh and his chariot and men are being engulfed in the waters. (*Roof Bosses*, CJP Cave, fig 152)

NOAH

Because Noah in the Ark was a symbol of Christian baptism and of Christ guiding the Church, and because the drunkenness of Noah prefigured the stripping and mocking of Christ, episodes from the life of Noah were frequently depicted in medieval art.

REPRESENTATIONS

1 **God's commandments and promises to Noah** In glass in Malvern Priory and on a Romanesque slab on the west front of Lincoln Cathedral, God is shown commanding Noah to build the Ark.

2 **Noah building the Ark** A quatrefoil on the west front of Wells Cathedral and a slab on the west front of Lincoln Cathedral (*Romanesque Sculpture 1140–1210*, G Zarnecki, fig 60) each show Noah building the Ark. The same episode is the subject of a boss in the nave of Norwich Cathedral. On the stone frieze of the chapter house of Salisbury Cathedral [1.56] is seen Noah, pausing from his labours to listen to the commandments of God.

3 **Entry into the Ark** In glass in Malvern Priory the entry into the Ark is shown in two stages. First the birds and animals are seen entering; these include a horse and mare, boar and sow, squirrel, lion and lioness and rabbit. They are followed by Noah and his family.

On a boss in the nave of Norwich Cathedral is seen a group entering the Ark.

On the frieze in Salisbury Cathedral [1.56] the Ark which is already afloat is being entered by a man by means of a ladder.

4 **The Ark afloat** On a misericord in Ely Cathedral [1.57] the Ark is depicted as a barque with three turrets which gives it an unseaworthy appearance.

1.58 *The sacrifice of Noah* (left) *and Noah working in his vineyard* Malvern Priory

The Salisbury Ark [1.56] is a two-storeyed structure; the upper storey is occupied by the birds and the lower by the animals.

On a boss in the nave of Norwich Cathedral Noah and his family and the animals look out from a three-tiered ark. (*Roof Bosses*, CJP Cave, fig 150)

5 **The raven**   On the supporter of the Ely misericord [1.57] and on a boss in the nave of Norwich Cathedral the raven is seen preying on a dead animal floating in the water.

6 **The dove**   On the other supporter of the Ely misericord and on another boss at Norwich the dove is seen with an olive branch in its mouth.

The return of the dove is depicted in glass in Malvern Priory.

7 **Leaving the Ark**   On a boss in the nave of Norwich Cathedral is seen Noah, staff in hand, and his wife, her hands folded across her breast, as they leave the Ark and step onto dry land.

8 **The sacrifice of Noah**   The rarely depicted subject of Noah's sacrifice occurs in glass in Malvern Priory [1.58]

where Noah is kneeling before an altar on which is a goat. It is also one of the episodes depicted in a window, in which is related the story of Noah, at St Neot [1.59, 1.60]. The last episode depicted, the death of Noah, is modern.

9 **Noah planting a vineyard**   Noah working in his vineyard is the subject of a boss in the nave of Norwich Cathedral, of glass in Malvern Priory [1.58] and it occurs in the Salisbury frieze [1.56].

10 **The drunkenness of Noah**   The drunkenness of Noah is depicted on a Norwich boss and on a tomb at Framlingham. In Malvern Priory two panels of glass are used to record this episode, the second panel is only fragmentary. In the first scene the sons bend over the drunken Noah; in the second only the heads of the sons remain, the lower part of the panel is confused. Presumably in the first scene one of the sons is covering Noah and in the second Ham is revealing his shame to the other brothers.

In the Salisbury frieze [1.61] Ham, covering his eyes, exposes their father to his brothers.

11 **The sons of Noah**   In glass in Canterbury Cathedral

1.59 *Disembarking from the Ark and the sacrifice of Noah* St Neot

1.60 *The drunkenness of Noah and the death of Noah* St Neot

the Church, represented as a woman holding a scroll, regards the three sons of Noah, Shem, Ham and Japheth, who hold a map of the world.

THE PASSOVER

In glass in Canterbury Cathedral two men are slaughtering a lamb; one of them holds a bowl into which the blood is gushing. A third bearded man with a bowl in his hand is shown marking with the sign 'T' the lintel of a doorway.

SAMSON

Apart from his conflict with the lion, episodes from the life of Samson are depicted infrequently.

REPRESENTATIONS

1 **Samson and the lion** On numerous misericords as at Norwich Cathedral [1.62], a man is depicted astride a lion, rending its jaws apart. It cannot be certain that Samson was intended in every case but when he was, the lion assumed the worse side of its dual nature and the episode symbolised Christ breaking open the gates of Hell.

2 **Samson and the Gates of Gaza** The carrying away of the Gates of Gaza was a type of the Resurrection. On the doorway of Malmesbury Abbey this incident is paralleled with Christ rising from the tomb. On a misericord in Ripon Cathedral [1.63], Samson carries one gate on his shoulder and the other under his arm from the gateway of a medieval walled city. On a boss in the nave of Norwich Cathedral Samson carries the gates in a similar way. (*Roof Bosses*, CJP Cave, fig 156)

3 **Samson and Delilah** Delilah, shearing off the hair of the sleeping Samson, is shown on a misericord in Gloucester Cathedral [1.64]. Two bosses at Norwich tell the same story. On the first Delilah is binding Samson's wrists and on the second is cutting off his hair.

4 **Samson pulling down the pillar of the house** This episode is recorded in a panel in the east window of York Minster.

5 **Samson slaying a Philistine** In glass at Fairford, Samson, holding the jaw bone of an ass behind his back, grasps the Philistine by the throat.

THE PRESENTATION OF SAMUEL

The presentation of Samuel prefigured the presentation of Christ. The incident is depicted in glass in Canterbury Cathedral where Hannah, accompanied by her husband Elkanah, is presenting Samuel to Eli in the Temple. Behind,

1.62 *Samson and the Lion* Norwich Cathedral

1.61 *Ham covers his eyes and exposes his father to his brothers*
Salisbury Cathedral

1.63 *Samson and the Gates of Gaza*
Ripon Cathedral

1.64 *Delilah cutting off the hair of Samson* Gloucester Cathedral

1.65 *The presentation of Samuel in the Temple* Worcester Cathedral

a woman servant holds a bottle of wine. In front are three baskets of corn and three bullocks.

On a misericord in Worcester Cathedral **[1.65]**, Samuel, with hands raised, stands before an altar; behind him stand Eli and Hannah, who carries a bottle of wine.

SOLOMON AND THE QUEEN OF SHEBA

The story of the judgment of Solomon between the two mothers is sufficiently dramatic to explain its appeal but the prominence given to the Queen of Sheba is only explained by her visit to Solomon being interpreted as the heathen seeking enlightenment.

REPRESENTATIONS

1 **The anointing of Solomon**   The anointing of Solomon by Zadok and Nathan is the subject of a boss in the nave of Norwich Cathedral.

2 **Solomon as builder of the Temple**   On another boss at Norwich, Solomon is seated on a throne and holds a sword in his left hand and a cruciform church in his right hand. (*Roof Bosses*, CJP Cave, fig 157)

3 **The judgment of Solomon**   This is found on a misericord in Westminster Abbey. Solomon sits on a throne with the dead child in front and a mother on either side of him. One supporting subject is each woman with a child; and the other,

1.66 *The judgment of Solomon* Worcester Cathedral

1.67 *The building of the Tower of Babel* Salisbury Cathedral

one woman with both children. Similarly on a misericord in Worcester Cathedral **[1.66]**, Solomon, with a counsellor on each side, sits on a throne beneath a canopy. On the left a woman holds a kicking child and on the right is the second woman with the dead child in swaddling clothes. On a capital in Westminster Abbey the crowned Solomon is giving his judgment to a woman holding a child and to a woman kneeling in supplication. (*English Medieval Sculpture*, A Gardner, fig 101)

4 **The visit of the Queen of Sheba** Solomon receiving the queen is depicted in glass at Fairford, where the king, seated on a throne, is accepting a jewelled casket from the queen. The room is grandly furnished and the occupants are richly attired.

5 **The Queen of Sheba** On a shaft of the jamb of the west doorway of Rochester Cathedral is a mutilated figure of the queen. An interesting feature is her long plaits of hair. In glass in Canterbury Cathedral Solomon, holding a sceptre, from his throne faces the queen. She is followed by two camels bearing gifts.

SUSANNA AND THE ELDERS

The story of Susanna and the two elders is recorded in the Apocryphal Daniel and Susanna. Two elders watched her bathing in her garden and conspired to seduce her. When forced to submit to their lust or face false accusations of infidelity she chose the latter. She was tried by the assembly and condemned by the false evidence of the two elders. Daniel, a devout young man, intervened and exposed the elders by examining them separately when they contradicted each other. They were put to death.

The story is recorded in Flemish glass at Bury St Edmunds. At Melton Constable in one panel Susanna is depicted in the garden with her two maids and in another is depicted the execution of the two elders. Other fragments of glass can be found elsewhere but no complete window remains.

THE TOWER OF BABEL

The building of the tower is depicted in glass in Malvern Priory. A load is being hoisted up to the top by a crane. Workmen ascend the tower by ladders and angels descend from the clouds. In the nave of Norwich Cathedral are two bosses; on the first a mason is shaping stone and on the second is shown the tower which is reminiscent of a medieval castle gateway and keep. At Salisbury Cathedral [1.67], on the frieze in the chapter house, men are busily engaged on the construction of the tower.

2
New Testament

WHEN THOSE SURVIVING representations of episodes recorded in the Gospels are regarded as a whole, it is apparent that a high percentage are related to either Christmas or Easter. We can assume that they constitute a fair sample of what originally existed. The great festivals dominated the Christian year and the choice of subject. There was a concentration on the infancy of Christ and the events of Holy Week and those following the Crucifixion. Apart from the baptism of Christ because of its sacramental significance, and the death of John the Baptist because of its dramatic character, the ministry of Christ received scant attention. The influence of the Apocryphal Gospels and devotional works, often vivid in their description of the New Testament events, is seen in interesting details which persisted throughout the period although the Apocryphal Gospels had ceased to be orthodox literature and the devotional works could not claim to be historical.

THE INFANCY OF CHRIST

THE ANNUNCIATION

As would be expected the Annunciation was a favourite, often repeated, subject in medieval art. The earliest form found in England is the two standing figures of the Archangel Gabriel and the Virgin Annunciate. Gabriel, the divine messenger, often carries a scroll bearing the words of the Annunciation. Later, modifications were made and interesting details were added. The three lilies in a pot by the side of the Virgin were introduced. This motif is usually taken to be a symbol of purity but other interpretations have been made. Emile Mâle has suggested that it served to associate the Annunciation with the spring, during which season it took place. GC Coulton in *Art and the Reformation* recounts the story of the Jew and the miraculous growth of the lily to convince him of the truth of the Incarnation, which he says became current as an explanation of the motif. The Holy Dove was introduced, sometimes in the breath of the Father, and a further addition was a miniature figure of the Holy Child bearing His Cross. In later representations the Virgin is kneeling or standing at a prayer desk, sometimes holding a book, 'No doubt derived from the apocryphal gospel of Pseudo-Matthew which says that Mary was instructed in the Law of God and the Psalms'. (*Medieval Christian Imagery*, GMcN Rushforth)

In the apocryphal *Protevangelium* it is recorded that when the angel appeared, Mary was weaving the purple and scarlet thread for the veil of the Temple. This led to her being depicted holding a distaff but no English example of this has been noted. Emile Mâle describes other details found in Continental art but which are not found in English representations of the Nativity.

2.1 *The Annunciation* Wells Cathedral

REPRESENTATIONS

The early form of the two standing figures of the Angel Gabriel and St Mary is found on the doorway of the chapter house of Westminster Abbey. (*English Medieval Sculpture*, A Gardner, figs 270 and 271.) The Virgin standing at a prayer desk, turning to greet the angel, with a pot of lilies nearby, is depicted on an alabaster panel in Wells Cathedral [2.1]. In glass at Fairford and in Malvern Priory, the Holy Dove is present. At Norwich, St Peter Mancroft, in glass and at Ross on Wye on the alabaster tomb of William Rudhall [2.2], the Holy Child, bearing His Cross, follows the descent of the Holy Dove.

Sometimes on the stem of the lily appears a miniature crucifix as on a misericord at Tong. Various explanations of this have been made but the exact origin and significance is somewhat obscure:

(i) Belief that the Annunciation and the Crucifixion both occurred on the same date, 27 March.

(ii) Devotions to the Seven Joys and the Seven Sorrows of the Virgin.

(iii) Prompted by descriptive devotional writings in the *Speculum Humanae*.

The events of the Annunciation are recorded in a simplified form on a series of bosses in the transept of Norwich Cathedral:

(a) Gabriel, holding a short staff, is in the presence of God who is encircled by an aureole of light.

(b) Gabriel is leaving Heaven, which is represented as a town, by a gateway.

(c) Gabriel stands by a smaller gateway.

2.2 *Holy Child follows descent of Holy Dove* Ross on Wye

2.3 *The Visitation* Ruthwell

2.4 *The Visitation*
Worcester Cathedral

(d) Gabriel in the house of Anne where Mary is reading at a lectern.
(e) The Annunciation by Gabriel in the presence of God, with His hand raised in blessing.
(f) Gabriel leaves the house escorted by Joseph.
(g) Joseph re-enters the house.
(h) God speaks to Joseph who takes Mary by the hand.
    These bosses and their relationship to the Mystery Plays are described in *Drama and Imagery* by MD Anderson.

AN ANGEL APPEARS TO ST JOSEPH
The annunciation to St Mary had a foremost place in medieval thought and art; in comparison little attention was paid to the annunciation to St Joseph.

In the transepts of Norwich Cathedral is a boss which depicts 'an angel appearing to St Joseph who is asleep on a green bank; the angel grasps his left arm and touches his right shoulder'. (*Archaeologia*, vol 83, CJP Cave)

THE VISITATION
There is little variation in the representation of the Visitation. One of the earliest examples is a small panel on the Ruthwell Cross [2.3]. A later example is found in a spandrel of the wall arcading in Worcester Cathedral [2.4], where the two figures clasp each other with animation. In East Anglian glass the subject received special treatment. At Norwich, St Peter Mancroft, the Visitation is represented in the tracery lights and in the main light and at East Harling in the main light. In each case 'the upper part of St Elizabeth's robe

shows what is meant to be a maternity garment. It is cut down the front and loosely laced'. The two figures face each other with dignity. At Norwich 'a woman dressed in a blue garment stands behind St Elizabeth. A piece of red cloth, edged with fur, hangs over her left arm and is held in place by her right hand. This detail must refer to the legend that St Elizabeth, when she heard of the Blessed Virgin's arrival, threw down a piece of scarlet cloth upon which she had been working and ran to meet her with the words here placed upon her scroll.' (*Norwich School of Glass-Painting*, C Woodforde, plate II)

At Malvern Priory the representation in the window devoted to the Gospel series follows the usual pattern; Mary and Elizabeth clasp each other. The representation in the Magnificat window includes an unusual feature. Elizabeth places her hand on the body of Mary and from the spot where her hand is placed spring golden flames, suggesting that the Divine Glory is already present. (*Medieval Christian Imagery*, G McN Rushforth, fig 172)

ZACHARIAS
In the transepts of Norwich Cathedral are a number of bosses on which Zacharias is figured. Amongst them are:
(a) The circumcision of St John the Baptist. The high priest is taking the child from the altar on which Elizabeth has placed him.
(b) Zacharias writing the name of St John. Zacharias points to a page in an open book held by a young man.
(c) Zacharias coming out of the Temple.
(d) His returning to his house.

THE NATIVITY
In addition to the simple account of the Nativity in the Gospel of St Luke, medieval artists were influenced by other writings: the Apocryphal Gospels. In the *Book of James*, or *Protevangelium*, is the story of the two midwives and how the hand of one, Salome, was withered because of her doubts and was healed by touching the Child. Although the healing incident is not depicted, this apocryphal account

2.5 *The Nativity* Worcester Cathedral

2.6 *The shepherds with an angel appearing* Exeter Cathedral

explains the inclusion of the midwife or midwives in some scenes of the Nativity and the Adoration of the Wise Men. In the *Gospel of Pseudo-Matthew*, after the description of the Birth in a cave in the presence of the two midwives, Zelomi and Salome, following the account in the *Book of James*, is written: 'On the third day Mary left the cave and went to a stable and put the child in the manger, and the ox and the ass adored him, fulfilling the prophecies of Isaiah and Habakkuk'. (*Apocryphal New Testament*, MR James)

In the *Meditations on the Life of Christ* (*Pseudo-Bonaventura*) the Birth of Christ is described as taking place without travail in a shelter, built by St Joseph, whilst awaiting a midwife. The animals recognised the Child and worshipped Him.

In the *Revelations of St Bridget of Sweden* St Bridget in her vision sees the Nativity in a cave, where St Joseph had lighted a candle whose light was overshadowed by the light surrounding the newly born Child to whom Mary knelt in adoration. The open thatched shed or stable, which replaced the cave of St Bridget's vision and the Apocryphal Gospels, 'seems to have been an Italian invention which was almost universally adopted by Northern Art in the fifteenth century'. (*Medieval Christian Imagery*, G McN Rushforth)

REPRESENTATIONS

In glass at Norwich, St Peter Mancroft, the Virgin with the Child is sitting up in a bed, placed in a stable. At the foot of the bed St Joseph sits. Near him is a fire at which a midwife is warming the swaddling clothes. Two adoring angels and the shepherds with their pipes are present. An ox and an ass are eating at a manger. The roof of the stable is thatched. 'On it are two angels, who have made a hole for the rays of the star to shine through.' (*Norwich School of Glass-Painting*, C Woodforde)

At East Harling, the Child is lying in a manger from which an ox is feeding. The Virgin kneels and St Joseph stands at the side of the manger. Two midwives are present and the star shines overhead.

At Malvern Priory two representations in glass show the influence of St Bridget's vision. The Virgin is adoring the Child, who lies on her cloak bathed in light and raises His hand in blessing. St Joseph stands nearby holding a lighted candle. In the background an ox and an ass peer over the doors of a stable.

The second representation at Malvern in the Magnificat window shows the same influence. 'A new detail here is the ruinous stable roof with its broken thatch, a way of suggesting the poverty of the shelter which was popular in fifteenth-century Flemish art.' (*Medieval Christian Imagery*, G McN Rushforth, figs 136 and 173)

At Worcester Cathedral [**2.5**], in a spandrel of the transept arcade, the Virgin lies on a bed with St Joseph at the foot. An ox and an ass watch over the Child lying in a crib.

At Fairford, in glass, the same influence is seen. The Virgin adores the Child, bathed in light, and St Joseph holds a lighted candle. 'Through an open doorway and

2.7 The Adoration of the shepherds
East Harling

window can be seen a landscape with fields and trees, and in the distance the tower of Micah's prophecy, that the Saviour should be born within sight of the Tower of the Flock. *Micah* IV 8.' (*Fairford Church*, OG Farmer)

On a boss in Tewkesbury Abbey the Child, in swaddling clothes, lies in a manger. The Virgin lies alongside with her head on a pillow; St Joseph leans on his staff. An ox and an ass look down on the manger. (*Roof Bosses*, CJP Cave, fig 210)

A similar representation is on a boss in the nave aisle of Worcester Cathedral.

In the transepts of Norwich Cathedral are three bosses each of which depicts the Nativity in a slightly different way. On the first, the Virgin holds the Child in the presence of St Joseph and two midwives. On the second, she adores the Child lying on a couch. On the third the Virgin lies on a bed and the midwife places the Child in a manger watched by two animals. A fourth boss shows St Joseph leading two beasts with the Virgin following. At Norwich, St Helen, on a boss, the Child appears to have been washed and the midwife is handing Him to His mother who holds a large towel. (*Roof Bosses*, CJP Cave, fig 166)

THE SHEPHERDS

Tradition maintained that there were three shepherds and that they were making music when the angel appeared.

REPRESENTATIONS

In Exeter Cathedral [2.6] is a group of shepherds, one of whom plays on the pipe. From above an angel appears and at their feet are the sheep.

In glass the Adoration of the shepherds is depicted at Norwich, St Peter Mancroft, and at East Harling (*Norwich School of Glass-Painting*, C Woodforde, plate XI), where a shepherd, cap in one hand and crook in the other, kneels before the Child on His mother's knee. Another shepherd holds a lamb and a third plays the pipes. In the background an ox and an ass feed from a manger [2.7]. In a medallion of glass at Lanchester is depicted 'the shepherds tending their flocks, the sheep being depicted in green grass'. (*Ancient Painted Glass*, P Nelson)

In the much faded wall painting at Ashampstead one of the shepherds holds a pipe.

On a boss at Salle (*Roof Bosses*, CJP Cave, fig 190) the whole adoration scene is beautifully depicted. In a series

2.8 *Shepherds* Gloucester Cathedral

2.9 *The Adoration of the Wise Men*
Long Melford

of bosses, devoted to the Nativity, in Norwich Cathedral are depicted:

    (a) The angel appearing to the shepherds.
    (b) The shepherds on the way to Bethlehem.
    (c) Their arrival at a house in Bethlehem.
    (d) The Adoration.
    (e) The shepherds leaving the Holy Family.

The shepherds also appear on a misericord in Gloucester Cathedral [2.8].

THE WISE MEN

St Matthew in his account is content to say 'there came wise men from the east to Jerusalem' with gifts of gold, frankincense and myrrh but tradition maintained that there were three and named them Melchior, Caspar and Balthazar. In art Melchior is represented as an old man with a beard, Caspar is younger and beardless, and from the fourteenth century Balthazar is depicted as a negro.

REPRESENTATIONS
1 **The journey of the Wise Men** This is depicted on

bosses in Tewkesbury Abbey and Norwich Cathedral. At Tewkesbury three crowned, bearded figures are being urged on from behind by an angel towards a star in front of them. At Norwich in the transepts are two bosses which show them on their journey. On one they are on horseback carrying gifts and the leader points to a star, as in glass in Canterbury Cathedral. On the other they are being led by an angel.

2 **The Adoration of the Wise Men** The traditional presentation is seen on an alabaster at Long Melford [2.9]. The Virgin rests on a couch and holds the standing figure of her Son. He stretches His hand towards a covered cup presented to Him by Melchior. Caspar holds a box and Balthazar a circular pyx. At the foot of the couch, St Joseph is seated, resting his head on a cross shaft. Behind, a midwife stands and adjusts a cushion. From under the drapings of the couch the heads of the ox and the ass emerge.

In glass at Norwich, St Peter Mancroft, and at East Harling are similar representations. At the latter Melchior removes the cover of his cup to show the gold coins marked with crosses. This may be a reference to the legend that they

2.10 *The Wise Men* Loddon

2.11 *The Adoration of the Wise Men* Lincoln Cathedral

2.12 *The Adoration* Bishopsteignton

were the origin of the thirty pieces of silver of Judas.

On the painted screen at Loddon [2.10], the Virgin, seated, holds the Child to face a kneeling king whose crown is on the ground. One of the other kings has also doffed his crown.

The adoration is found on bosses at Tewkesbury Abbey and in the transepts of Norwich Cathedral and on a misericord in Lincoln Cathedral [2.11].

A primitive representation of the Adoration occurs on the Norman tympanum at Bishopsteignton [2.12]. An early, simple representation is found on the Norman font at Sculthorpe [2.13] where the Virgin and Child, St Joseph and each of the Wise Men occupy one of the arched panels.

3 Herod and the Wise Men In the transepts of Norwich Cathedral are bosses depicting Herod's interest.

(a) 'Herod inquiring of the Magi. On the sinister Herod sits with his ankles crossed, on the dexter are the three Magi holding cups, one of them is speaking with Herod.

(b) 'Herod charging the Magi to return. Herod sits with his left leg crossed over his right knee; there is

another figure behind, in front are the Magi, one of them shakes hands with Herod.' (*Archaeologia*, vol 83, CJP Cave)

In glass in Canterbury Cathedral the Magi are warned in a dream not to return to Herod. The three kings, each wearing a crown, lie side by side in a bed over which appears an angel with the warning. At Glastonbury, on the north doorway, are three medallions in each of which one of the kings is receiving the warning.

HEROD ANTIPAS

Herod is depicted in glass at Fairford, holding a child in one hand and a sword in the other.

On the bosses in the transepts of Norwich Cathedral are depicted several incidents from his life. A full description is given by CJP Cave in *Archaeologia*, vol. 83.

Among the incidents are:

(a) The Feast of Herod. The king with Herodias and others is sitting at a table.

(b) The daughter of Herodias dancing in contortionist fashion.

2.13 *The Adoration of the Magi*
Sculthorpe

(c) Herod marrying Herodias.
(d) Herod demanding to be told where Christ should
be born.
(e) Herod, pulling his beard, is exceeding wroth.
(f) Herod ordering the slaughter of the Innocents.
(g) The death of Herod who lies in bed.

THE FLIGHT INTO EGYPT

The Flight into Egypt is represented as early as the Ruthwell
Cross. It is depicted on bosses in the transepts and in
the nave of Norwich Cathedral. On one transept boss,
the Virgin, holding the Child, is coming out of a doorway
towards St Joseph; on others, carrying the Child, she rides
upon a horse led by St Joseph. On a nave boss, she rides
an ass and the Child is wrapped in swaddling clothes.

In a medallion of glass at Lanchester 'the Holy Mother
and Child ride upon an ass, whilst St Joseph walks beside
them, carrying a wallet hung from his staff.' (*Ancient Glass*,
P Nelson)

The representation in glass at Fairford shows the influence
of the *Gospel of Pseudo-Matthew* in which is related the
story that the Virgin, resting under a tall palm, wished
to eat the fruit and that Jesus commanded the tree and it
bent low so that she could gather the fruit. Also at His
ordering a spring of water arose at its roots. Here at Fairford,
the Virgin, nursing the Child, feeds Him with fruit; whilst
St Joseph reaches to the fruit on the bough of a tree which
an angel is bending down. The legend that at Sontinen,
the Holy Family rested in a heathen temple and that the
idols fell down is included in the wall-painting representations at Brook and at Hardham.

Two more bosses in the transept of Norwich Cathedral
continue the story to Egypt. 'There is an unusual scene
of the arrival in Egypt; in the background Our Lady can
be seen upon the ass; in the front St Joseph speaks to a
young man and at the side is a seated figure in a striking

2.14 *The circumcision* Loddon

2.15 *The Presentation in the Temple*
Malvern Priory

head-dress, probably intended for Pharaoh, while in the background is a house. Finally comes the scene when the angel tells St Joseph that Herod is dead.' (*Roof Bosses*, CJP Cave)

THE MASSACRE OF THE INNOCENTS

The earliest example of this subject is on the Norman doorway of Glastonbury Abbey. It is represented in glass at Norwich, St Peter Mancroft, where the scene is set before the throne of Herod who joins in the massacre with the soldiers. One soldier has impaled a child whose mother appears to be attempting to strangle him.

At Fairford, again in glass, three soldiers are in the act of killing. The subject is also depicted in a panel of glass in the Jerusalem Chamber of Westminster Abbey.

Several bosses in the nave and transept of Norwich Cathedral show a soldier plunging a sword into a child, sometimes with the mother intervening.

THE CIRCUMCISION

In glass at Norwich, St Peter Mancroft, the circumcision is included in an Infancy series. Before the High Priest, holding a knife and seated on a throne, sits the Virgin on a low stool suckling the Child. Behind her is St Joseph.

The circumcision is depicted in similar fashion on a boss at Salle. (*Roof Bosses*, CJP Cave, fig 191)

On the painted screen at Loddon [2.14] the Virgin has placed the Child on an altar behind which, facing them, is a priest who holds a knife. On a boss at Tewkesbury and on one in the nave of Norwich Cathedral the same pattern is followed.

THE PRESENTATION IN THE TEMPLE
THE PURIFICATION OF THE VIRGIN

These two events were celebrated at Candlemas, so called because during the procession a lighted candle was carried, symbolising the entry of Christ into the Temple. In his account St Luke makes no mention of Simeon being at the ceremony but art assigned to him the role of receiving Christ when He was presented.

REPRESENTATIONS

In glass at East Harling, Simeon, standing behind an altar, holds the Child. The Virgin is facing him and behind her is St Joseph holding a candle and a basket containing two doves.

One representation at Malvern Priory [2.15] is similar. G McN Rushforth has suggested that another representation

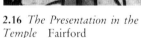

2.16 *The Presentation in the Temple* Fairford

2.17 *The Presentation* Loddon

in glass at Malvern which is divided into two parts shows the Purification of St Mary and the traditional Presentation as separate events. (*Medieval Christian Imagery*, G McN Rushforth, figs 38 and 39)

At Fairford in glass [2.16], the Virgin is offering the Child to Simeon. St Joseph is present but it is a female attendant who is holding a candle in one hand and two doves in a cage in the other.

The representation at Canterbury Cathedral is similar to that at East Harling.

In Norwich Cathedral in the transepts is a boss on which the Virgin, behind whom is St Joseph, holds the Child in swaddling clothes; in the nave on one boss is the Presentation at the altar and on another is St Joseph with a basket containing two doves. Part of a painted screen panel has survived at Loddon [2.17] on which is depicted the Presentation, as is the circumcision on an adjacent panel. Simeon is holding the Child and behind is His mother. The remainder of the scene is missing.

CHRIST AMONG THE DOCTORS IN THE TEMPLE

In a panel of glass in the east window at East Harling [2.18] this subject is depicted in its usual form. (*Norwich School of Glass-Painting*, C Woodforde, plate XIII.) Christ is seated on an elaborate throne facing the doctors. On the left is the Virgin. At Fairford the scene which is placed in a Gothic church is divided into two parts. On the right Christ looks down, from a raised dais, on the doctors. On the left stand the Virgin and St Joseph. At Malvern Priory, Christ, on a high seat, is encircled by the doctors, who wear cap and gown. The Virgin and St Joseph, holding his crutch, are entering on the left. (*Medieval Christian Imagery*, G McN Rushforth, fig 174)

In glass in Canterbury Cathedral, and in a quatrefoil on the west front of Wells Cathedral, Jesus is depicted disputing with the doctors, in the traditional manner. (*English Art*, P Brieger, fig 11A.) The subject occurs on bosses in the transept and the nave of Norwich Cathedral.

2.18 *Christ among the doctors* East Harling

2.19 *St John the Baptist with book and lamb* Blythburgh

THE MIRACLE OF THE CLAY BIRDS

In the *Apocryphal Gospel of St Thomas* is recorded how on the Sabbath the infant Jesus 'having made soft clay, he fashioned thereof twelve sparrows'. When reproved by Joseph 'Jesus clapped his hands together and cried out to the sparrows and said to them: "Go". And the sparrows took their flight and went away chirping'.

It has been suggested that this story is the subject of a wall painting at Shorthampton.

THE MINISTRY OF CHRIST

ST JOHN THE BAPTIST

The rugged figure of St John the Baptist and the story of his violent death appealed to the medieval mind and he is frequently represented. Often he is wearing a skin or a tunic made of camel's hair. The Agnus Dei became his attribute. In the fifteenth century he was depicted holding a book on which rested the Lamb.

REPRESENTATIONS

1 **Holding a book on which rests the Lamb** This is seen on the desk front at Blythburgh [2.19], and in glass in Malvern Priory.

2 **His death and Herod's feast** Salome danced and asked at the instigation of her mother, Herodias, for the head of St John on a charger. This is recorded on a misericord in Ely Cathedral [2.20], on a boss in the cloisters of Norwich Cathedral [2.21], and on a mutilated alabaster table in Ripon Cathedral [2.22], where Herodias thrusts a knife into the head of St John which rests on a charger.

In a wall painting at Idsworth are included incidents surrounding his death:

(a) His arrest by two men.

(b) His imprisonment, he is being pushed through the door of a prison.

(c) The dance of Salome.

(d) Herodias and Salome both crowned and attended by two women stand at a table to receive the head of St John.

2.20 *Salome asks for the head of St John the Baptist* Ely Cathedral

2.22 *Herodias thrusts knife into the head of St John the Baptist* Ripon Cathedral

2.21 *Salome dancing* Norwich Cathedral

3 **Life of St John** On bosses in the transepts of Norwich Cathedral is depicted a series of scenes in which St John is the central figure:

(a) Preaching in the synagogue.
(b) Pointing out Christ to the people.
(c) With the Pharisees and Sadducees.
(d) Rebuking Herod.
(e) Being put in prison.
(f) His head being placed on a charger.
(g) His birth. 'A woman is lying on a bed, behind another woman is holding a child, in front an angel speaks to a man, no doubt Zacharias; above is the roof of a building with two little angle turrets with bosses carved as roses below. The absence of St Joseph and of any sign of a manger debars this from being Christ's nativity, and the building is represented as the Temple and not as the stable.' (*Archaeologia*, vol 83, CJP Cave)

At Gresford [2.23], in one panel of glass an executioner looks down on the stretched-out figure of St John, with his head on a block. Salome, holding a dish, is standing in readiness in the background. The feast is depicted in a second panel. Salome presents the head of St John on a dish to Herodias who is sitting at table with Herod.

THE BAPTISM OF CHRIST

The baptism of Christ appears frequently; not surprisingly two of the best examples are found on fonts.

At Castle Frome [2.24] Christ is naked with His hands on His breast. He stands in the river with the water up to His waist. St John the Baptist, with a maniple or stole on his right arm, places his hand on Christ's head. Four fishes are shown swimming in the water. The presence of the Trinity is indicated by the inclusion of the Hand of God and the Holy Dove.

At Bridekirk Christ is again naked and waist deep in the

(e) The head is shown to Herod.

In the Jerusalem Chamber of Westminster Abbey is a panel of glass in which is depicted the beheading. Above the blood-stained saint is a soldier with uplifted sword. A second soldier stands guard.

2.23 *Executioner with head on block* (left); *Salome presents head on a dish* (right)   Gresford

water which is heaped around Him. St John places his hands on Christ's shoulders and not on His head which is the more usual. The Holy Dove is exceptionally large.

The baptism is represented on bosses in the nave and transept of Norwich Cathedral. In each case Christ is naked and waist deep in water and St John pours water from a vase over His head. On two nearby bosses in the nave are angels holding garments and perhaps a towel. Sometimes the eighth panel of a Seven Sacraments font is used to depict the baptism of Christ as at Gresham [2.25]. Here Christ is knee-deep in water and St John is pouring water from a vase over His head. A third figure is holding a towel or His garments. Above is the crowned figure of God the Father and the descending Dove.

An angel holding a garment is shown on the font at West Haddon.

At Kirkburn [2.26] is a Norman font with a number of crude carvings. One may represent the baptism of Christ although the nimbus is absent and a curious-shaped font is being used. The Holy Spirit descends in the form of a dove.

On the left is the baptism and on the right a figure holding an aspergillum. Here there seems to be a mixture of the baptism of Christ and the sacrament of baptism.

An unusually placed representation is on a capital of the Norman chancel arch at Adel. Here the water is made to rise in an odd way; perhaps due to the limited and awkward space.

THE TEMPTATION OF CHRIST

The Temptation is rarely depicted. Only a fragment in glass remains at Malvern Priory and the other examples are found on bosses. In the transepts of Norwich Cathedral are four bosses depicting this subject.

(a) A devil in the form of a grotesque figure, holding stones, stands beside Christ.

(b) The devil in the form of a dragon turns away.

(c) Christ, holding an orb, confronts a large and grotesque devil. Two tables and four animals are introduced into the picture, the precise significance of which is not apparent.

2.24 *The baptism of Christ*   Castle Frome

2.26 *Crude carving of Christ's baptism*   Kirkburn

(d) Christ and a devil appear on the turret of the Temple.

In the nave of the same cathedral on one boss a grotesque devil is holding stones, on another Christ 'holds a white scroll which bears a long inscription, intended no doubt to represent the words with which the tempter was defeated'. (*Norwich Roof Sculptures*, EM Goulburn and E Hailstone)

On a boss in Peterborough Cathedral 'the devil appears as a very strange figure with a second face on his belly; one leg is flexed at the knee and a wooden stump is strapped onto it; in his hand he holds a stone'. (*Roof Bosses*, CJP Cave)

At Malvern Priory [2.27] Christ is seated on a pinnacle of the Temple with the towers of the city in the background.

THE MIRACLE AT CANA

The miracle at Cana is depicted in glass at East Harling, Malvern Priory and Canterbury Cathedral. At East Harling [2.28] the bride, wearing an elaborate turban, is seated at a table. On her right is the groom and Christ is on her left. On the table are plates and food. In front of the table on the right, is a man (the ruler of the feast) who is strangely nimbused and holds a palm and a covered cup. The crowned Virgin, on the left, points to six water vessels into which a boy is pouring water.

At Malvern, Christ, with His hand raised in blessing, His mother, the bride and bridegroom are seated at a table. On a smaller table, in front of which is a boy holding a covered cup, are three vessels. A touch of realism is seen in the inclusion in the picture of a dog lying under the table. (*Medieval Christian Imagery*, G McN Rushforth, fig 175)

At Canterbury Cathedral Jesus is seated at a long table, on His right is His mother and on His left the bride and bridegroom. The governor of the feast sits at the end of the table. A servant is handing wine to him. In front of the table is a row of water pots one of which is being filled by a servant. (*Ancient Glass of Canterbury*, B Rackham, fig 19d)

In Norwich Cathedral the miracle is recorded on bosses. In the transept are two similar bosses. Christ, His mother

2.25 *The baptism of Christ*   Gresham

2.27 *The Temptation of Christ seated on a pinnacle* Malvern Priory

2.28 *The miracle at Cana* East Harling

and several other people are clustered round a table on which are cups which servants are filling. Three bosses in the nave may relate to this incident. On the first, Christ and His mother are seated at a table. On the second, a servant is filling a water pot and on the third, a servant holds a cup.

CHRIST CALLS ST PETER AND ST ANDREW
Two bosses in the transept of Norwich Cathedral refer to this episode. On the first, Christ, standing on the shore, looks towards a ship over the side of which the two apostles are lowering a net. St Peter is holding a key and behind St Andrew is a saltire cross.

On the other, St Andrew, again recognised by his saltire cross, standing by the side of Christ is pointing to St Peter who has his attribute, two keys.

THE CALLING OF NATHANAEL
In glass in Canterbury Cathedral this episode is depicted in two parts. In the first, Philip directs the attention of Nathanael, sitting under a fig tree, by pointing towards Jesus. In the second Jesus, accompanied by Peter and Andrew, confronts Nathanael who bears a scroll with the words 'Whence knowest thou me'. (*Ancient Glass of Canterbury*, B Rackham, fig 6a)

NICODEMUS
The encounter between Christ and Nicodemus is illustrated in glass at North Tuddenham. Nicodemus, with raised hands expressing wonder at His words, stands before the figure of Christ.

THE SERMON ON THE MOUNT
In the transept of Norwich Cathedral is a boss showing Christ surrounded by seven figures. This has been interpreted as illustrating the Sermon on the Mount. (*Archaeologia*, vol 83, CJP Cave)

CHRIST ASLEEP IN THE SHIP
On a boss in the transept of Norwich Cathedral is a ship in which are the twelve disciples, all of whom have a beard except one. Christ, resting His head on His arm, is asleep. On another boss appears the same ship with the twelve disciples but Christ is now standing and preaching.

THE WOMAN OF SAMARIA AT THE WELL
The only representation of the Woman of Samaria at the Well is found in glass at North Tuddenham where the woman, holding a pitcher, faces Christ who sits on the wall of the well.

2.29 *Charging of Peter with the keys*   Kirkburn

2.30 *Christ walking on the water*   Wenlock Abbey

2.31 *The Transfiguration*
Fairford

2.32 *Christ with hands raised*
Westhall

THE CHARGING OF ST PETER WITH THE KEYS

This rare subject is represented on the Norman font at Kirkburn [2.29], where St Peter is being presented with two enormous keys. It is also found on the tympanum of the Norman doorway at Siddington. (See also *St Peter*)

THE JEWS ACCUSE CHRIST OF CASTING OUT DEVILS BY BEELZEBUB

A boss in the transepts of Norwich Cathedral may refer to this incident in the ministry of Christ. 'Christ on the dexter side; in the centre is a man in a high-crowned gold hat and voluminous robes, looking back at Christ, but pointing to two mis-shapen figures.' (*Archaeologia*, vol 83, CJP Cave)

CHRIST WALKING ON THE WATER

On the lavatorium at Wenlock Abbey [2.30] is depicted Christ walking on the water. In each of two small boats are two disciples. In each case one of them is rowing with a

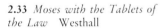

2.33 *Moses with the Tablets of the Law* Westhall

2.34 *Elijah in a turban* Westhall

2.35 *The Anointing of the Feet* Ruthwell Cross

small paddle. Christ, standing on the water, has taken one of the disciples, in the nearer boat, firmly by the hand.

PETER WALKING ON THE WATER

At Norwich, St Peter Mancroft, is depicted in glass a number of incidents from the life of Peter; amongst them is this incident told in the Gospels. Christ is standing on the shore at the water's edge and Peter, walking on the water, approaches Him. (*Norwich School of Glass-Painting*, C Woodforde, plate V)

THE TRANSFIGURATION

The best recording of this rare subject is in glass at Fairford [**2.31**]. The figure of Christ, surrounded by an aureole of golden light, appears in the sky. Above are angels. Rays of light spread from a sacramental wafer on His breast. Three rays are directed towards the three disciples at the base of the window. At the feet of Christ are Elijah and Moses. Elijah holds a rod and Moses the Tablets of the Law.

A primitive representation occurs on painted screen panels at Westhall [**2.32, 2.33, 2.34**]. One panel shows Christ with hands raised. On one side, on an adjacent panel, is Moses with the Tablets of the Law. On the other side, on a third panel, is Elijah, wearing a turban.

THE ANOINTING OF THE FEET OF CHRIST

In the Western Church the 'woman which was a sinner' was identified with Mary Magdalene and with Mary the sister of Martha and Lazarus, whom Christ raised from the dead. The attribute of Mary Magdalene is a box of ointment and she is shown with long flowing hair.

The Anointing of the Feet is depicted as early as the Ruthwell Cross [**2.35**]. A later example occurs on a Norman capital at Leonard Stanley [**2.36**] and in glass at West Horsley.

On a boss in the nave of Norwich Cathedral, Martha is offering a cup to Christ who is seated at a table. Mary, with

2.36 *The Anointing* Leonard Stanley

2.37 *The healing of the deaf and dumb*
Malvern Priory

characteristic long hair, kneels and clasps the feet of Christ. A worn example in stone at Tiverton follows the same pattern but Martha is absent. Judas, demonstrating against the act, stands in the background.

ACTS OF HEALING

The earliest representation of an act of healing by Christ is found on the Ruthwell Cross where He is healing the blind man.

On the bosses in the transepts of Norwich Cathedral several acts of healing have been identified. These are simplified illustrations with little iconographical detail. Among the representations are:

1 **The raising of the widow's son**   Christ faces the widow who holds the wrist of her son.

2 **The halt and the lame**   Christ is in the centre of a group of four lame men. One has a staff and one a wooden leg.

3 **Casting out a devil**   The devil, in the form of a naked figure, issues from the mouth of a kneeling man.

4 **The healing of a deaf and dumb man**   At Malvern Priory [2.37] in glass is recorded the healing of a deaf and dumb man. Christ is touching the ear of a man with His left hand.

5 **The healing of the infirm**   A second panel [2.38] in the same window shows the infirm being brought to Christ. One man is being transported in a wheelbarrow and another on the shoulders of a companion.

6 **The healing of a leper and the centurion's servant**   A third, incomplete, panel [2.39] has been interpreted as the representation of two of these miracles, which are recorded together because they follow each other in the Gospel account. (*Medieval Christian Imagery*, G McN Rushforth)

CHRIST IN THE HOUSE OF PETER'S WIFE'S MOTHER

This rare subject is depicted on two bosses in the transepts of Norwich Cathedral. On the first, Peter, recognised by his attribute, a key, which he is holding, is sitting beside Christ at a table. A woman holding a dish, probably Peter's wife's mother, is waiting on them. On the second boss we see the healing of the mother; she is being raised from a bed by two companions. Christ stands on one side of the bed and Peter on the other.

2.38 *Healing the infirm* Malvern Priory

2.39 *The healing of the leper and the centurion's servant* Malvern Priory

THE POOL OF BETHESDA

In glass at Malvern Priory the Pool of Bethesda is represented as a stone tank. A number of men stand nearby and in front is a fragmentary figure of Christ. 'On its far side an angel with his left hand resting on the margin "troubles the waters" with his right hand.' (*Medieval Christian Imagery*, G McN Rushforth)

THE RAISING OF JAIRUS'S DAUGHTER

A fine example of this rare subject is the twelfth century wall painting at Copford. At the entrance to his house stands Jairus, showing his great agitation, with his weeping wife. They are dwarfed by the figure of Christ standing between them.

THE RAISING OF LAZARUS

The raising of Lazarus is the subject of two early bas reliefs in Chichester Cathedral. On the first, Christ, accompanied by His disciples, is seen arriving at the house of Mary and Martha who kneel with clasped hands to receive Him. On the second Lazarus rises erect from the tomb which has been opened by two servants. On the right, Christ is in the act of commanding and in the background are the sorrowing women. (*English Medieval Sculpture*, A Gardner, figs 77 and 78)

On the Saxon font at Lenton [**2.40**] Lazarus, in swaddling clothes, still lies in the grave the lid of which a servant has just raised and over which Christ stands in an attitude of command.

The miracle is also the subject of a boss in the nave of

2.40 *The raising of Lazarus* Lenton

2.41 *The entry into Jerusalem* Haddon Hall

2.42 *Christ's entry into Jerusalem* Aston Eyre

Norwich Cathedral where Christ stands by an open coffin and draws aside the grave clothes of a figure arising from it.

THE PARABLE OF DIVES AND LAZARUS

This parable is recorded at Lincoln Cathedral, on two sections of the Romanesque relief on the west front. On the first, Dives, with his cup bearer at his side, is feasting with his friends. On the second section, an angel is receiving the soul of Lazarus but Dives is being thrust into Hell. (*English Medieval Sculpture*, A Gardner, figs 152 and 153)

The parable is also recorded in glass at Great Milton, and in a wall painting at Ulcombe.

THE PARABLE OF THE GOOD SHEPHERD

This parable is represented in glass at Thorpe St Mary, Chertsey.

THE PARABLE OF THE PRODIGAL SON

In glass in a lancet window in the south transept of Lincoln Cathedral is depicted a feast. A number of figures, two of whom are holding drinking cups, are seated at a table.

A standing figure is playing a musical instrument. This may represent the feast which was made on the return of the Prodigal Son.

THE PARABLE OF THE SOWER

Among the medallions of early glass in Canterbury Cathedral are two, each of which contains a representation of the Parable of the Sower. The sower with his seed box slung round his neck walks the field as did the medieval worker.

THE PARABLE OF THE WISE AND THE FOOLISH VIRGINS

This parable became associated with the Judgment of Christ. At Lincoln Cathedral the central figure of the south doorway is Christ in Judgment. On the outer order of the doorway on one side are depicted the wise and the foolish virgins encircled in foliage. The foolish virgins are distinguishable from the wise ones by their holding their lamps upside down to denote the lack of oil.

HOLY WEEK AND BEYOND

THE ENTRY INTO JERUSALEM

There is little variation in the representation of this subject, apart from when an attempt is made to depict it on bosses where conditions of space cause modifications in the usual pattern.

On an alabaster panel in the chapel of Haddon Hall [2.41], Christ rides upon an ass in front of which a boy is spreading a garment. He is surrounded by disciples and followers; spectators look down from the city walls.

On a tympanum at Aston Eyre [2.42] Christ is riding upon an ass which is followed by its foal.

In glass at Fairford, three boys on the battlements of the gateway hold scrolls with the words of the antiphon sung in procession on Palm Sunday.

At Malvern Priory, a panel in the east window shows Christ, riding upon an ass and followed by Peter and two other disciples, about to enter the gateway of the city. Just within the gateway, two men are throwing down richly worked garments and from above the gateway three children

2.43 *Simple rendering of the entry into Jerusalem*   Gayton

2.44 *The Last Supper*   Brighton, St Nicholas

2.45 *The Last Supper*   Somerton

are throwing flowers and branches. This is a reference to the words of Pilate's messenger recorded in the *Gospel of Nicodemus*: 'I saw Jesus sitting upon an ass, and the children of the Hebrews held branches in their hands and cried out and others spread their garments beneath him.' (*Medieval Christian Imagery*, G McN Rushforth, fig 12)

On a boss at Salle the scene is beautifully depicted. Space limits the crowd to a few figures. (*Roof Bosses*, CJP Cave, fig 192)

The representation at Tewkesbury Abbey follows the same pattern but at Norwich Cathedral the scene is reduced to Christ riding upon an ass.

At West Haddon the episode is depicted on the Norman font in a simple way. Christ, seated upon an ass, is being offered a palm. A misericord at Gayton [2.43] has been interpreted as depicting a simple rendering. The central figure is seen as a boy shouting 'Hosannah' from the battlement.

THE LAST SUPPER

Representations of this subject are not as common as would be expected and the emphasis appears to be on the treachery of Judas rather than on the sacramental significance. One of the best examples is on the font at Brighton, St Nicholas [2.44], where Christ, with three apostles arranged on either side of Him, sits on one side of a long table. The tablecloth is shown in detail. On the table in front of Christ are a cup and a loaf of bread. Other loaves and a jug are placed elsewhere on the table.

The reredos at Somerton [2.45] consists of Christ in the centre, flanked by five apostles on each side, sitting at a long table covered with a cloth. The apostles are without attributes.

A similar arrangement is seen in a wall painting at Ashby St Ledgers where Judas appears to be hiding a fish under the tablecloth.

At Malvern Priory the Last Supper is twice recorded in glass. A panel in the east window shows Christ with eight disciples seated round a table. John, in characteristic pose, is lying across Him. On the table is a dish containing two

2.46 *The Agony in the Garden*   Bosbury

2.47 *The betrayal of Christ*   Haddon Hall

2.48 *Christ being led away*   Lincoln Cathedral

fishes and loaves of bread. One disciple is drinking, one is cutting bread, another is eating but the emphasis is on Christ and Judas who sit opposite each other. Christ is offering an embossed wafer to Judas who opens his mouth to receive it. At the same time Judas is trying to hide a fish which he has taken. This is a reference to the sop which he had taken and would serve to emphasise his reputed gluttony. The prominent display of fishes and bread 'are a survival of the primitive symbolic representation of the Eucharist in the Catacomb art by fishes, loaves, and a vessel of wine, the former being an allusion to the miracle of the loaves and fishes as a type of the sacrament'. A panel in the Magnificat window shows Christ with the disciples at the table. Judas is receiving the sop. The fish of the previous example is replaced by a joint from the paschal lamb which was more usual in late medieval representations. (*Medieval Christian Imagery*, G McN Rushforth, figs 13 and 186)

Representations on bosses show some modification in the arrangement and number of disciples present because of the limitation of space. In most cases emphasis is placed on John's inclination to Christ. Examples are to be found at Salle, Tewkesbury Abbey and Norwich Cathedral.

2.49 *Judas embraces Christ; St Peter cuts off the ear of Malchus*   East Harling

The preparation for the Supper may be intended in the carving of a man carrying a pitcher on a boss in the nave of Norwich Cathedral. (*Norwich Roof Sculptures*, EM Goulburn and E Hailstone)

CHRIST WASHING THE FEET OF THE APOSTLES
The subject is not common. The earliest example depicted on a Romanesque slab at Wirksworth shows Christ bending over to wash the feet of Peter behind whom are grouped other disciples.

Similar treatment is seen on a boss in the nave of Norwich Cathedral. 'St Peter is seated and is lifting his robe in his right hand as high as the knee. . . . Our Lord is kneeling and holding the feet of the disciple, which are covered with black shoes. Under them stands a round pan of water.' (*Norwich Roof Sculptures*, EM Goulburn and E Hailstone)

The incident was included in the Passion Series in the east window of Malvern Priory but little now remains.

THE AGONY IN THE GARDEN
This subject does not occur as frequently as would be expected. It is recorded in glass at Fairford where Christ kneels in prayer in front of a tall rock on which is placed the cup of the Passion. Nearby are three sleeping disciples. On a pulpit panel at Bosbury [2.46] Christ is depicted kneeling before the cup. Three sleepy disciples are in the foreground and an angel, bearing a cross, appears in the clouds. On a boss in the nave of Norwich Cathedral, Christ kneels in front of a chalice which contains the eucharistic wafer. This is a confusion between the chalice of the Last Supper and the cup of the Passion. Emile Mâle notes the introduction into late representations of a barricade of hurdles due to the influence of the miracle plays. Remnants of these can be seen in the representation of the Agony in the Passion Series in the east window of Malvern Priory.

THE BETRAYAL AND ARREST OF CHRIST
The betraying kiss of Judas, the cutting off of the ear of Malchus, servant of the high priest, by Peter and the healing act of Jesus are the distinctive features in the representations.

At Hawkley, in an alabaster panel, Christ is in the act of healing Malchus who lies on the ground. St Peter, with key, holds a large sword and Judas places his hand on the chest of Christ. A similar alabaster is at Yarnton.

2.50 *The mocking of Christ*   Haddon Hall

An alabaster panel in the chapel of Haddon Hall [2.47] shows Christ stretching His hand towards the servant who leans on a lantern. Judas is embracing Him and one of the soldiers has grasped His robe. Peter is sheathing his sword.

In Lincoln Cathedral [2.48] is a station of the cross (probably of foreign origin) in which Christ, a rope round His neck, is being led away. In the foreground is an upturned lantern and Malchus is defending himself with a club from the sword of Peter.

The story is recorded in glass at Malvern Priory and at East Harling [2.49] where Judas embraces Christ who is almost surrounded by soldiers whilst St Peter cuts off the ear of Malchus.

On a boss at Tewkesbury, Judas kisses Christ whilst St Peter severs the ear of Malchus.

At Norwich in the nave the various incidents are recorded on several bosses.

THE APPEARANCE OF CHRIST BEFORE PILATE
St Luke relates two appearances before Pilate with an intervening appearance before Herod and he makes no reference to Pilate's hand-washing. The other evangelists mention only one appearance before Pilate.

In glass at Fairford, Christ, bound by a rope, is led by a soldier before Pilate. An attendant pours water from a ewer into a bowl for Pilate to wash his hands. The High Priest stands near Pilate.

On a boss in the nave of Norwich Cathedral Christ is shown standing before seated Pilate with soldiers and attendants crowding round.

At Malvern, two fragmentary panels are in the east window. They are separated by the panel depicting the appearance before Herod. The first panel, it would seem, represents the first appearance before Pilate and the second, the second appearance when He was condemned.

CHRIST BEFORE HEROD
A fragment of glass indicates that Christ before Herod was once a subject in the east window of Malvern Priory.

An alabaster panel has survived in the chapel of Haddon Hall which illustrates this incident more fully. Christ, bound, stands before Herod who sits on his throne holding a sceptre. He is being accused by a scribe. Judas is an uncomfortable spectator. (*Archaeological Journal*, vol 74, P Nelson)

THE BLINDFOLDING AND MOCKING OF CHRIST BY THE SERVANTS OF THE HIGH PRIEST
This episode preceded the scourging and the crowning with thorns. In glass at Malvern Priory Christ, blindfolded, is seated and holds a bulrush. The servants make vulgar gestures.

On a boss in the nave of Norwich Cathedral, Christ is seated and is blindfolded. He is flanked by two servants, one of whom has his tongue out in derision.

An alabaster panel in the chapel of Haddon Hall [2.50] shows Christ seated with His hands tied. A servant on each side of Him holds a cloth over His eyes. Behind are three figures one of whom is striking Christ on the head with a club and another has his hand raised ready to strike.

THE SCOURGING OF CHRIST
The subject is rare in early art but is found more frequently and in a realistic form as men dwelt more, during the latter part of the Middle Ages, on the suffering of Christ.

REPRESENTATIONS
1 In glass at Fairford the High Priest and Pilate, from a window, watch two men scourging Christ who is bound to a pillar.
2 At Malvern Priory sufficient glass remains to show that Christ was bound to a pillar and scourged by four men.
3 At Norwich Cathedral, in the nave, are two bosses depicting men with scourges, and in the cloisters on a boss Christ is flanked by men wielding scourges.
4 On a misericord at Boston the Pillar of Flagellation is entwined with rope on to the ends of which angels are holding. Censing angels form the supporters.
5 An alabaster panel in the chapel of Haddon Hall [2.51]

2.51 The flagellation of Christ Haddon Hall

2.52 Christ carries the Cross followed by man with nails in his hand Norwich Cathedral

shows Christ tied to a slender post. Four men are in the act of striking Him with scourges.

THE CROWNING WITH THORNS

The crowning with thorns was part of the mocking by the Roman soldiers and is sometimes shown independently of the scourging. In glass at Norwich, St Peter Mancroft, two soldiers place a crown of thorns on the head of Christ whilst three men with hooked sticks attempt to fix it over His brow. The High Priest, seated, points an accusing finger at Christ.

On a boss in the nave of Norwich Cathedral, Christ, seated on the ground, is flanked by two soldiers each with spears in their hands.

JEWS DISPLAYING THE WARRANT FOR THE CRUCIFIXION

It has been suggested that a boss in the nave of Norwich Cathedral refers to this subject which is not recorded elsewhere. A turbaned figure, accompanied by two companions, one of whom carries a sword, displays a scroll from which

hang five seals. (*Norwich Roof Sculptures*, EM Goulburn and E Hailstone)

JUDAS RETURNING THE THIRTY PIECES OF SILVER

This rare subject is combined with Christ before Pilate at Tiverton. In the presence of one of the chief priests, recognised by his mitre-shaped head-dress, Judas is returning the thirty pieces of silver. Judas still carries the money bag but the silver lies on a table over which a second priest is bending.

CHRIST CARRYING HIS CROSS

During the Middle Ages interest in the incident of Christ carrying His Cross grew with the increasing interest in His Passion.

REPRESENTATIONS

1 An early example is on a Romanesque stone cross at Leek which shows Christ succumbing to the weight of the Cross.
2 At Tiverton, Simon of Cyrene is relieving Christ of the weight.
3 In glass at Fairford, a portion of the Crucifixion window shows a Roman soldier leading Christ, who bears the Cross, by a cord fastened round His neck.
4 At Yarnton on the alabaster reredos, the soldiers are pressing upon the Cross to increase the burden.
5 At Blunham a broken alabaster panel shows His mother trying to relieve Him of the weight.
6 On a boss in the cloisters of Norwich Cathedral [2.52] Christ, clad in loin cloth, carries the Cross on His shoulders and is followed by a man with the nails in his hand.

2.53 *Carrying the Cross*   Haddon Hall

2.54 *Agnus Dei in centre of a cross*   Durham Cathedral

2.55 *Christ triumphant*   Romsey Abbey

2.56 *Christ bearing pain*   Langford

7 An alabaster panel in the chapel of Haddon Hall [**2.53**] shows Christ carrying His Cross on the arm of which a man rests a hand. He is preceded by a man with a scourge and followed by another with a scourge and some nails. In the background can be seen the head of a woman, presumably His mother, and the head of a man, probably St John.

CHRIST DISROBED FOR THE CRUCIFIXION
This rare subject is depicted in glass at Norwich, St Peter Mancroft. Two men take away Christ's garments. An onlooker is holding two nails. In the lower part of the panel one man is throwing dice and two others are fighting.

THE NAILING OF CHRIST TO THE CROSS
The tradition that the Cross was first erected and that

Christ was then nailed to it is not reflected in any English representation. The usual composition is the Cross laid diagonally with Christ being nailed to it. The tradition that His arms were fastened with ropes, because His hands would not reach to where the holes had been made for the nails, may have influenced the representation on a Saxon cross at South Church, St Andrew, Bishop's Auckland, where Christ has been attached to the Cross by ropes but there is no suggestion of nailing.

The depiction in the east window at Malvern Priory, although much damaged, is typical of most examples. The Cross is laid diagonally on the ground with His executioners grouped around it.

A boss in the nave of Norwich Cathedral shows Christ lying on the Cross, which is flat on the ground. He appears

2.57 *Christ wearing long robe*   Langford

2.58 *Crucifixion group*   Taunton, St James

to have been tied to it but a soldier is driving a nail through one of His hands. (*Roof Bosses*, CJP Cave, fig 160)

THE CRUCIFIXION

An early form of the Crucifixion was the Agnus Dei carved in the centre of a cross. An example of this is the Saxon cross in the cathedral library at Durham [**2.54**] and the Saxon slab at Wirksworth.

Christ appeared alone as a solitary figure on the Cross or flanked by figures. A dual tradition existed and persisted for some time. One tradition was Byzantine in origin and the other was Eastern. These two traditions are seen in two Saxon works both executed early in the eleventh century. The Romsey Rood [**2.55**] shows Christ as a dignified figure, triumphant over death. His arms are outstretched parallel with the arms of the Cross and there is no suggestion of suspension or suffering. 'The conception we see here is exactly that which dominated in the Byzantine area from the tenth to the twelfth century.' (*English Art*, D Talbot Rice)

At Langford [**2.56**] is a small crucifixion, now wrongly re-assembled, in which Christ is seen with bent arms and contorted neck, bearing pain and agony. 'This is the conception that was in early times dominant in Syria and Palestine, but not in Constantinople or the central part

of the Byzantine world where Greek ideas of elegance were never subordinated to eastern realism.' (*English Art*, D Talbot Rice)

When supplementary figures were included the two traditions again became apparent. In the Byzantine tradition Christ was flanked by His Mother and St John; whereas in the Eastern tradition their places are taken by Longinus and Stephaton. In this respect the Eastern tradition is seen in the Crucifixion on a slab at Daglingworth, where the flanking figures are Longinus and Stephaton, and the Byzantine tradition is seen in the Crucifixion on a slab at Stepney, St Dunstan, where the Virgin and St John appear on either side of the Cross.

A larger Crucifixion at Langford [**2.57**] is unusual in that Christ wears a long robe tied at the waist instead of the more usual loin cloth. In the thirteenth century, Christ as the Suffering Servant became the more usual form and in the fourteenth century the crown of thorns became common.

The presence of the Virgin and St John in the Crucifixion Group became traditional and was emphasised in the Great Rood which all medieval churches had in some form. What is almost a miniature rood is seen on a font panel at Taunton, St James [**2.58**].

In more realistic and detailed representations other

2.59 *Christ with the good and the bad thief* Lenton

2.60 *Longinus blind and healed* East Harling

figures are included. On the right hand of Christ is the Good Thief and on the left hand the Bad Thief. On the font at Lenton [2.59] the soul of the first is shown ascending as an angel and the soul of the second as a devil.

Longinus and Stephaton continue to be represented, often with the Virgin and St John. Longinus, holding a spear, was placed on the left and Stephaton, holding a sponge on a reed, was placed on the right. Longinus, according to tradition, was blind when he pierced the side of Christ but was healed by His blood. In a wall painting at Peakirk and in glass at East Harling [2.60], one of his eyes is closed and he is pointing to it.

Another figure, the centurion (Matthew 27 v 54), is sometimes included, often on horseback as at East Harling where he holds a scroll 'Vere filiu dei erat'. The centurion and Longinus were in some cases confused and their identities were merged.

The crucifixion scene is shown as a composite picture in glass in five lights at Fairford.

In addition to Christ, His Mother, St John, the two thieves, Longinus and the centurion on horseback, are included Pilate and the High Priests. Above the Cross is the title INRI being the initial letters of St John's version 'Jesus Nazarenus Rex Judaeorum'. At the foot of the Cross are a human skull and cross bones. These appeared in late medieval representations as an allusion to 'the place of a skull'.

In glass in Malvern Priory the scene occupies three lights. In the centre light on each side of Christ is an angel catching the stream from the five wounds in a gold cup. On His right

are His Mother and St John and on His left the centurion, holding a scroll bearing the confession of the soldier. Similarly at Windermere in glass three angels are holding golden cups to receive the sacred blood.

On a bench end *c* 1500 at Osbournby [2.61] is a crucifixion which seems to indicate some return to an earlier form.

THE DESCENT FROM THE CROSS

The descent from the Cross is depicted in glass at East Harling [2.62]. The Virgin, who is flanked by St John and St Mary Magdalene, holds the body of Christ in her lap. In the background is the Cross on which can be seen the nails and from which hang two scourges. A spear and a two-pronged fork are crossed in front of it.

The representation on an alabaster panel in the chapel of Haddon Hall [2.63] shows the influence of the Meditations. A tall ladder is being used. Joseph of Arimathea supports the weight of the body whilst Nicodemus removes the nail from His foot, and a second man, up the ladder, removes a nail from His left hand. The Virgin is holding His right hand which has been freed. The same tradition is followed in glass at Fairford. The example in the east window at Malvern Priory is fragmentary but it would appear to follow the same tradition. The earliest representation of the descent is on a Romanesque slab at Wirksworth.

THE ENTOMBMENT

An adjacent panel to the one depicting the descent from the Cross in the chapel of Haddon Hall [2.64] continues

2.61 *The Crucifixion* Osbournby

2.62 *The descent from the Cross*
East Harling

the story. The same figures, St Joseph of Arimathea and Nicodemus, are seen laying the body of Christ into a stone coffin. His Mother, with clasped hands, bends over Him and St Mary Magdalene, in front of the tomb, holds His right hand.

A similar scene is depicted in glass at Fairford where, in the distance, can be seen the crosses on Calvary.

Also in glass at Norwich, St Peter Mancroft, the body is being lowered into the tomb. St Mary, accompanied by St John, holds her Son's hand. Two other men, presumably St Joseph and Nicodemus, are assisting.

In glass in Canterbury Cathedral two disciples are lowering the body of Christ, which St Joseph of Arimathea is anointing, into a tomb in the form of a sarcophagus. The two Marys watch.

In the nave of Norwich Cathedral are two bosses. 'On the first two figures are laying the body of the Saviour in the tomb, which has somewhat the form of a coffin.' On the second are two figures which have been identified as the Virgin and St John. 'St John is a youthful figure, kneeling at the left side of the Virgin, apparently entreating her to come home with him.' (*Norwich Roof Sculptures*, EM Goulburn and E Hailstone)

2.63 *The descent from the Cross using a ladder* Haddon Hall

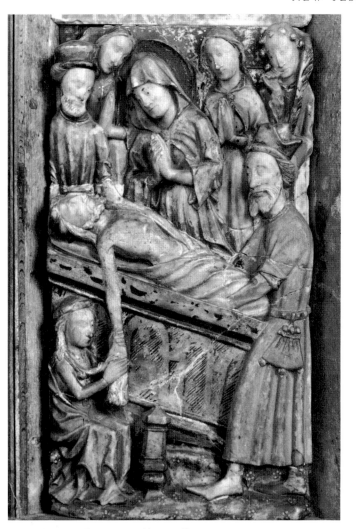

2.64 *The entombment*   Haddon Hall

2.65 *The sealing of the tomb*   Norwich Cathedral

THE SEALING OF THE TOMB

On a boss in the cloisters of Norwich Cathedral [2.65] is depicted the sealing of the tomb. The tomb itself, shown as a coffin tomb with a floriated cross on the lid, occupies the centre of the boss. It is surrounded by a number of armed soldiers some of whom are touching the tomb and a group of civilians one of whom carries a bag and appears to be sealing the tomb.

The sealing of the tomb may have been the subject of one of the panels in the Passion series in the east window of Malvern Priory but not sufficient glass remains for exact identification.

THE HARROWING OF HELL

The Harrowing of Hell is based on a passage in the Apocryphal *Gospel of Nicodemus*. Christ stormed the gates of Hell and liberated from bondage Adam and the Old Testament Prophets.

It is depicted in a simple form on a grave slab in Bristol Cathedral [2.66] where Christ is thrusting down into Hell's mouth a tall processional cross. On the Norman tympanum at Quenington [2.67] Christ is opening the gates of Hell

with a long cross and a large sun hovers in the sky, perhaps a reference to the words of Karinus 'suddenly there shone upon us a great light, and Hell did tremble, and the gates of death'. (*Apocryphal New Testament*, MR James)

In Malvern Priory a more elaborate form did exist. Although the figure of Christ has disappeared and the glass is disarranged, what does remain shows a devil crushed beneath the gates of Hell and the nude figures of Adam and Eve. (*Medieval Christian Imagery*, G McN Rushforth, fig 177)

In glass at Fairford, Christ has descended, accompanied by angels, through a cleft rock and Adam and Eve are coming to meet Him.

At Stowlangtoft [2.68] is a wood carving (not English in origin). Christ is calling naked figures from the mouth of Hell in the form of a monster's gaping jaws. A demon, custodian of the gates, has a large key suspended over his shoulder.

On a boss in the nave of Norwich Cathedral, Christ, holding a cross staff, stands at the mouth of Hell which is crowded with naked figures. (*Roof Bosses*, CJP Cave, fig 162)

2.67 *Christ opening the gates of Hell* Quenington

2.66 *Christ thrusting cross into Hell's mouth*
Bristol Cathedral

2.68 *Christ calling naked figures from the mouth of Hell* Stowlangtoft

THE RESURRECTION

In the thirteenth century there appeared a representation of
the Resurrection in Western art which became universal in
the fifteenth century. Christ with the cross staff in His left
hand and His right hand raised in blessing, steps out of a
chest tomb onto a prostrate soldier. This form may reflect
the influence of the Mystery Plays and the Easter Sepulchres
some of which, as at Hawton [**2.69**], had the sleeping
soldiers at their base and some of which were actual tombs.
This form is found as an alabaster at Ripon Cathedral
[**2.70**], on a bench-end at Bishop's Hull [**2.71**], and on a
misericord in Lincoln Cathedral. In glass at East Harling
[**2.72**] Christ's robe is parted and the wound in His side is
exposed to view. The same motif is seen on a boss in the
nave of Norwich Cathedral.

An interesting detail is included in the depiction of
the Resurrection in glass at Wrangle 'three soldiers are
represented as sleeping by a tent, the figure of a lion being
on the left'.

An alabaster panel in the chapel of Haddon Hall [**2.73**] is
similar to the one in Ripon Cathedral, with the addition of
censing angels.

2.70 *Stepping out of the tomb*
Ripon Cathedral

2.69 *Easter sepulchre* Hawton

2.71 *The Resurrection* Bishop's Hull

2.72 *Robe parted showing wound in His side*
East Harling

2.73 *The Resurrection with censing angels* Haddon Hall

2.74 *Empty grave revealed* Norwich Cathedral

2.75 *Three seated women – the three Marys at the tomb(?)* Gayton

THE MARYS AT THE TOMB

An early representation of the subject occurs on the Saxon font at Lenton. (See 'The Raising of Lazarus' [2.40].) The women are seen approaching the tomb which is a domed classical building.

At Fairford in glass the tomb of fifteenth-century style is placed in a cave situated in the garden of Joseph of Arimathea beyond which can be seen the city. The women are carrying spices for the anointing. They gaze at the empty tomb on which kneels an angel who informs them of the Resurrection. The lid of the tomb has been displaced and the burial clothes are draped on it in a disorderly way.

On a boss in the cloisters of Norwich Cathedral [2.74] the women, bearing spices, stand by a Gothic altar tomb. At the head is an angel and at the foot are two soldiers one of whom has his hand on the tomb. The lid, bearing a foliated cross, has been pushed to one side to reveal the emptiness of the grave.

Another boss in the nave depicts St Mary with a vase and a ewer. On·a misericord at Gayton [2.75] are three women seated before the entrance to an arcaded structure. Lost details might have shown this to be the three Marys at the tomb.

2.76 *Appearance of Christ to Mary* Norwich Cathedral

2.77 *Mary kneels before Christ who is shown as a gardener* Haddon Hall

2.78 *Christ with the disciples at the table* Norwich Cathedral

THE APPEARANCE OF CHRIST TO MARY MAGDALENE

The appearance of Christ to Mary Magdalene is depicted in glass at Bledington where, with hands raised, she kneels before Him as He raises one hand in a gesture of address and points to a wound in His side with the other. At Fairford a similar scene is part of the representation of the women's visit to the tomb.

At Norwich Cathedral on a boss in the nave, St Mary Magdalene kneels before Christ, bearing the Resurrection banner and, in the cloisters on one boss, she stands by Him. He is dressed as a gardener with His hand on a spade and on another [2.76], with her hair on the ground, she kneels at His feet. Christ is in His grave clothes bearing the banner and displaying His wounds. On a misericord in Lincoln Cathedral the central subject is the Resurrection and one supporter is St Mary Magdalene bearing a pot of spices and the other Christ as a gardener with a spade.

An alabaster panel in the chapel of Haddon Hall [2.77] shows St Mary Magdalene holding a vase and kneeling

2.79 *The appearance of Christ to His Mother at the house of St John* Fairford

2.80 *The supper at Emmaus* Norwich Cathedral

THE APPEARANCE OF CHRIST TO HIS MOTHER

In the Golden Legend is recorded the appearance of Christ to His Mother in the house of St John. This rare subject is depicted in glass at Fairford [**2.79**]. In the foreground of the sparcely furnished room Christ, holding a processional cross, faces the Virgin. On a scroll are the words '*Salve sancta parens*'. Beyond this room can be seen a second chamber.

THE SUPPER AT EMMAUS

The journey to Emmaus and the supper itself are shown together on a boss in the cloisters of Norwich Cathedral [**2.80**]. On the left the house is depicted as an elaborate and ornate building which Christ with the disciples is about to enter. On the right the interior of the house is shown. Christ is seated at a long table with two disciples and is in the act of breaking bread. Above the building is a host of angels.

The same scene occurs in glass at Fairford, where again Christ is seated in a richly furnished room between two disciples who show their astonishment at His revealing of Himself in the act of breaking bread. The representation is in two parts. Through an open doorway is seen the arrival of Christ with the disciples, dressed as pilgrims. In the east window of Malvern Priory it is the journey which is depicted. Christ and the two disciples are dressed as pilgrims with staff, wallet and pilgrim's hat displaying the scallop shell. The representation of Christ and the disciples as pilgrims 'seems to have originated in the word *peregrinus* used in the Vulgate of Luke 24/18 (art thou a stranger in Jerusalem)'. (*Medieval Christian Imagery*, G McN Rushforth)

before Christ carrying a cross staff and with His left hand on the handle of a spade. Here is a combination of two traditions. In early medieval art Christ holds the Resurrection banner; in the fifteenth century He is shown as a gardener with a spade, probably because of the influence of the Mystery Plays. Here the two motifs appear together.

CHRIST'S APPEARANCE TO THE ELEVEN

On a boss in the cloisters of Norwich Cathedral [**2.78**] is depicted Christ, wearing His grave clothes, appearing to the disciples, 'as they sat at meat'. St John can be recognised on His right and on the table are three dishes containing fish, bread and knives.

2.81 *St Thomas feels wound in Christ's side* Norwich Cathedral

2.82 *The incredulity of St Thomas* Fairford

THE INCREDULITY OF ST THOMAS

The incredulity of St Thomas is not a common subject. It occurs in glass at York, All Saints North Street as a two-light subject. In one light is a figure of St Thomas facing a figure of Christ, in the second light is a figure of Christ displaying His wounds.

On a boss in the cloisters of Norwich Cathedral [2.81] St Thomas kneels at the feet of Christ who guides his hand to the wound in His side.

On a bench end in Launcells, a hand touches a wounded heart and may have a reference to this episode.

At Fairford in glass [2.82] the incident is depicted as taking place in a Gothic church. St Thomas in the presence of other disciples kneels before Christ who draws aside His robe to display the wound which St Thomas touches.

THE MIRACULOUS DRAUGHT OF FISHES

This post-Resurrection miracle is recorded in glass at Norwich, St Peter Mancroft. Peter appears to be leading other disciples along a plank into a boat. (*Norwich School of Glass-Painting*, C Woodforde, plate VI)

At Fairford two disciples are pulling a net full of fish into a boat. Peter standing in the prow looks towards the shore on which is seen the figure of Christ. A second boat follows. In the foreground is an open fire on which are cooking two fishes.

In Canterbury Cathedral there are two boats. In the stern of the first, Christ, accompanied by Peter and Andrew, sits with His hand raised. In the second boat are James and John. The disciples are pulling in the net filled with fishes. (*Ancient Glass of Canterbury*, B Rackham, fig 18)

2.83 *The Ascension* East Harling

2.84 *Christ supported in an aureole* Kirkburn

2.85 *The Ascension with censing angels* Lincoln Cathedral

THE ASCENSION

The Ascension was depicted in a stereotyped way. Christ, His body hidden in cloud and only His feet showing, ascends into Heaven. Frequently He ascends from a rock which bears the imprint of His feet. Around the rock are gathered His Mother and a varying number of apostles who gaze upwards. This pattern is probably based on presentations in religious drama.

The subject is represented in this way in glass at East Harling [2.83], and in a companion panel to that in which the Pentecost is depicted in the Jerusalem Chamber in Westminster Abbey. At Fairford the Mount of Olives is depicted as a tall pillar above which can be seen the feet of Christ showing the nail marks and the lower part of His robe as they disappear into the clouds. The apostles with the Virgin grouped round the pillar, gaze upwards at the ascending figure.

On the Norman font at Kirkburn [2.84] is a primitive representation. The figure of Christ, with nimbus and upraised hands, is being supported in a horseshoe-shaped aureole by an angel on each side.

It is depicted on a misericord in Lincoln Cathedral [2.85] where censing angels form the supporters.

In a similar way it is found on bosses at Tewkesbury Abbey, Salle and Norwich Cathedral [2.86], where the footprints of Christ on the rock can be plainly seen.

THE PENTECOST

Representations of the descent of the Holy Spirit all follow the same pattern. The Holy Spirit, in the form of a dove, descends upon the apostles grouped round the Virgin. It is shown in glass in this way at Fairford [2.87], East Harling, and in a panel in the Jerusalem Chamber of Westminster Abbey. (*Royal Commission*, plate 19d.) In Canterbury Cathedral Christ is seated on a rainbow and rays descend from below His feet to touch the heads of the apostles.

The subject is depicted on two bosses, one in the nave and one in the cloisters, of Norwich Cathedral [2.88].

2.86 *The Ascension with footprints of Christ on the rock* Norwich Cathedral

2.87 *The descent of the Holy Dove – Pentecost* Fairford

2.88 *Pentecost* Norwich Cathedral

THE DOOM

In the Middle Ages each church would have its Doom painting, associated with the Great Rood, painted on a tympanum in the chancel arch, above the chancel arch or around it as at Salisbury, St Thomas. The essential feature was Christ sitting on a rainbow in judgment, His hands raised and the wound in His side displayed. Then could be added all or some of the following details:

   (a) The dead rising naked from their tombs.
   (b) The weighing of souls by St Michael.
   (c) The intercession of the Virgin and, opposed to her supplication, the trickery of Satan.
   (d) The departure of the redeemed to Paradise.
   (e) The dragging away of the damned to Hell.
   (f) The presence of apostles and saints.

REPRESENTATIONS

1 At Wenhaston [2.89] Christ sits on a rainbow; on His left the dead ascend naked from their tombs. Below, St Michael is weighing a soul in the presence of Satan; St Peter meets the redeemed represented, rather unfairly, by a bishop and three crowned persons; the redeemed entering the gates of Paradise and the damned being led in chains into the mouth of Hell.

2 At Penn [2.90] Christ, on a rainbow, is flanked by angels, one of whom carries His Cross. Below, the dead are leaving their graves. On His right are His Mother and apostles and on His left other apostles.

3 At Chaldon, in addition to the usual features, the ladder of salvation is introduced; up this the redeemed ascend to Paradise and the damned descend, sometimes falling headlong, to the torments of Hell.

4 In the nave of Norwich Cathedral is a series of bosses on which the traditional features of the Doom are depicted. These are fully described in *The Ancient Sculptures in the Roof of Norwich Cathedral*, EM Goulburn and E Hailstone.

2.89 *Doom painting* Wenhaston

2.90 *Doom painting* Penn

2.91 *Remains of Doom over chancel arch* Cawston

2.92 *Christ sitting on a rainbow* Sherborne Abbey

2.93 *Dead man carried to his burial* Worcester Cathedral

5 In glass at Fairford the subject is treated in the greatest detail. (See *Fairford Church*, OG Farmer)

6 A picture of the nave roof at Cawston [2.91] shows, by the remains above the chancel arch, the position occupied by the Doom painting in relation to the rest of the church.

7 A simple treatment of the judgment is shown on a misericord at Sherborne Abbey [2.92]. Christ, with hands raised and an orb between His feet, sits on a rainbow. On each side the dead are leaving the grave.

8 In Worcester Cathedral the spandrels of the arches of the arcade in the transepts are filled with carvings. A number of these combine to relate the Doom cycle of events.

   (a) A dead man is being carried to his burial [2.93].

   (b) The dead are seen rising from their tombs [2.94].

   (c) Christ, showing the wounds of the Crucifixion, sits enthroned in judgment [2.95].

   (d) St Michael is weighing souls and a devil is pulling down the scale [2.96].

   (e) An angel is leading the righteous souls to Paradise [2.97].

   (f) The mouth of Hell and the damned in the custody of devils [2.98].

   (g) A damned soul is being roasted by two devils [2.99].

At Salisbury, St Thomas [2.100] is a restored painting of the Doom. Here Christ sits on a rainbow with upraised hands. The dead are rising from their graves and the saved and the damned have been separated into two groups. On a misericord at Gayton [2.101] Christ sits in judgment on a throne; on each side of Him is a group of small naked figures.

THE APOSTLES PREACHING

The rare subject of the apostles preaching may be what is recorded on a boss in the cloisters of Norwich Cathedral [2.102]. On either side of a tree stands an apostle talking to a group of listeners.

THE REVELATION OF ST JOHN

In the cloisters of Norwich Cathedral there are nearly four hundred bosses, about a quarter of this number depict

2.94 *Dead rising from their tombs* Worcester Cathedral

2.97 *Righteous souls led to Heaven* Worcester Cathedral

2.95 *Christ, showing the wounds of His Crucifixion, sits enthroned in judgment* Worcester Cathedral

2.98 *The mouth of Hell* Worcester Cathedral

2.96 *St Michael weighing souls* Worcester Cathedral

2.99 *The damned being roasted by devils* Worcester Cathedral

2.100 *Restored painting of the Doom*   Salisbury, St Thomas

2.102 *The Apostles preaching*   Norwich Cathedral

2.101 *Christ sitting in judgment*   Gayton

2.103 *St John receives the Revelation*
Norwich Cathedral

2.104 *The vision of the Son of Man*
Norwich Cathedral

2.105 *The Lamb with seven horns and seven eyes and book between its feet*
Norwich Cathedral

2.106 *Opening the fourth seal; Death rides on a horse followed by Hell*
Norwich Cathedral

2.107 *Opening the sixth seal; stars of Heaven falling unto the earth*
Norwich Cathedral

2.108 *Salvation to our God and unto the Lamb* Norwich Cathedral

2.109 *Sounding the second trumpet; mountain of fire cast into the sea*
Norwich Cathedral

scenes from the Apocalypse. The Revelation of St John has been translated into a visual form. It is a unique series which is worthy of a study in itself. By viewing the bosses in order it is possible to see how the text is followed and transcribed into stone. This is illustrated by the following selection:

(a) St John, facing an angel, receives the Revelation [**2.103**].
(b) The vision of the Son of Man in the midst of the seven candlesticks; in his right hand seven stars, and out of his mouth a sharp two-edged sword [**2.104**].
(c) The adoration of the Lamb with seven horns and seven eyes and the book between his feet [**2.105**].
(d) Opening of the fourth seal. Death rides upon a horse followed by Hell [**2.106**].
(e) Opening of the sixth seal. The stars of Heaven fall unto the earth [**2.107**].

2.110 *Sounding the sixth trumpet; God before the golden altar*
Norwich Cathedral

2.111 *The army of horsemen*
Norwich Cathedral

2.112 *Woman with wings of a great eagle chased by serpent* Norwich Cathedral

2.113 *The beast which rose out of the sea*
Norwich Cathedral

2.114 *The song of Moses and of the Lamb*
Norwich Cathedral

2.115 *The sixth angel pours out his vial*
Norwich Cathedral

2.116 *The fall of Babylon*
Norwich Cathedral

(f) Salvation to our God which sitteth upon the throne, and unto the Lamb **[2.108]**.

(g) Sounding of the second trumpet. A great mountain burning with fire was cast into the sea **[2.109]**.

(h) Sounding of the sixth trumpet. God in glory before the golden altar and the loosening of the four angels **[2.110]**.

(i) The army of horsemen **[2.111]**.

(j) The woman with the wings of a great eagle chased by the serpent casting water out of its mouth **[2.112]**.

(k) The beast which rose out of the sea **[2.113]**.

(l) The song of Moses and of the Lamb **[2.114]**.

(m) The sixth angel pours out his vial, to prepare the way of the kings of the East **[2.115]**.

(n) The fall of Babylon **[2.116]**.

3
The Life of the Virgin Mary

THE VIRGIN WAS a central figure in scenes of the Infancy of Christ. The New Testament is silent about her life before her marriage to Joseph and about her life after the Crucifixion. As veneration of the Virgin increased so did the desire for more information about her parentage and the nature of her death. This information was supplied by the Apocryphal Gospels and the *Golden Legend*. Accounts of the posthumous miracles increased during the Middle Ages and these received the attention one would expect of the medieval artist. Some representations have survived but at the Reformation these were particularly vulnerable and destruction was almost universal. The extent of this destruction is demonstrated by the mutilated carvings in the chapter house of Ely Cathedral.

THE EARLY LIFE OF ST MARY
The early life of St Mary, of which nothing is said in the Gospels, was a subject of much speculation so it is not surprising that in the *Golden Legend* a number of incidents are described. Representations of these are rare in English churches.

THE BIRTH OF ST MARY
In glass in Malvern Priory there are two representations of the birth of St Mary. In the first St Anne is sitting up in a bed which is covered with a richly worked bedspread. She is holding out her hands to receive the swaddled infant, Mary, from the midwife.

The second example is smaller and not in such a good state of preservation. (*Medieval Christian Imagery*, G McN Rushforth, figs 40 and 163)

At Fairford St Anne is seen propped up in bed by pillows. An attendant is passing the infant, Mary, to her.

In glass at Gresford [3.1] St Anne lies in bed with one of her breasts exposed. St Joachim stands behind the bed and a woman holds the child. In front a girl stirs the contents of a saucepan.

THE PRESENTATION OF ST MARY
In the *Golden Legend* it is recorded that, when only three years old, St Mary at the time of her Presentation in the Temple climbed without any assistance the fifteen steps up to the altar.

Associated with each of the representations of her birth in glass at Malvern is one of this episode but both are now fragmentary.

At Fairford, St Mary is climbing the steps which lead to the Temple. Through the open door can be seen the altar under a baldachin. On the left-hand side of the steps stand St Anne and St Joachim.

At Gresford ('Birth of St Mary' [3.1]) St Anne is presenting St Mary to the High Priest, who stands behind a table.

ST ANNE TEACHING THE CHILD MARY TO READ
According to the *Book of James*, St Mary was brought up in the Temple where 'she danced with her feet and all the house of Israel loved her'. From the thirteenth century St Anne was depicted teaching St Mary to read. The usual presentation is seen in a figure in the Chapel of Henry VII, Westminster Abbey, where the Child Mary faces an open

3.1 *The birth of the Virgin Mary* (left); *St Anne presents St Mary to the High Priest* (right) Gresford

3.2 *St Anne teaching the child Mary to read* Almondbury

book under the watchful eye of St Anne. (*English Medieval Sculpture*, A Gardner, fig 477)

This subject is frequently found depicted in glass as at Almondbury [**3.2**].

THE REFUSAL OF ST MARY TO MARRY AND THE CHOICE OF A HUSBAND

St Mary was brought up in the Temple and when, as was the custom, it was the time to choose her husband she refused to marry. The priests prayed for guidance and the choice was made by the suitors bringing rods to the altar. When that of St Joseph flowered and a dove alighted upon it, he was chosen. These events are recorded in three panels of glass in Malvern Priory.

- (a) Mary refuses to marry.
  St Mary accompanied by priests stands before an altar.
- (b) The priests pray for guidance.
  The priests gazing upwards lift their hands in prayer.
- (c) A priest returns to St Joseph his rod which has flowered and on which has descended the dove. (*Medieval Christian Imagery*, G McN Rushforth, figs 160, 161 and 164)

ST ANNE AND ST JOACHIM

The apocryphal *Gospel of James* gave Anne and Joachim as the names of the Virgin's parents. As devotion to the Virgin increased so did the stories connected with her parents. Not all of these found representation in medieval art. Apart from those in which the Virgin herself occurs, the following are some of the representations of St Anne and St Joachim:

1 The Annunciation to St Joachim After his offering had been refused by a priest because he was childless, St Joachim retired to the desert where an angel assured him that his aged wife would bear the Virgin and that they would meet at the Golden Gate as a sign. This is depicted in glass in Malvern Priory where an angel bears an inscribed scroll

3.3 *The Annunciation to St Joachim* Gresford

3.4 *The Annunciation to St Anne* Gresford

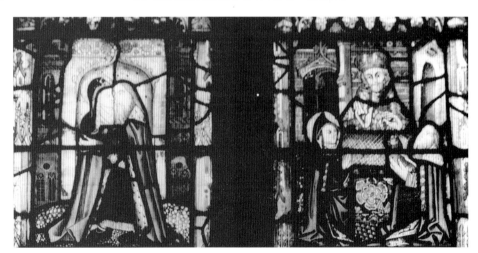

3.5 *Anne and Joachim meeting at the Golden Gate* (left); *the marriage of Joachim and Anne* (right) Gresford

to him. (*Medieval Christian Imagery*, G McN Rushforth, fig 43)

At Gresford **[3.3]** the angel is presenting a scroll to the kneeling St Joachim.

2 The Annunciation to St Anne A similar promise was made to St Anne. This is also depicted in glass at Malvern Priory, where an angel flies down to her with a scroll. In a tree a bird is feeding her young in a nest. This is probably a reference to St Anne's comparing her childless state to the fruitfulness of the fowls of the heaven.

At Gresford **[3.4]** St Anne, with uplifted hands, prays before an open book. Two angels hover in the background.

3 The meeting at the Golden Gate At Fairford St Anne and St Joachim are embracing near the Golden Gate with the Temple in the background. At Gresford **[3.5]** and at Malvern Priory they are again in a characteristic embrace.

4 The blessing by the High Priest At Gresford **[3.5]** St Anne and St Joachim kneel on either side of the High Priest who stands behind an altar. St Joachim is offering a lamb.

5 The marriage of St Anne and St Joachim The ceremony

3.6 *The marriage of Joachim and Anne*   Malvern Priory

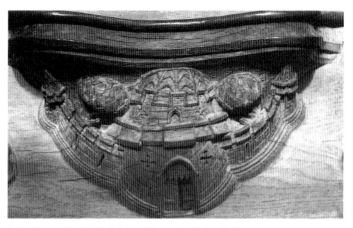

3.7 *The castle of virginity*   Norwich Cathedral

3.8 *The coronation of the Virgin*   Ripon Cathedral

3.9 *The coronation of the Virgin*   Norwich Cathedral

is depicted in glass in Malvern Priory [3.6] where the priest is joining their hands. She is attended by a woman and he is attended by a man.

THE HOLY KINDRED

In order to reconcile scriptural references to the brethren of Jesus and belief in the virginity of the Virgin a legend grew up which gave St Anne three husbands to each of whom she bore a daughter called Mary.

(a) St Joachim and a daughter, St Mary the Virgin.

(b) Cleophas and a daughter, St Mary Cleophas, who married Alphaeus and had four sons: St James the Less, St Simon, St Jude and St Joseph Justus Barsarbas (*Acts* 1 v 23).

(c) Salome and a daughter, St Mary Salome, who married Zebedee and had two sons: St James the Greater and St John.

It will be seen that this legend made it necessary to suppose that Salome was a man.

THE CASTLE OF VIRGINITY

The closed door and the fortified castle were used by writers and preachers of the Middle Ages to symbolise the virginity of Mary. They drew elaborate analogies in typical medieval manner.

Not all castles found in medieval carving need have this significance but some, such as the misericord in Norwich Cathedral [3.7], may have such intended symbolism.

THE CORONATION OF THE VIRGIN

The coronation of the Virgin was depicted in most media but was most frequently chosen by the boss carvers. CJP Cave (*Roof Bosses*) distinguishes five different ways in which it was presented.

(a) 'The figures of Christ and the Virgin are seated, and Christ is placing the crown on Our Lady's head; Christ has either a book in, or a globe in or under, his left hand.' Examples are found on bosses in Ely and Exeter Cathedrals.

(b) 'Very similar to (a), but Our Lady is already crowned and Christ is blessing.' Examples are found on bosses at Lincoln Cathedral and Tewkesbury Abbey. An alabaster of the same type is found in Ripon Cathedral [3.8].

(c) 'Christ and Our Lady are seated side by side and an angel is placing a crown on the Virgin's head.' Examples are found on bosses in Westminster Abbey and at Beverley Minster.

(d) 'The Father and the Son are seated on a throne with the Virgin on a lower seat between them, while above is the Dove.' Examples are found on bosses in York Minster and in the cloisters of Norwich Cathedral [3.9].

(e) 'The three Persons of the Trinity as three old men, and the Virgin is in front of them.' CJP Cave cites two examples on bosses at Worcester and Christchurch. It occurs in glass at York, Holy Trinity Goodramgate.

(f) In a simplified form the subject is found on misericords

3.10 *The coronation of the Virgin by angels*   Carlisle Cathedral

as at Boston and Carlisle Cathedral [3.10] where an angel is placing a crown on the Virgin's head, and in Norwich Cathedral where the Virgin is nursing her Son who is holding a dove.

In glass at Malvern Priory were two representations. The first, of which only fragments now remain, was the early type in which only Christ and His mother appear. The second, a more elaborate form, in the Magnificat window has also suffered damage. The Father and the Son unite in the crowning in the presence of the Holy Dove. The scene is set in a vesica of golden light which is flanked by Old Testament patriarchs.

THE DEATH AND ASSUMPTION OF ST MARY

A cycle of stories concerning the death of the Virgin was formed, most of which are recorded in the *Golden Legend*.

The main episodes of the stories are:

(a) In her old age the Virgin prayed for death. She was visited by an angel who presented her with a palm from Heaven and told her that her prayers would be answered.

(b) She presented the palm to St John with the request that he should carry it before her bier.

(c) The apostles were miraculously gathered to her death bed.

(d) Christ appeared with a host of angels and carried her soul to Heaven.

(e) The funeral cortege was led by St John carrying the palm.

(f) A Jew laid his hand on the bier to stop the procession. His hand was withered but he beseeched St Peter to pray for him. St Peter demanded that first he should profess the Christian faith. This he did and his hand was healed.

(g) The body was placed in the tomb.

(h) The apostles kept watch for three days.

(i) The Assumption of the Virgin. After three days her body left the grave and was united with her soul in Heaven.

(j) The gift of her girdle to St Thomas.

3.11 *The death of the Virgin*
Norwich Cathedral

3.13 *The Assumption*   East Harling

3.12 *The Assumption* Fairford

3.14 *The Virgin protecting souls*   Gayton

St Thomas was not present at her Assumption which he refused to believe and demanded that the grave should be opened. Standing by the empty open grave he saw the body of the Virgin being transported upwards and to convince him she flung her girdle down to him.

REPRESENTATIONS

1 The gift of the palm to St John   In glass in Norwich, St Peter Mancroft, is depicted St Mary seated on a throne presenting a palm to St John.

One of the scenes in a wall painting at Croughton is an angel presenting a palm to the Virgin. This is followed by a scene showing her giving the palm to St John.

2 The gathering together of the apostles   In a reproduction of the original panel of glass at St Peter Mancroft, Norwich and in the wall painting at Croughton are depicted the apostles miraculously assembled in a cloud at the bidding of an angel.

3 The death   On a boss in the cloisters of Norwich Cathedral [3.11] the death of the Virgin is depicted. She is lying on a bed at which kneel two apostles. Two angels are carrying her naked soul to Heaven in a napkin.

4 The Jew halting the bier   This episode is depicted in another panel of glass in Norwich, St Peter Mancroft. The Jew is dressed in armour and places two hands on the coffin which is carried by two apostles. A companion lies on the ground.

This episode was also one included in the series of wall paintings in Eton College Chapel but has now disappeared. It is described by MR James in *Publications of the Walpole Society*, vol XVII.

At Gresford in glass is depicted the entombment in the presence of the Trinity. The body of the Virgin and the coffin are surrounded by the apostles. The funeral cortege is depicted in a second panel. The apostles are carrying the coffin on which the wicked Jew has placed his hands. The same episode is represented in glass at North Moreton, Berks and in the wall painting at Croughton.

5 The Assumption   This subject is depicted at an early date on a grave slab at Wirksworth. It is depicted in stone on the Speke Chantry Chapel in Exeter Cathedral and in glass at Fairford [3.12] and East Harling [3.13]. At Fairford the Virgin is being transported upwards to be crowned by two angels in the presence of God who holds an orb and a cross.

THE VIRGIN PROTECTING SOULS

At Gayton [3.14] on a misericord a female figure in a long flowing robe stands with outstretched arms. On either side of her, under her outstretched arms, is a small group of naked figures. This has been interpreted as the Virgin protecting souls.

THE SEVEN JOYS AND THE SEVEN SORROWS OF THE VIRGIN

The seven joys of the Virgin are the Annunciation, Visitation, Nativity, Adoration of the Wise Men, Presentation, Finding of Christ among the doctors and the Assumption. The

3.15 *Romanesque Madonna and Child*   York Minster

seven sorrows are the Prophecy of Simeon, Flight into Egypt, Loss of Jesus on the return journey from the Temple, Betrayal, Crucifixion, Deposition and Ascension. These episodes are each considered under their individual headings.

THE TRIAL OF ST MARY

In glass at Hessett is depicted 'hell and the trial of the Blessed Virgin, the latter mentioned in the *Gospel of the Pseudo St Matthew*'.

THE VIRGIN AND CHILD

Representations of the Virgin suffered severely at the hands of the iconoclasts and the few examples that survive of the Virgin and Child from the large and varied number which must have existed are usually in a mutilated condition.

3.18 *Christian of Constantinople*
Norwich Cathedral

3.19 *Christian casting the casket; the Jew picking it up* Norwich Cathedral

3.16 *Crowned Virgin and Child*
Willoughby on the Wolds

3.17 *Virgin and Child* Stewkley

REPRESENTATIONS

Two of the earliest examples that have survived are the headless figure in York Minster **[3.15]**, which in spite of mutilation retains much of its power, and the figure in the tympanum at Fownhope. At Fownhope the Virgin and Child are flanked by a bird and a winged lion. At York the Virgin's right arm supports the Child, whose hand is raised in blessing. (*English Medieval Sculpture*, A Gardner, fig 95)

On a panel of an alabaster tomb at Willoughby on the Wolds **[3.16]** is a crowned figure of the Virgin and Child (head missing). She holds the stem of a rose bush in which the Holy Dove is resting. On an alabaster table at Stewkley **[3.17]** there are flanking angels with censers and at Shrewsbury a symposium of the Trinity and a Virgin and Child are receiving the prayers of a monk.

Even bosses did not escape the general destruction. Good examples remain at Worcester Cathedral (restored), where both figures are crowned and the Child holds an orb; Chester Cathedral, where there are censing angels; and at Ottery St Mary, where the Virgin is giving a fruit. (*Roof Bosses*, CJP Cave, figs 284, 72 and 172)

THE CHRISTIAN OF CONSTANTINOPLE

The story is that a Christian of Constantinople borrowed money from a Jew and gave a statue of the Virgin to him for surety. When it was time for redeeming the debt the Christian was abroad, so he placed the money in a casket and threw it into the sea. The casket was found on the shore by the Jew but he refused to return the surety. The image came to life and convicted the Jew of fraud. The story is related on three bosses in the cloisters of Norwich Cathedral.

On the first the bargain is being made **[3.18]**. Between the Christian on the right and the Jew on the left is a negro servant with an open bag of money. Behind on a pedestal is a figure of the Virgin.

3.20 *Virgin facing Jew* Norwich Cathedral

3.21 *The vision of Basil* Norwich Cathedral

On the second boss two parts of the story are combined: on the left the Christian is casting the casket from a boat into the sea, and on the right the Jew is picking it up off the sea shore [**3.19**].

On the third boss [**3.20**] is depicted the final episode. In the centre is the statue of the Virgin and facing it is the Jew with several companions.

ST BASIL AND THE EMPEROR JULIAN

The story of St Basil and the Emperor Julian is recorded on four bosses in the cloisters of Norwich Cathedral.

On the first boss St Basil, vested in a cope, is presenting three loaves to the Emperor Julian who, outraged at the humble gift offered to him, threatens to destroy the city. On the second boss [**3.21**] is depicted the vision of St Basil which followed, for he saw the Virgin surrounded by a host of angels. The third boss [**3.22**] continues the story. The Virgin raised from the dead Mercurius, a Christian knight. The open grave is seen in the foreground beside which is Mercurius, mounted on a charger. In the background is a figure of the Virgin surrounded by angels. The final scene is depicted on the fourth boss [**3.23**]. It is the conflict between Mercurius and the Emperor. Mercurius, who is thrusting his spear at Julian and unmounting him, is supported by an angel whilst Julian is accompanied by a devil.

In the legend St George sometimes takes the place of St Mercurius and in the 'St George Window' at St Neot the following incidents are recorded:

(a) St George fights against the Gauls.

(b) Kneeling before an altar he is about to be beheaded.

(c) The Virgin raises him from the tomb.

(d) She arms him.

(e) St George fights the dragon.

(f) He is arrested and brought before the king for denouncing pagan idolatry.

(g) He is torn with rakes.

(h) On his hands and knees he is ridden by the Emperor's son.

(i) He is hung from a gibbet with a millstone tied to his feet.

(j) He is thrown into a cauldron of molten lead.

(k) He is fastened to the feet of wild horses.

(l) He is beheaded.

THE MIRACLE OF THE JEW OF BOURGE

A Jewish boy received the Eucharist with his Christian companions and was put into an oven by his irate father, but was protected by the Virgin who wrapped him in her girdle so that he emerged from the oven unhurt.

This miracle of the Virgin is depicted on a boss in the cloisters of Norwich Cathedral. In the centre of the boss a priest, with his back to an altar on which is an open book and a chalice with a corporal, is administering the sacrament to three small boys. On the left a man is seizing a boy and another man is pushing him into an oven with a fork. On the right are two men, one with his hand on an oven.

In Eton College Chapel and in Winchester Cathedral are wall paintings which show a similar scene where a priest is

3.22 *The Virgin raising Mercurius from the dead* Norwich Cathedral

3.23 *Mercurius and the Emperor Julian* Norwich Cathedral

giving the sacrament and a second scene where the Virgin stands by an oven in which can be seen a boy.

In Lincoln Cathedral this miracle is recorded in a panel of glass, in two parts. In the first part the Virgin is watching a man standing in a furnace. In the second half a man is about to thrust a boy into a furnace under which are faggots.

THEOPHILUS

Theophilus was a medieval Faust who sold his soul to the Devil for personal profit. When the Devil had fulfilled his part of the bargain, Theophilus repented. After a period of prayer and fasting, he was visited by the Virgin who returned to him the odious contract.

This legend is depicted on a damaged capital of the altar screen at Beverley Minster, where Theophilus is making the bargain with the Devil.

In glass in Lincoln Cathedral a fuller account of the legend is recorded. Theophilus bargains with the Devil, the Virgin retrieves the bond from a horned devil, and the liberated Theophilus takes the contract to the bishop.

4

The Godhead

THE TRANSLATION OF the concept of the Trinity into a visible image was not found to be easy. The attempts, some more successful than others, are illustrated by the quoted examples.

The Almighty was rarely depicted as an isolated figure. When He appears as part of an Old Testament subject He is usually shown as an old man with a beard. Christ was more frequently depicted, especially as the main character in New Testament episodes. Apart from these scriptural representations there were specialised representations which are considered under their respective headings.

The presence of the Holy Spirit was indicated in symbolic form.

THE TRINITY
Representations of the Trinity occur in several forms:
1 A geometrical design as in glass at Woolley [4.1].
2 The Father crowned and seated holds the Son, hanging on the Cross, between His knees. In some cases the Holy Dove hovers above. This form is found on an alabaster tomb in Wells Cathedral [4.2] and at Willoughby on the Wolds [4.3].
3 A rather grotesque arrangement of three united heads under a single crown as on a misericord at Cartmel Priory [4.4].
4 The Three Persons are depicted side by side as in glass at Doddiscombsleigh and at York, Holy Trinity.

GOD THE FATHER
The representation of God the Father as a human figure is confined, for the most part, to Old Testament incidents where His form is based on the description taken from the vision of Daniel. The 'Ancient of Days' is depicted as an old man with a beard and long hair. This is seen in glass at Malvern Priory. (See 'Abraham' [1.4] and 'Creation' [1.27])

In those cases as at Malvern and St Neot where He holds a pair of compasses He is measuring out the universe in an act of creation.

Elsewhere in Old Testament scenes, a symbolic representation is used in the form of the 'Hand of God'. Here the Hand of God intervenes in order to protect, or to denote the Divine Presence. The former is well illustrated in the

4.1 *The Trinity emblem* Woolley

4.2 The Godhead Wells Cathedral

4.3 The Trinity Willoughby on the Wolds

4.4 Three heads
Cartmel Priory

Sacrifice of Isaac (See 'Abraham' **[1.2]**) and the latter in the Baptism (See 'Baptism of Christ' **[2.24]**) as depicted on the font at Castle Frome and in the early Crucifixion at Romsey Abbey. (See 'Crucifixion' **[2.55]**)

In representations of the Trinity, God the Father is depicted in human form wearing a papal crown. The finial of the gable of the Percy Tomb in Beverley Minster **[4.5]** consists of a seated figure of the Father who is receiving the souls of the departed in a cloth on His knees supported by two angels. In glass at St Neot is a similar representation of the Almighty. Here He is crowned.

GOD THE SON

CHRIST

In the early Church, Christ was at first represented as Orpheus and then as the Good Shepherd but neither form persisted. In English medieval art, apart from heads on bosses, and other than in a New Testament scene, representation is restricted for the most part to single Romanesque figures, where He is usually in the act of blessing; and in tympana, where He is usually depicted in Glory.

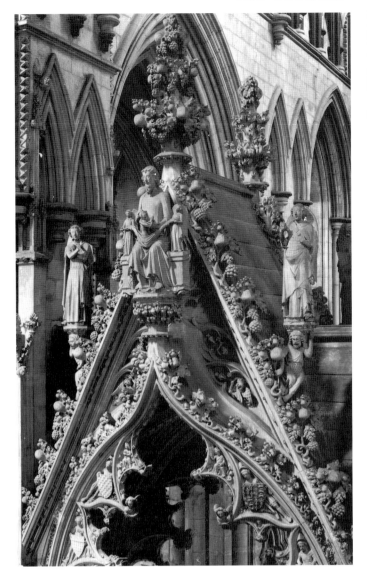

4.5 *God the Father receiving souls* Beverley Minster

4.6 *Christ* Ruthwell

REPRESENTATIONS

1 On bosses Christ is depicted at Lincoln Cathedral in the act of blessing; at Ottery St Mary, holding an orb; in Ely Cathedral, wearing a crown of thorns; and in Gloucester Cathedral, displaying His wounds.

2 Romanesque representations are to be seen on the Bewcastle and Ruthwell Crosses [4.6]. At Beverstone is a slab of the eleventh century showing a full figure of Christ, holding a long cross in His left hand and His right hand raised in blessing.

At Jevington, Sussex, He has a cruciform halo and tramples on the asp and the basilisk.

3 At Ely Cathedral [4.7] in the Romanesque tympanum, He is seated in an aureole supported by angels: His right hand is raised in blessing and He holds a book and an orb in the left hand. Similarly in a tympanum at Rowlstone, Hereford, He is depicted in Glory.

4 In a spandrel of the choir arcading of Lincoln Cathedral is a full figure of Christ. He is drawing aside His clothing to display His wound and an angel is bringing a soul to Him.

5 The emblematic symbol of a fish arose because the initial letters of His title 'Jesus Christ, the Son of God, the Saviour' in Greek formed the Greek word for a fish. This symbol is rarely seen in English churches. At St Just-in-Roseland is a boss with three fishes painted on it and the word IXθYE.

CHRIST OF PITY

A representation of Christ displaying His wounds is known as the Pity of Christ. Its popularity was increased by the indulgences granted to those who prayed before the image. Frequently it is associated with St Gregory to whom Christ revealed Himself in this way whilst he was saying mass. (See 'St Gregory'.) The Pity of Christ is depicted on a painted screen panel at Roxton, and in glass at Diddington.

This devotion to the Passion of Christ was enhanced by the many woodcuts which appeared towards the end of the Middle Ages. Here the same theme of Christ displaying His wounds is found and not surprisingly, the Emblems of the Passion are incorporated into the picture, often in the border.

4.7 *Christ seated in aureole* Ely Cathedral

4.8 *Pietà* Breadsall

PIETA

The mourning figure of the Virgin with the figure of her dead Son lying across her knees is usually referred to by the Italian term: a *pietà*. Few examples have survived apart from a fine alabaster figure at Breadsall **[4.8]**, a relief as a font panel at Orford, and a mutilated example in wood at Battlefield.

SIN AND CHRIST'S PASSION

The individual sins which men commit were associated with Christ's Passion. Writers and preachers emphasised that the Agony and the Crucifixion were re-created by the sinfulness of men.

This theme is illustrated in wall paintings. At Broughton, the Virgin holds the dismembered body of Christ. Around the two figures are fashionably dressed young courtiers, holding the severed parts of His body. At the foot of the picture are two men quarrelling over their gambling.

At Breage is depicted what is popularly known as the 'Christ of the Trades'. The figure of Christ, naked, bleeding and displaying His wounds, but crowned, is surrounded by implements of various trades. Whilst this picture could be a commentary on the social conditions of the time it could also be a reminder that the working day can be wrongly used.

At Hessett is shown Christ of the Trades in association with the Tree of Deadly Sins. The presence of a dice box and a playing card suggests the relationship between the two subjects.

GOD THE HOLY SPIRIT

The Third Person of the Trinity was only depicted in human form when the Trinity was represented by three similar human figures. (See 'Coronation of the Virgin' (e).)

Elsewhere the presence or the intervention of the Holy Spirit was depicted in the symbolic form of the Holy Dove. This is frequently found in representations of the Annunciation and the Baptism.

5
Saints

THE NUMBER OF saints recognised by Western Christendom is so great that any attempt to include all would result in a lengthy account, a large part of which would be of little interest to the visitor to English churches. Choice has been restricted to those saints who found favour with the medieval artist and who have a distinctive attribute by which they were recognised by medieval men and women, and can be as easily recognised today. Because of this basis of selection some well-known saints are ignored or receive but brief mention, whilst others, perhaps due to local popularity, were frequently represented and hence appear to receive undue attention.

Saints were depicted wearing the clothes of their calling. The bishop is represented wearing a mitre, the king with his crown, the knight in armour, and the martyr carrying the palm of victorious martyrdom. These are generic attributes and in addition, to make individual recognition possible, to each was assigned a personal distinctive attribute. Such an attribute was usually derived from the manner of the martyrdom or from some well-known episode in the saint's life. On the Continent saints were sometimes given attributes, examples of which are unknown in this country. These have been ignored as their inclusion would be more confusing than helpful.

Main consideration has been given to a saint's place in medieval iconography rather than his or her reputation in the Church for other reasons. The short biography of each is intended to explain the derivation of an attribute or the reason for a representation of an episode in the saint's life. No attempt has been made to distinguish between historical fact and fiction. Rather the aim has been to see with the eyes of the artist, and to understand what remains of his work today.

Where no recognition is given for a quotation it is from the *Golden Legend*, a collection of stories made in the thirteenth century by Jacobus de Voragine, which enjoyed great popularity and influenced iconography.

THE APOSTLES AND THE CREED

From the belief that the Apostles' Creed was the product of the apostles as a corporate body, arose the practice of associating a phrase of the Creed with each of the apostles. At the same time a particular Old Testament prophet was associated with each of the apostles thus forming a link between the glorious company of the apostles and the goodly fellowship of the prophets. The best remaining example of this scheme is in glass at Fairford. In three windows are depicted the twelve apostles ([5.1] and [5.2] show eight of them). Each apostle has his own attribute and carries a scroll bearing the phrase of the Creed accredited to him. In three other windows on the other side of the church are depicted twelve prophets carrying scrolls bearing a quotation which predicted the corresponding article of the Creed. All representations of this theme would follow this pattern although there would no doubt be variations in the attributes of the apostles and the associated prophecy.

The scheme at Fairford can be summarised as follows:

5.1 *St Thomas, St James the Less, St Philip, St Bartholomew* Fairford

5.2 *St Matthew, St Simon, St Jude, St Matthias* Fairford

St Peter, holding keys. On his scroll: 'I believe in God the Father Almighty, maker of heaven and earth.'
Jeremiah: 'Thou shalt call me, My Father' (*Jeremiah* 3 v 19); 'Thou hast made the heaven and the earth.' (*Jeremiah* 32 v 17)

St Andrew, holding a saltire cross. On his scroll: 'And in Jesus Christ, His only Son, our Lord.'
David: 'The Lord hath said unto me, Thou art my Son, this day have I begotten thee.' (*Psalm* 2 v 7)

St James the Greater, wearing a pilgrim's hat and carrying a staff. On his scroll: 'Who was conceived by the Holy Ghost, born of the Virgin Mary.'
Isaiah: 'Behold a virgin shall conceive and bear a son.' (*Isaiah* 7 v 14)

St John, holding a chalice from which emerges a dragon. On his scroll: 'He suffered under Pontius Pilate, was crucified dead and buried.'
Zechariah: 'I have raised up thy sons.' (*Zechariah* 9 v 13)

St Thomas, holding a book and a spear. On his scroll: 'He descended into hell; the third day he rose again from the dead.'
Hosea: 'O death I will be thy plagues; O grave I will be thy destruction.' (*Hosea* 13 v 14)

St James the Less, holding a club. On his scroll: 'He ascended into heaven and sitteth on the right hand of God the Father Almighty.'

Amos: 'It is he that buildeth his stories in the heaven.' (*Amos* 9 v 6)

St Philip, holding a cross. On his scroll: 'From thence He shall come to judge the quick and the dead.'
Zephaniah: 'I will come near to you to judgement; and I will be a swift witness.' (*Malachi* 3 v 5)

St Bartholomew, holding a book and a knife. On his scroll: 'I believe in the Holy Ghost.'
Joel: 'In the valley of Jehoshaphat; for there will I sit to judge all the heathen round about.' (*Joel* 3 v 12)

St Matthew, holding a cross. On his scroll: 'He descended into hell; the third day He arose again from the dead.'
Micah: 'They may all call upon the name of the Lord to serve Him.' (*Zephaniah* 3 v 9)

St Simon, holding a book and a saw. On his scroll: 'The forgiveness of sins.'
Malachi: 'If thou feelest anger put it away from thee.' (*Malachi* 2 v 16)

St Jude (Thaddeus), holding three loaves, an attribute more usually assigned to St Philip. On his scroll: 'The resurrection of the body.'
Daniel: 'O my people I will open your graves and cause you to come up out of your graves.' (*Ezekiel* 37 v 12)

5.3 *St Andrew*
Blythburgh

5.4 *St Andrew* Ranworth

5.5 *St Andrew* St Neot

St Matthias, holding a book and a halberd. On his scroll:
'and the life everlasting.'
Obadiah: 'The Kingdom shall be the Lord's.' (*Obadiah* 21)

(*Fairford Church*, OG Farmer)

APOSTLES

ST ANDREW
The popularity of St Andrew was due to the legends about
his missionary exploits rather than the little that is recorded
about him in the Gospels. Of him it was said: 'he was fair
in his life, answering in wisdom and in doctrine, strong in
pain and converted high in glory.'

There seems to be no clear reason why a cross saltire
should have been chosen as his attribute.

REPRESENTATIONS
1 With his attribute, the cross saltire, as on the desk front
at Blythburgh [5.3], on the painted screen at Ranworth
[5.4], and in glass at St Neot [5.5].

5.6 *Martyrdom of St Andrew* Norton

2 His martyrdom is depicted on a misericord at Norton
[5.6] where four men appear to be affixing him in a saltire
position.
3 The *Apocryphal Acts of Andrew and Matthias* tell of
St Andrew's visit to St Matthias when he had been imprisoned by cannibals. This story is recorded in ten panels

5.7 *St Andrew's visit to St Matthias when he had been imprisoned* Greystoke

5.8 *St Andrew visits St Matthias (following* **[5.7]***)* Greystoke

of glass in the east window at Greystoke **[5.7, 5.8]**. A detailed description of the panels and the possible association with a lost miracle play is given in *Drama and Imagery in English Medieval Churches* by MD Anderson.

St Bartholomew

Nothing is recorded in the Gospels about St Bartholomew except his name. According to legend he was engaged in missionary work in India 'which is the end of the world'. Here he overthrew idols and enraged the king who sent armed men against him. Finally he was martyred by being

5.9 *St Bartholomew holding a flaying knife* Blythburgh

flayed alive. The flaying knife became his attribute and by association he became patron saint of the tanners.

REPRESENTATIONS
1 Holding a flaying knife and sometimes a book in addition as on the desk front at Blythburgh **[5.9]**, and on a painted panel of the screen at Southwold and Ranworth **[5.10]**.
2 With his skin over his arm as in the Chapel of Henry VII, Westminster Abbey (Royal Commission, plate 123d). A similar figure is found on the west front of Exeter Cathedral and he is similarly depicted in glass at Grappenhall.

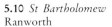

5.10 *St Bartholomew*
Ranworth

5.11 *St James the Greater*
Sherborne Abbey

5.12 *St James the Greater*
Blythburgh

5.13 *St James the Greater*
Ranworth

ST JAMES THE GREATER

St James, the son of Zebedee, has his place in the Gospels as one of the three most privileged disciples. 'He was sent into Spain for to sow there the word of Jesus Christ.' It was his legendary exploits in Spain fighting against the Moors, and his church at Compostela as a place of pilgrimage, which endeared him to the Middle Ages.

REPRESENTATIONS

1 As a pilgrim with a wallet, scallop shell in his hat, and staff in hand, he is depicted in the figure in Sherborne Abbey [**5.11**], and on the desk front at Blythburgh [**5.12**]. In glass at Doddiscombsleigh his cloak is powdered with shells. On the painted screen at Ranworth [**5.13**] he is not dressed as a pilgrim but he carries a staff and a book.

In glass in Malvern Priory, Norwich, St Peter Hungate, and All Souls College, Oxford, he is depicted as the traditional pilgrim holding a staff to which has been tied a small stick. It has been suggested that this represents a souvenir collected during the pilgrimage. (*Medieval Glass at All Souls College,* FE Hutchinson, plate III)

2 In conflict with the Moors as on the tympanum at Fordington 'a knight on horseback is overthrowing armed foot soldiers. He is nimbed and is usually described as St George, but more probably is St James who appeared according to the Spanish Legend and helped to rout the

5.14 *St James appears before King Herod*   Norwich Cathedral

5.15 *St James the Less* Blythburgh

5.16 *St James the Less*
Ranworth

5.17 *St John holding a cup* Blythburgh

5.19 *St John in cauldron over blazing
furnace* Norwich Cathedral

5.18 *St John before the Latin Gate* Lincoln Cathedral

5.21 *St John holds the poisoned cup*
Norwich Cathedral

5.20 *The Assumption of St John*
Norwich Cathedral

Spanish Host in the great battle of Clavijo in 939.' (*English Medieval Sculpture*, A Gardner, fig 134)

3 On a boss in the cloisters of Norwich Cathedral [5.14] St James appears before King Herod who is crowned and seated on a throne surrounded by attendants.

4 On an adjacent boss is shown the saint's martyrdom. His headless body lies before the mutilated figure of a throned ruler, flanked by two attendants and two praying men.

ST JAMES THE LESS

James the son of Alphaeus (*Mark* 3 v 18) was confused with James the Lord's brother (*Galatians* 1 v 19) and was venerated as St James the Less. His attribute is a fuller's club because legend relates that, after being thrown from the pinnacle of the temple, he was struck on the head with a club. Josephus relates that he was stoned to death.

REPRESENTATIONS

1 Holding a fuller's club as on the desk front at Blythburgh [5.15], and on a painted screen panel at Ranworth [5.16].
2 Holding a knife as in glass in the chapel of All Souls College and New College, Oxford. (*Medieval Glass at All Souls College*, FE Hutchinson, plate VII)

ST JOHN

St John the Evangelist shared with St Peter and St James a privileged position which is recorded in the Gospels. He was acknowledged as the author of the Fourth Gospel and the Book of Revelation. It was mainly from the legends that the medieval artist drew. Tradition relates his arrest and boiling in a cauldron of oil before the Latin Gate, from which he emerged unharmed; his encounter with the priest of Diana at Ephesus and his expulsion, in the form of a demon, of the poison from a cup of poisoned wine; his exile to Patmos and the gift of the Virgin's palm, brought to her by an angel prior to her death to be carried before her bier. His special attributes are a cup with a demon emerging, a palm, and sometimes his evangelistic emblem, the eagle.

REPRESENTATIONS

1 Holding a cup as on the desk front at Blythburgh [5.17].
2 Holding a palm as in glass at York, All Saints North Street and on a tomb at Harewood where he also has a cup. His having a palm as an attribute may be a reference to his gift of the Virgin's palm.
3 His arrest and exile to Patmos is illustrated in glass in Norwich, St Peter Mancroft.
4 **Before the Latin Gate** Domitian 'made him to be cast into a vat or ton full of hot oil in the presence of the senators, of which he issued out by the help of God'. This episode is recorded on a misericord in Lincoln Cathedral [5.18] where

5.22 *St Jude holding a boat*   Blythburgh

5.23 *St Jude with a boat*
Ranworth

5.24 *St Matthew with a sword*
Ranworth

a cauldron is on blazing faggots which a man is blowing with bellows. It is also depicted in glass at Lincoln where the saint is seen in a cauldron over a blazing furnace, and on a boss in Norwich Cathedral [5.19].

5 Writing his Gospel 'Part of the figure of St John writing with a pen and pieces of four of the seven golden candlesticks' is in glass in Norwich, St Peter Mancroft. (*Norwich School of Glass Painting*, C Woodforde)

6 His assumption is depicted on a boss in the cloisters of Norwich Cathedral [5.20], where two angels bear him over an open grave.

7 St John's encounter with the Priest of Diana Aristodemus challenged him with the words: 'I will give to thee venom to drink, and if it hurt not thee, then thy Lord is very God'. The episode is depicted on a boss in the cloisters of Norwich Cathedral [5.21]. St John on the left holds the poison cup; on the right are the bodies of the two men who have also been forced to drink the poison and have died. In the centre is Aristodemus who has taken hold of St John's cloak prior to placing it over the corpses and restoring them to life.

8 In glass in Lincoln Cathedral is seen a man, with raised hammer, in front of a long table on which are numerous small objects. This may refer to the episode when St John restored to its original form the broken jewellery which Crato had destroyed in vainglory.

St Jude

St Jude (Thaddaeus) receives no special mention in the Gospels but legend tells of his taking a letter to Edessa from Our Lord and that with St Simon he preached in Persia where he was martyred.

His usual attribute is a boat but other attributes more common to other apostles are sometimes assigned to him.

REPRESENTATIONS

1 Holding a boat as on the desk front at Blythburgh [5.22], and on the painted screens at Southwold and Ranworth [5.23].

2 In glass at Fairford he is depicted holding three loaves which is the usual attribute of St Philip. Again in glass in the chapel of All Souls, Oxford: 'the apostle holds with both hands three hexagonal objects (yellow stain), the conventional form of a loaf of bread in medieval church art'. (*Medieval Glass at All Souls College*, FE Hutchinson)

5.25 *St Matthew holding a carpenter's square* Blythburgh

5.26 *St Matthew wearing spectacles* Cawston

5.27 *St Matthias with an axe* Blythburgh

ST MATTHEW

Apart from his calling to be a disciple from the receipt of customs and the feast he made, nothing is recorded in the Gospels. Legend tells of his missionary work in Ethiopia and his death by the sword after refusing to marry a princess vowed to chastity.

His attribute varies; it can be a sword or spear, the instrument of his martyrdom, a money box or bag, a reference to his one-time occupation, and a carpenter's square. There was repeated confusion between St Matthew and St Matthias.

REPRESENTATIONS
1 With a sword as on the painted screen panels at Southwold and Ranworth [5.24].
2 Holding a carpenter's square as on the desk front at Blythburgh [5.25].
3 In the Chapel of Henry VII, Westminster Abbey is a figure of him wearing spectacles. He is writing (his Gospel) in a book which is held by an angel who also holds an inkwell. On the painted screen panel at Cawston [5.26] he is also depicted wearing spectacles.
4 In glass in Malvern Priory he is holding a money box.
5 The call of St Matthew is depicted in a medallion of glass in the south aisle of Lincoln Cathedral.
(See also 'Emblems of the Four Evangelists')

5.28 *St Matthias* Wiggenhall St Mary

5.29 St Matthias with St Jude, on left with boat Worstead

5.30 St Peter with his key Blythburgh

5.31 St Peter Ranworth

ST MATTHIAS

St Matthias was chosen by lot to take the place of Judas. He met his death in Treves. He was first stoned and 'finally he was slain with an axe after the manner of the Romans'. His usual attribute is an axe or a halberd but sometimes another of the apostolic attributes is assigned to him. When the apostles are depicted as a body his place is sometimes taken by St Paul.

REPRESENTATIONS

1 With an axe as on the desk front at Blythburgh [5.27]. A figure of a saint with an axe and a book on a bench end at Wiggenhall St Mary [5.28] could be St Matthias but, as it is an isolated figure, identification is uncertain.

2 On a painted screen panel, bearing the inscription 'Matthias' at Worstead [5.29] is a saint carrying what may be a bag. If it is a bag it is more likely to be St Matthew. This is not an uncommon confusion.

ST PETER

To St Peter were given the Keys of the Kingdom of Heaven. He was leader of the Church in the days after the Resurrection and later worked in Rome where he met his death. 'Thirty-six years after the Passion of Our Lord he was crucified by Nero turned the head downwards, for he would be so crucified.' His attribute is a key or keys.

5.32 St Peter with his key Kilpeck

5.33 *St Peter wearing a papal crown and holding a key* Wenhaston

5.35 *Martyrdom of St Peter, head downwards*
Norwich Cathedral

5.36 *St Philip with loaves* Blythburgh

5.34 *Christ seated on a throne hands key to St Peter* Siddington

REPRESENTATIONS

1 Holding a key as on the desk front at Blythburgh [**5.30**], the painted screen panel at Ranworth [**5.31**], and on the chancel arch at Kilpeck [**5.32**].

2 In glass at Norwich, St Peter Mancroft, are depicted a number of episodes from his life.

(a) The encounter with Simon Magnus.

This encounter and its consequence are depicted in two panels. In the first are seen St Peter and Simon Magnus against the background of a walled city. In the second panel St Peter is held before the agitated Nero who clutches at his beard.

(b) St Peter stands in a wooden medieval pulpit and preaches to an audience of five.

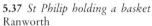

5.37 *St Philip holding a basket*
Ranworth

5.38 *St Philip holding a basket* Marsham

5.39 *St Simon with an oar* Blythburgh

5.40 *St Simon with
a saw* Milverton

(c) In another panel St Peter is pouring water on the head of a kneeling man (probably Cornelius).

3 In the Doom painting at Wenhaston [5.33] St Peter, wearing a papal crown and holding a key, is receiving the Blessed.

4 At Siddington [5.34], on the tympanum of the Norman doorway, is depicted the bestowal of the keys. Christ, seated on a throne, hands a large key to the kneeling St Peter.

5 His martyrdom by crucifixion, head downwards, is depicted on a boss in the cloisters of Norwich Cathedral [5.35].

ST PHILIP

St Philip was the disciple who, at the feeding of the multitude, asked the question 'where are we to buy bread that these may eat?' and for this reason three loaves of bread or a basket are his attributes. He sometimes holds a cross-staff, 'this refers to the legend of his having slain a dragon by holding up a cross before it'. (*Medieval Glass at All Souls College*, FE Hutchinson.) *The Golden Legend* relates that he was crucified in Asia Minor.

REPRESENTATIONS

1 With loaves as on the desk front at Blythburgh [5.36].

2 Holding a basket as on the painted screen panel at Ranworth [5.37], and at Marsham [5.38].

5.41 *St Simon with a saw* Wiggenhall St Mary

5.42 (Right) *St Simon holding a fish* Ranworth

5.43 (Far right) *St Thomas holding a spear* Ranworth

ST SIMON

Of St Simon nothing but his name in the list of apostles is recorded in the Gospels. Tradition makes him a missionary in Egypt and the companion of St Jude in Persia. His attribute can be a fish, an oar, a saw, or through confusion, another apostolic attribute.

REPRESENTATIONS

1 With an oar as on the desk front at Blythburth [5.39], and on a painted screen panel at Southwold, Suffolk.

2 With a saw as on the desk front at Milverton [5.40], and on a bench end at Wiggenhall St Mary [5.41].

3 Holding a fish as on a painted screen panel at Ranworth [5.42].

4 In glass in the chapel of All Souls College, Oxford to both St Simon and St Jude, the apostle associated with him, is assigned an unusual attribute. If the names have been transposed, as has been suggested (*Medieval Glass at All Souls College*, FE Hutchinson), St Simon is holding a club which is usually attributed to St James the Less.

ST THOMAS

St Thomas, one of the twelve, is best known because of his doubts of the Resurrection. Legend relates his being taken to India as a carpenter, his work as missionary and healer, and his martyrdom by a spear. The spear became his attribute.

REPRESENTATIONS

1 Holding a spear as on the painted screens at Southwold and Ranworth [5.43], and on the desk front at Blythburgh [5.44].

SAINTS, OTHER THAN APOSTLES

ST ADRIAN

St Adrian a knight of Nicomedia embraced the Christian faith and refused to offer sacrifices. After he was imprisoned, his wife Natalia encouraged him to remain steadfast and kissed the chains which bound him. He was tortured and died after his limbs had been crushed on an anvil before being severed from his body.

5.44 *St Thomas holding a spear* Blythburgh

5.46 *St Adrian holding an anvil(?)* Wolborough

5.47 *St Agatha with a knife thrust into her breast* Wiggenhall St Mary

5.45 *St Apollonia, St Christopher, St Adrian* Bradninch

5.48 *St Agatha and St Lucy* Ugborough

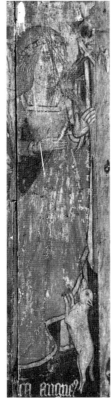

5.49 *St Agnes with long hair holding a lamb* Plymtree

5.50 *St Agnes with sword in her throat and lamb at her feet* Westhall

5.51 *St Agnes with her lamb* Eye

5.53 *St Alexis carrying a ladder* Torbryan

5.52 *Martyrdom of St Alban* St Albans Abbey

He is represented on the painted screen at Bradninch [5.45] as a knight in armour holding a sword and at Wolborough [5.46] in civilian clothing holding what may be an anvil.

St Agatha

St Agatha, a virgin of Cantania in Sicily, repulsed the advances of the pagan provost Quintianus, and refused his commands to sacrifice to idols. In revenge he tortured and imprisoned her. Her breasts were cut off but were miraculously healed. After her death a stream of lava from Mount Etna, which threatened the city, was diverted by her silken veil on a staff.

REPRESENTATIONS

1 Holding her breasts in pincers, or on a salver, or she may have a knife thrust into them as on a bench end at Wiggenhall St Mary [5.47]. On a painted screen panel at Heavitree she is depicted with a sword thrust through both breasts. On an adjacent panel is St Lucy with a sword piercing her neck. At Ugborough [5.48] are two similar adjacent panels.

2 In Norfolk glass as at Wighton and Cley-next-the-Sea she is represented holding a fleshhook. This is an unusual attribute and peculiar to this county.

3 Sometimes she is represented with a flowing veil as she is in glass in Winchester Cathedral.

5.54 *St Ambrose* Ashton

5.55 *St Anthony of Egypt* Ashton

5.56 *St Anthony and his pig* Westhall

St Agnes

The son of a Roman prefect sought to win St Agnes in marriage by gifts of jewels and precious stones. When she refused to marry him because she was a Christian she was stripped naked but 'the hairs of her head became so long that they covered all her body to her feet'. She survived an attempt to burn her but was martyred by stabbing. She is depicted holding a sword or with a sword driven into her neck. Because of the etymology of her name the lamb became her attribute.

REPRESENTATIONS

1 With long hair holding a lamb as on the painted screen panel at Plymtree [5.49], and in glass at Fairford.
2 As on the painted screen at Westhall [5.50] where a sword is in her throat and a lamb jumps up at her feet. Similarly at Eye [5.51], where her long tresses reach almost to her feet.

St Alban

St Alban, the first Christian martyr in England, was a Roman who, after his conversion, refused to offer sacrifice to pagan gods. Because of his refusal he was beheaded where the town of St Albans now stands. The eyes of his executioner are reputed to have fallen out. His attributes are a tall cross or a sword.

REPRESENTATIONS

1 Holding a cross and a sword on a brass in St Albans Abbey, and in glass at Wintringham.
2 On his mutilated shrine in St Albans Abbey [5.52] his martyrdom is depicted.
3 At Norwich, St Peter Mancroft, in glass he holds a sceptre and wears a coronet.

St Alexis

After spending seventeen years as a pilgrim in the East, St Alexis returned to Rome to his father's house where he obtained work as a servant. Here he was despised and ill-treated by the other servants and was forced to live under the stairs. He bore this with humility and was steadfast in prayer and fasting. After his death a voice from Heaven pronounced his sanctity. On the painted screen at Torbryan [5.53] he is carrying a ladder which refers to his abode in his father's house under the stairs.

St Alkelda

Little is known about St Alkelda; she is reputed to have been a Saxon princess who was strangled by the Danes.

Two churches are dedicated to her in Yorkshire, and it is recorded that at Middleham she was depicted in a fragment of glass. She has a towel round her neck and her stranglers are represented by two female heads.

St Alphege

St Alphege was Archbishop of Canterbury during the reign of Ethelred the Unready. When the city was attacked by the Danes he was captured and held to ransom at Greenwich. He refused to allow the Church to pay his ransom and was stoned to death by his captors.

REPRESENTATIONS

1 St Alphege is depicted in glass in Canterbury Cathedral. His capture is shown in two roundels. In the first the city is being attacked, and in the second armed knights are taking the saint aboard a ship.
2 In glass in the chapel of New College, Oxford he wears a white alb and chasuble and at Malvern he is depicted in mitre and cope without any distinctive attribute.

St Ambrose

St Ambrose, Bishop of Milan, gained a reputation as a scholar and administrator. He is one of the four Western Doctors of the Church. His attributes are a beehive, because a swarm of bees settled on his face when he was a baby, and a scourge because of the penance he gave to the Emperor Theodosius.

REPRESENTATIONS

1 St Ambrose is depicted in glass in the chapel of All Souls College, Oxford, where, vested as a bishop, he reads from a book held by an angel, and at Fairford, where he holds a pastoral staff.
2 On the painted screen at Ashton [5.54] he holds a crozier and a book.
3 In the chapel of Henry VII, Westminster Abbey, is a figure of him as a bishop holding an open book and a scourge.
(See also *The Church: Western Doctors*)

St Anastasia

St Anastasia was a Roman lady who was imprisoned by her pagan husband, Publius, because of friendliness towards the persecuted Christians, whom she visited in prison. While herself imprisoned, she was miraculously fed. When still adamant in her Christian faith she was burned to death.

REPRESENTATIONS

St Anastasia is depicted in glass in the chapel of All Souls College, Oxford. 'St Anastasia is not distinguished by any emblem, but she holds a book in her covered right hand and a pomander, or possibly a reliquary, hangs from her girdle. If it is a pomander, it may be intended to indicate her being a great lady.' (*Medieval Glass at All Souls College,*

FE Hutchinson.) She is also found depicted in glass at Torbryan, Devon and in Wells Cathedral.

St Anthony of Egypt

St Anthony of Egypt, son of wealthy parents, embraced poverty at eighteen and retired to the desert where he spent the next twenty years in solitude, leading an ascetic life and struggling against the sins of the flesh. Later he taught a few disciples who were attracted by his holy life. When an old man, he visited St Paul the Hermit. The two old men lived together fed by a raven which brought a loaf of bread each day. When St Paul died, St Anthony returned to his former dwelling near the Nile.

St Anthony is usually considered to be the father of monasticism and is depicted in a monk's habit with a theta on the shoulder and holding a crutch. Two other attributes of St Anthony are of uncertain origin. The pig at his feet has been explained by his being patron of an order of Hospitallers who enjoyed special privileges in the keeping of pigs; by its being the emblem of gluttony; by one of the demons he overcame; and by its being his companion in the desert. The bell which he carries has been attributed to his power in the exorcism of evil spirits.

REPRESENTATIONS

1 With his attribute the pig as on a painted screen panel at Ashton [5.55], and at Westhall [5.56].

In Westminster Abbey he is found twice, in a niche in Henry VII's Chapel with pig, book, bell and T-staff, and again on a plaque in association with St George on Henry's tomb.
2 The visit of St Anthony to St Paul the Hermit is depicted on the Ruthwell Cross.
3 At Gresford [5.57] are two panels of glass. In the first is depicted St Anthony in monk's habit, from which a small pig pokes its snout. He is being received by three monks. The monastery he is about to enter can be seen in the background. On the second panel is depicted his burial. The monks are lowering his body into a coffin.

St Apollonia

St Apollonia, a deaconess in the church of Alexandria in the third century, suffered in the persecution of the Emperor Decius. She was bound to a column and her teeth were broken by blows on the jaw or were pulled out by pincers. Afterwards she cast herself on the fire prepared for her martyrdom. Her attribute is a tooth held in a pair of pincers. She was often invoked to cure toothache.

REPRESENTATIONS

Holding a tooth in a pair of pincers as on the painted screens at Kenn [5.58], Barton Turf [5.59], and Westhall [5.60]; and in glass at Norwich, St Stephen and Norton.

St Armiel (Armagilus)

St Armiel is one of the saints famous for his successful conflict with a dragon. Near Rennes, in Brittany, a dragon was laying waste the countryside. St Armiel bound it with

5.57 *St Anthony as a monk* (left); *his burial* (right)   Gresford

5.58 *St Apollonia with tooth in forceps*
Kenn

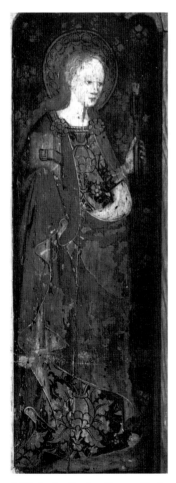

5.59 *St Apollonia*   Barton Turf

5.60 *St Apollonia*   Westhall

his stole and led it up a hill where he commanded it to plunge into the river below

REPRESENTATIONS
In Henry VII's Chapel, Westminster Abbey is a statue of him, wearing a chasuble over his armour; he leads a dragon by his stole. (*English Medieval Sculpture*, A Gardner, fig 494.) He is leading the dragon by a chain on a painted screen panel at Torbryan [**5.61**], and by his stole at Litcham.

St Augustine of Hippo
St Augustine, one of the Four Western Doctors, is famous as bishop and theologian.

REPRESENTATIONS
1 St Augustine is represented in glass in the chapel of All Souls College, Oxford. He is dressed as an Augustinian canon and holds a pen in his right hand, with his other hand resting on an open book which is supported by an eagle.
2 In glass at Fairford he is vested as a bishop and holds a staff in one hand and a heart in the other as a symbol of his zeal and devotion.
3 With the other three Doctors he occurs, in doctor's robes, on the painted screen at Ashton.

5.61 *St Armiel (Armagilus)
leading a dragon by a chain*
Torbryan

5.62 *St Barbara with her tower*
Barton Turf

5.63 *St Barbara with tower in
background* Kenn

5.64 *St Barbara holding a
miniature tower* Torbryan

ST BARBARA

St Barbara was confined in a tower by her father 'to the end
that no man should see her because of her great beauty'.
She was sought in marriage by many but refused to wed.
One day she ordered workmen to insert not two but three
windows in a fountain they were building for her father.
When he questioned her, she replied that they symbolised
the Trinity. Outraged at finding that she was a Christian
he delivered her to the authorities. In spite of torture she
adhered to her faith and was finally slain by her father
who was himself killed by lightning, 'a fire from heaven
descended on him and consumed him in such wise that
there could not be found only ashes of all his body'. She was
invoked for protection against lightning and thunderstorms.
Her attribute is a tower.

REPRESENTATIONS

With her attribute, a tower, as on a painted screen panel at
Barton Turf [5.62]; at Kenn [5.63] where she holds a book
and the tower is seen in the background; Torbryan [5.64]
where she holds a miniature tower and a book; and at Eye
[5.65] where she stands by a tower holding a palm.

ST BENEDICT

St Benedict is one of the best-known saints, mainly because,
at Monte Cassino, he drew up a rule of life for his companions which became the Benedictine Rule and was the
beginning of organised Western monasticism. Much is
made of his confrontation, during life, of the power of evil
in the form of devils which he successfully repulsed.

REPRESENTATIONS

He is usually depicted vested as an abbot holding a crozier
as on the painted screen panel at Burlingham St Andrew
[5.66].

ST BERNARD

St Bernard, the famous Cistercian monk and preacher,
is rarely found depicted in medieval art in England. He was
first abbot of Clairvaux, active in promoting the Second
Crusade, and was the author of theological works and hymns.

REPRESENTATIONS

1 A painting on a screen panel at Torbryan [5.67], of a
monk with a crozier, has been thought to represent St
Bernard.

5.65 *St Barbara stands by tower holding a palm* Eye

5.66 *St Benedict holding a crozier* Burlingham St Andrew

5.67 *St Bernard with a crozier* Torbryan

5.68 *St Blaise holding woolcomber's iron comb* Ashton

5.69 *St Bridget of Sweden, crowned abbess, writing on a scroll with dove above* Kenn

2 A poppy head of a monk with a dog at Fressingfield could be intended for St Bernard. Prior to his birth his mother 'saw in her sleep a dream which was a demonstration of things to come. Her seemed that she had in her belly a whelp, all white and red upon the back'. This was later interpreted as being a forecast of the Cistercian habit which her son was to wear.

3 Wearing a habit he is depicted in glass in the chapel of New College, Oxford.

St Birinus

St Birinus was a seventh-century missionary who worked in Wessex. In glass at Dorchester, Oxon, where he established his see, are depicted incidents from his life. He is represented in one scene saying mass, 'in his right hand a chalice and a flagon and in his left the sacred wafer'.

In a second scene he is 'obtaining authority from an enthroned archbishop'. (*Ancient Painted Glass*, P Nelson)

St Blaise

St Blaise was a bishop is Asia Minor who was martyred during the Diocletian persecutions for refusing to adore idols. He was 'torn with combs of iron' and was beheaded.

Because of the unusual instrument of torture he became the patron of the wool trade. He was invoked to cure throat diseases because, on the way to prison, he extracted a fish bone from a child's throat and because, prior to his death, he promised that all who offered a taper in his memory should be free from throat infections.

His atribute is an iron comb.

REPRESENTATIONS
1 He is usually depicted vested as a bishop and holding a woolcomber's iron comb as on the painted screen at Ashton [5.68].
2 On the restored screen at Exeter, St Mary Steps he holds a comb and what may be a repainted taper.
3 He is depicted in glass, without an attribute, in Malvern Priory and Christchurch Cathedral, Oxford.

St Blida
St Blida was the mother of St Walstan; little is known about her. At Norwich, St James on a painted screen panel is St Walstan; the crowned female figure holding a book and a palm on an adjacent panel has been identified as St Blida.

St Brannock
St Brannock is the patron saint of Braunton where on a bench end 'he is represented with a chalice in his left hand and in the base is a bullock. The latter refers to the legend of St Brannock restoring to life the animal of a poor man which had been killed and consumed by robbers.' (*Bench Ends*, JC Cox, fig 77)

St Bridget of Sweden
St Bridget was Queen of Sweden until her husband's death when she left the court and became foundress of the Brigettine Order of nuns. Her Revelations, which were widely read, had an influence on art, especially representations of the Nativity.

REPRESENTATIONS
1 She is depicted on several painted screen panels. At Kenn [5.69] she is shown as a crowned abbess writing on a scroll, above hovers the Holy Spirit in the form of a dove; at Westhall [5.70] she holds a crozier and a heavy chain hangs from her right wrist.
2 At Horsham St Faith she is seated with an open book; above, appears a vision of the Godhead.

St Catherine of Alexandria
St Catherine was one of the most popular saints in the Middle Ages and one of the most frequently represented. She was a wealthy Christian woman who lived in Alexandria. She chose a simple life and withstood the lustful advances of the emperor, Maximinus. The story of her encounter with the emperor was expanded to include many incidents. She defeated him in argument and when he 'saw that in no manner he could resist her wisdom, he sent secretly by letters for all the great grammarians and rhetoricians'.

5.70 *St Bridget of Sweden holding crozier with heavy chain hanging from her right wrist* Westhall

5.71 *St Catherine of Alexandria crowned, with sword* Ashton

5.72 *St Catherine of Alexandria with long sword, a miniature wheel at the tip* Eye

When she was confronted with them 'they were all abashed and wist not what to say, but were all still'. She was tortured by being tied to 'four wheels of iron, environed with sharp razors'. Finally she was beheaded and it was said her body was transferred to Mount Sinai by angels.

5.73

5.74

5.75

5.76

5.73 to **5.76** *St Catherine of Alexandria:
Story of the saint from her encounter with
Maximinus to her martyrdom and burial*
Lydiate

5.77 *St Catherine of Siena wearing a crown of thorns and holding a heart* Torbryan

5.78 *St Catherine of Siena holding a heart and a book* East Portlemouth

5.79 *St Cecilia with wreaths of flowers* North Elmham

REPRESENTATIONS

1 On the painted screen at Ashton [5.71] she is crowned and holds a sword; at Eye [5.72] she holds a long sword at the tip of which is a miniature wheel.

2 In the Roman Catholic church at Lydiate [5.73, 5.74, 5.75, 5.76] is a series of alabasters which depict the story of the saint from her encounter with Maximinus and the philosophers to her martyrdom and burial. The relationship between these and the Miracle Plays is discussed in *Drama and Imagery*, MD Anderson.

St Catherine of Siena

St Catherine was a fourteenth-century ascetic and mystic who had great influence on Church and State. She advised the leaders of her day and after her death the Dominican Order was reformed according to her counsel.

She is represented on the painted screen at Torbryan [5.77] as a mystic wearing a crown of thorns and holding a heart; at East Portlemouth [5.78] she holds a heart and a book. At Horsham St Faith she holds a flaming heart.

St Cecilia

St Cecilia was the daughter of Christian Roman parents. She was married to Valerian with whom, by mutual consent, she did not consummate the marriage. An angel, it is said, brought a garland of flowers for her and her husband. When she refused to sacrifice to Jupiter she was placed in a burning bath. An attempt was made to behead her; after three strokes she was left half alive. She lingered for three days. Due to a mistaken reading of her Acts she was represented with an organ and became the patron saint of musicians. Her attribute is a garland of flowers.

REPRESENTATIONS

1 With a chaplet of flowers as on a painted screen panel at Yaxley. At North Elmham [5.79] she is wearing a wreath of flowers on her head and holds a second wreath in her hand.

2 At Eye [5.80] on a painted screen panel, a figure of a female saint may be intended for St Cecilia. A sword is thrust through her neck which could be a reference to her form of martyrdom.

3 At Holne [5.81] on the screen she is playing on a stringed instrument. The panel appears to have been over-painted and this could be a later interpretation.

4 Among the small figures of saints in the tracery lights at Wrangle is St Cecilia holding a portable organ.

5.80 *St Cecilia with sword through her neck* Eye

5.81 *St Cecilia playing a stringed instrument* Holne

5.82 *St Christina holding an arrow and trampling on a pagan* Kenn

5.83 *St Christina holding a millstone* Alphington

ST CHRISTINA

St Christina was a noble maiden of whom little is known apart from the many tortures she endured for refusing to sacrifice to idols. She was accused of witchcraft and her tongue was cut out. When attempts to burn and to drown her had failed, she was shot by an arrow.

Her attributes are an arrow and a millstone.

On a painted screen panel at Kenn [5.82] she holds an arrow and tramples on a pagan, and at Alphington [5.83] she holds a millstone.

ST CHRISTOPHER

St Christopher, of whom little is known, enjoyed great popularity. Because of the belief that those who looked at St Christopher should not suffer sudden death that day, most churches had a statue or painting of him, usually placed opposite the south door.

He is reputed to have been a giant who wished to serve the greatest king in the world. On the advice of a hermit he lived on the bank of a dangerous river near a ford and helped travellers across. One day, a child he was carrying became heavier and heavier so that only with difficulty did he reach the other side, where the Child revealed Himself as Christ who was bearing the sins of the world.

St Christopher is usually depicted as a giant holding his ragged staff, sometimes miraculously bearing leaves, and carrying the Child on his shoulder.

5.85 *St Clare — an abbess holding a monstrance* Trimingham

5.86 *St Clement robed as a pope carrying an anchor* Ashton

5.84 *St Christopher — his temptation in prison* Norwich Cathedral

REPRESENTATIONS
1 At Little Missenden is a typical wall painting of him.
2 In the Chapel of Henry VII, Westminster Abbey, is a figure of him with his staff but the hand of the Child is lost.
3 In glass at Malvern Priory he wears a turban (perhaps indicating an Eastern origin of the story) and carries the Child who blesses with His right hand and holds an orb in His left. He rarely appears on a boss but one is in the cloisters of Norwich Cathedral.
4 One of the best examples on a painted screen is at Bradninch. (See 'St Adrian', [5.45])
5 On a boss in the cloisters of Norwich Cathedral [5.84] is depicted the lesser-known story of his temptation in prison. King Dagnus, hoping to make him sacrifice to the gods, tempted him when in prison by sending two women to the prison. The subsequent episode in the story is the one shown. When the attempt had failed and the women had been converted, St Christopher was brought before the king who, holding a large sword, sits on a throne before which two men hold the saint. One of the women is seen in a doorway.

ST CLARE
St Clare is one of the Franciscan saints. Due to the influence of the Order and of St Francis himself, she adopted a life of poverty and founded the Order of Poor Clares. When confronted by the Saracens at her nunnery she saved it by appearing with a monstrance.

REPRESENTATIONS
On a painted screen panel at Trimingham [5.85] she is depicted as an abbess holding a monstrance.

ST CLEMENT
St Clement was an early pope celebrated for his writings. He was banished to the Crimea by order of the Emperor Trajan. Here he and his followers suffered from thirst. A lamb led St Clement to a spot which he struck and water gushed forth. His enemies, enraged by the miracle, tied an anchor round his neck and threw him into the sea. The waters of the Black Sea parted revealing to his followers the saint's body in a marble shrine not made by mortal hands.

He is depicted as a pope with an anchor as an attribute.

REPRESENTATIONS
1 Robed as a pope carrying an anchor as on the painted screens at Ashton [5.86], and Westhall [5.87].
2 The miracle of the finding of water is depicted on a boss in the cloisters of Norwich Cathedral [5.88]. In the centre of the boss is a lamb perched on a rock around which is a group of figures.
3 His martyrdom is the subject of a boss in Chester Cathedral

5.87 *St Clement robed as a pope carrying an anchor* Westhall

5.88 *St Clement* Norwich Cathedral

5.89 *St Clement with anchor round his neck being thrown from a boat* Norwich Cathedral

5.90 *St Cornelius holding horn and cross* East Portlemouth

5.91 *St Cosmas holding pestle and mortar* Wolborough

5.92 *St Damian holding a glass phial* Wolborough

5.93 *St Cuthbert in the act of blessing* Lydiate

5.94 *St Denis – his martyrdom and miraculous journey* Norwich Cathedral

and in the cloisters of Norwich Cathedral [5.89], where St Clement, with a papal crown on his head and an anchor round his neck, is being thrown from a small boat by two men.

ST CORNELIUS

St Cornelius was pope in the third century when there was a rival pope. His attribute is a horn, derived from his name.

He is represented on the painted screen at East Portlemouth [5.90] where, wearing the papal crown, he holds a horn and a cross.

ST COSMAS AND ST DAMIAN

The two Arabian saints are usually considered together as they worked together as physicians healing both men and animals without payment. 'They were learned in the art of medicine and leechcraft, and received so great grace of God that they healed all maladies and languors, not only of men but also cured and healed beasts.'

They are said to have been beheaded for refusing to sacrifice to idols. They are rarely found depicted but each is found on the painted screen at Wolborough [5.91, 5.92]. St Cosmas is holding what may be a pestle and mortar and St Damian is holding up a glass phial.

ST CUTHBERT

St Cuthbert was a shepherd when he had a vision of angels bearing St Aidan's soul to Heaven. He joined the monks at Melrose and spent his life teaching and preaching, often taking long difficult journeys. In 644 he was made Prior of Lindisfarne but after twelve years he retired to Farne Island where he lived a life of solitude and extreme asceticism until 685 when he was made Bishop of Lindisfarne. He was only bishop for two years before returning to Farne Island where

he died. No distinctive attribute is given to him.

REPRESENTATIONS

1 In the Chapel of Henry VII, Westminster Abbey, there is a statue of him crowned and bearing a sceptre and supporting the crowned head of St Oswald in his hand. This form of representation arose because when his body was transferred to Durham, the head of St Oswald was included in the coffin.
2 The life of St Cuthbert is recorded in glass in York Minster. The scenes include his boyhood with St Columba, his conversion, his life of teaching and miracles, and his death. (A full description is given in *The Painted Glass of York*, F Harrison)
3 In the Roman Catholic church at Lydiate [5.93] there is an alabaster figure of him as a bishop in the act of blessing.
4 On the stalls of Carlisle Cathedral are seventeen painted panels on which are recorded incidents from his life.

ST DENIS

St Denis was identified with Dionysius of Athens who was 'converted to the faith of Jesus Christ by Saint Paul the Apostle'. He was first Bishop of Paris and patron saint of France. He was beheaded for refusing to sacrifice to idols. After his decapitation he was reputed to have walked, carrying his head, from Montmartre to St Denis, where he was buried. He is depicted as a headless bishop bearing his head in his hands.

REPRESENTATIONS

1 On a painted screen panel at Hempstead he is depicted as a vested bishop with crozier holding his mitred head. In the Chapel of Henry VII, Westminster Abbey, there is a figure of him holding his mitred head in his hands. (*English*

5.95 *St Dominic – half figure*
East Portlemouth

5.96 *St Dorothy with basket of flowers and holding a palm* Ashton

5.97 *St Dorothy with flowers and palm* Eye

Medieval Sculpture, A Gardner, fig 470)
2 His martyrdom and subsequent miraculous journey are the subject of a boss in the cloisters of Norwich Cathedral [5.94]. On the left-hand side an executioner is about to strike off the head of St Denis who kneels in prayer. On the right the saint, holding his severed head, approaches a church at the door of which awaits a cleric to receive him.

St Dominic

St Dominic, the founder of the Dominican Order of Black Friars and one of the outstanding figures of medieval christendom, is almost unknown in English art. He is included in the saints recorded on the beautiful painted reredos at Thornham Parva with St Peter Martyr who was a member of the Dominican Order.

A half figure of him appears on a painted screen panel at East Portlemouth [5.95].

St Dorothy

St Dorothy was a highborn maiden of Caesarea known for her beauty and humility. During the Diocletian persecutions she proclaimed herself a Christian and refused an offer of marriage from the prefect Fabricius. She was tortured and when she referred to the fruits and flowers of paradise a jesting notary, Theophilus, said: 'I pray thee to send me some of thy roses and apples ... and she granted to him his desire.' After her martyrdom by beheading, an angel appeared to Theophilus with a basket of roses and apples saying it was a gift sent by St Dorothy from paradise. He was converted and in turn suffered martyrdom. A basket of flowers is her attribute.

REPRESENTATIONS

She is frequently depicted on painted screen panels, displaying a basket of flowers and holding the palm of martyrdom, as at Ashton [5.96], Eye [5.97], and at Westhall [5.98]. A figure of her with a basket on her arm and holding

5.98 *St Dorothy* Westhall

5.99 *St Dunstan* (top right)
Cockayne Hatley

a book is in the Chapel of Henry VII, Westminster Abbey.

ST DUNSTAN

St Dunstan was Abbot of Glastonbury, Bishop of Worcester and later Archbishop of Canterbury. He was both scholar and administrator and throughout his life he showed a reforming spirit and combatted the laxity of the tenth century. He was also skilled as a metalworker. When he was making a chalice, the Devil appeared to him in the form of a woman. 'He supposed that she was a wicked spirit, and anon caught her by the nose with a pair of tongs of iron, burning hot, and then the devil began to roar and cry and fast drew away but Saint Dunstan held fast.'

Because of the popularity of this story a pair of tongs or a pair of pincers became his attribute.

REPRESENTATIONS

1 He is depicted in glass at Ludlow where, in mitre and chasuble, he holds a cross and a pair of pincers. At Malvern Priory, in a choir clerestory window, he is similarly vested but is without the pincers attribute. In the Chapel of Henry VII, Westminster Abbey, is a figure of him as a bishop, holding a crozier in one hand and a demon in a pair of pincers with the other.

2 At Canterbury Cathedral, in medallions of glass, are recorded episodes from his life. These include:

  (a) The release of King Edwy from Hell.
    St Dunstan is stretching his hands to the crowned king amidst the flames and demons in Hell's mouth.
  (b) St Dunstan's vision of Christ.
    The saint lies in bed asleep and Christ appears between two angels.
  (c) The conflict with the Devil at Glastonbury.
    St Dunstan kneels before an altar in the locked church which he had entered through the roof assisted by an angel. Outside, the Devil retreats confronted by an angel.
  (d) The miraculous escape at Calne.

5.100 *St Edmund holding an arrow*
Barton Turf

5.102 *St Edmund: the finding and guarding of the head*   Norwich Cathedral

5.101 *St Edmund*
Wiggenhall St Mary

During an argument the floor of an upper room collapsed. St Dunstan remained safe but his opponents were cast to the ground. He bends down to assist one of them.

A figure of St Dunstan in glass is in Cockayne Hatley [5.99].

St Eanswyth

St Eanswyth was a seventh-century princess who founded a nunnery at Folkestone. Her attribute is a fish.

In the British Museum is an ivory figure of her standing on a fish. She occurs as an abbess, with a crozier flanked by two fishes, on the seal of Folkestone.

St Edmund

St Edmund, King of East Anglia in the ninth century, was defeated and captured by the Danes. When he refused to renounce the Christian faith, he was bound to a tree and wounded with arrows. Finally he was beheaded. His head was cast aside but was recovered; it retained its ability to cry out. When found, it was guarded by a wolf which reverently followed it to its burial before returning to the woods. The king's attribute became an arrow.

REPRESENTATIONS

1 Holding an arrow as on the painted screen at Barton Turf [5.100], where crowned and robed he holds an arrow and a sceptre; and possibly on a bench end at Wiggenhall St Mary [5.101].

2 The martyrdom of St Edmund is shown on two bosses

5.103 *The crowned King Edmund flanked by archers*   Norton

5.104 *King Edmund guarded by a wolf*
Walpole St Peter

in the cloisters of Norwich Cathedral. On one the king is on one side of the boss, a man with bow and arrows on the other, and a wolf is in the foreground. On the other boss the king is bound to a tree and pierced with an arrow, and three men with bows confront him.

3 The finding and guarding of his head is shown on a third boss at Norwich [5.102], where a wolf guards the head between its forelegs. One man is about to pick it up; two others are spectators.

On a misericord at Norton [5.103] the crowned king is flanked by diminutive archers carrying bows. Each supporting subject is an archer who directs an arrow towards the saint.

At Walpole St Peter [5.104] on an elbow rest a wolf is guarding the crowned head of a king. There is a similar elbow rest at Hadleigh.

ST EDWARD THE CONFESSOR

St Edward is best remembered for his piety and devotion rather than for his statesmanship. 'For this holy king Edward was ever full of meekness and virtue, and never lifted up by vainglory.' The best-known story of his piety is the giving of his ring to a beggar who asked for alms. Later the beggar appeared to two pilgrims in Palestine, and gave them the king's ring saying that he was St John the Evangelist. He told them to return to St Edward and say that in six months time the king would die. His attribute is a ring.

REPRESENTATIONS

1 He appears on a number of painted screen panels holding a ring as at Plymtree [5.105], Eye [5.106], and at Barton Turf [5.107].

The story of St Edward's ring is recorded in glass at Ludlow where the pilgrims have become members of the Ludlow Palmers Guild. The main episodes depicted are:
    (a) The king's gift of a ring to a beggar.
    (b) St John's appearance to the palmers.

5.105 *St Edward the Confessor* Plymtree

5.106 *St Edward the Confessor*
Eye

5.107 *St Edward the Confessor*
Barton Turf

(c) The return of the ring to the king.

(d) The granting of a charter to the palmers.

(e) The palmers' return to Ludlow and the ensuing feast.

2 Of his abbey at Westminster it was said: 'and he did do cast down the old work, and did do build it up new, and endowed that monastery worshipfully with livelihood and jewels.' In the abbey are representations of him and records of episodes of his life, the chief of which are:

(a) In the Chapel of Henry VII a figure of him, crowned, holding a sceptre in his left hand and a ring in his right hand.

(b) In the same chapel a bronze plaque on which St Edward, holding a ring, is associated with St Vincent.

(c) In the chapter house is a tile on which are St Edward and the pilgrim.

(d) On the east side of the screen of the high altar is a series of carvings depicting scenes from his life:

   (i) The oath of fealty to Edward's mother. Ethelred and Parliament decided that Edward, not yet born, should succeed him. 'A general oath was made to perform the same in time coming.'

   (ii) The birth of St Edward.

   (iii) The coronation.

   (iv) The danegelt.

Under pressure from his counsellors St Edward raised money as danegelt but he 'saw the devil in the likeness of an ape, sitting upon the treasure' so he ordered its return to the people.

(v) The thief warned to escape.

When the king was sick a clerk entered his room and stole money. When he returned a second time, the king warned him against the wrath of the treasurer and advised him to flee.

(vi) The appearance of Christ to St Edward.

During mass at the consecration Christ appeared to St Edward and 'blessed the king with his right hand'.

(vii) The vision of the King of Denmark's shipwreck.

During mass the king laughed and afterwards explained that he had seen the King of Denmark, who was preparing an invasion of England, fall into the sea and drown.

(viii) The quarrel of Harold and Tostig.

The king saw a friendly game between the two turn into a fight and saw this as foreshadowing their future enmity.

(ix) The vision of the Seven Sleepers of Ephesus.
On Easter Day St Edward saw the Seven Sleepers of Ephesus turn in their sleep from the right side to the left side.

(x) The giving of his ring.

(xi) The healing of a blind man.
Reluctantly, the king allowed a blind man to bathe his eyes in the water which he had used to wash his hands and the man's sight was restored.

(xii) St John's return of the ring to the two pilgrims.

(xiii) The pilgrims' return of the ring to the king.

(xiv) The dedication of Westminster Abbey by St Peter.
St Peter appeared to a fisherman and told him he had consecrated the abbey and that he was to tell this to the Bishop of London. The bishop refused to believe this but on entering the church he saw signs and tokens of its recent consecration. (*Royal Commission*, plates 42 and 43)

3 In the cloisters of Norwich Cathedral [5.108] is a boss, the subject of which is the Vision of St Edward during mass. A priest is saying mass at an altar on which is a chalice and an open book. One server is holding a book and another a candle and crozier; above the latter is a sanctus bell. The king, crowned, kneels at a prayer desk and raises his hands and head. An angel hovers above.

4 On a second boss [5.109] is depicted the birth of St Edward. A crowned queen lies on a bed at the foot of which is a woman to whom a crowned king (Ethelred) is talking. Another woman holds a child (St Edward) to which the Divine Hand points from amongst the clouds. Under the bed is a monk gazing at a snake.

St Edward (King and Martyr)

St Edward was King of Wessex in the tenth century. His stepmother, Elfrida, who wanted the throne for her own son, enticed her brother to murder him at Corfe Castle. The king was offered a goblet of wine and whilst drinking he was stabbed with a dagger.

His attributes are a goblet and a dagger.

REPRESENTATIONS

1 At Westminster Abbey in the Chapel of Henry VII is a figure of St Edward. It is mutilated so that no attribute is recognisable.

2 On the west front of Wells Cathedral is a figure of him holding a goblet and standing on Queen Elfrida.

3 In glass in the chapel of All Souls College, Oxford is a figure of a king entitled *Edwardus Martir* but there is no distinguishing attribute.

Edward II

Edward was proclaimed a saint by popular consent because of the miracles performed at his tomb, but he was never officially canonised.

REPRESENTATIONS

1 In Worcester Cathedral is a figure of him holding a spit.

5.108 *Vision of St Edward the Confessor* Norwich Cathedral

5.109 *Birth of St Edward the Confessor* Norwich Cathedral

5.111 *St Elizabeth of Hungary* Torbryan

5.112 *St Elizabeth of Hungary with crippled boy* Bury St Edmunds Museum

5.110 *St Elizabeth of Hungary* Barnham Broom

2 He is depicted on the painted screen at Strensham.

3 In the north transept of Bristol Cathedral are two bosses depicting a king 'one is completely naked except for his crown, the other partially so; I have no hesitation in ascribing these to Edward II in his death agony; in one boss the king is actually pointing with his finger to the exact spot where was inserted the red hot iron which killed him'. (*Roof Bosses*, CJP Cave, fig 29)

St Egwin

St Egwin was a seventh-century bishop of Worcester. To atone for his sins he went on a pilgrimage to Rome with his legs locked in fetters. He threw the key into the river. He found the key in the entrails of a fish; this he took to be a sign of his forgiveness and he returned to his see at Worcester. A chain and fetterlock is his attribute.

REPRESENTATIONS

In a much mutilated window at Little Malvern his attribute is still discernible but little else remains.

St Elizabeth of Hungary

St Elizabeth, a king's daughter, found no satisfaction in court life, so she devoted herself to prayer and acts of charity. 'She entended with all her power to the seven acts of mercy.' One day her husband uncovered a basket of food which she was taking to the poor and miraculously found only roses in the basket.

She is usually depicted wearing a crown and her attributes are a cup, a loaf, or roses.

REPRESENTATIONS

1 On a painted screen panel at Barnham Broom [5.110] she holds a covered cup and some loaves; at Fulbourn she is carrying a loaf and a basket. A female saint holding a large vessel in front of her at Upton could be intended to represent St Elizabeth.

2 It has been suggested that a female saint, holding a crown in both hands, on the painted screen at Torbryan [5.111] is St Elizabeth but identification is uncertain.

3 In glass at Ludlow she is crowned and holds a sceptre in one hand and a rose in the other.

4 A panel of glass at Norwich, St Peter Mancroft, depicting a saint distributing loaves marked with a cross to a crowd of beggars, may represent an episode from her life.

5 A statue in wood in Bury St Edmunds Museum [5.112] shows her holding a crown on a book, with a crippled boy clutching at her robes.

5.113 *St Eloy (Eligius) shown as a bishop with a hammer* (right); *St Leonard* (left)   Hempstead

5.114 *St Erasmus (Elmo) holding a windlass* Ashton

ST ELOY (ELIGIUS)

St Eloy was a goldsmith of Limoges who later became Bishop of Noyon, renowned for his charitable works. He is reputed to have cut off a horse's leg before shoeing the hoof and then, when the operation was completed, to have replaced the leg.

His attributes are a horseshoe and a hammer.

REPRESENTATIONS

1 In Westminster Abbey in Henry VII's Chapel is a figure of him as a mitred bishop, holding a large horseshoe.

2 He is depicted, as a bishop holding a hammer, on painted screen panels in Norfolk at Potter Heigham, Hempstead [5.113] and Tunstead. A boss at Ugborough showing a man shoeing a horse may refer to St Eloy. A wall painting at Slapton depicts a bishop, vested and holding a crozier with one hand and the leg of a horse with the other.

ST ERASMUS (ELMO)

St Erasmus is said to have been a bishop in Italy who was martyred by Maximian. He was the patron saint of sailors and his figure holding a windlass and rope often stood on the prow of ships. This may have given rise to the story that he suffered martyrdom by having his bowels drawn out by a windlass. A windlass is his attribute.

REPRESENTATIONS

1 On a painted screen panel at Ashton [5.114] and at Hennock he holds a windlass, as he does in glass at Sandringham. In the Chapel of Henry VII, Westminster Abbey, is a figure of him as a mitred bishop reading from a book and holding a windlass.

2 At Lullingstone his martyrdom is depicted in a panel of glass now much weathered. A group of men are gathered round St Erasmus who is lying on his back on the ground. A windlass protrudes from his abdomen.

5.117 *St Eustace kneeling before a stag carrying a crucifix in its horns* Norwich Cathedral

5.115 *St Etheldreda crowned* Blythburgh

5.116 *King Anna (adjacent to* [**5.115**]*) said to be father of St Etheldreda* Blythburgh

St Etheldreda

St Etheldreda, a Saxon princess, was one of the daughters of King Anna. She left the court of her husband and became the foundress and abbess of the restored church at Ely, where she died in AD 679. She was famed for her ascetic life, and miracles were wrought by her uncorrupted body which attracted large numbers of pilgrims to Ely.

She is usually depicted as a crowned abbess.

REPRESENTATIONS

1 She appears on several painted screen panels in Norfolk as at Barnham Broom and Horsham, St Faith, where she is depicted as an abbess holding a crozier. A crowned figure of her occurs on a desk front at Blythburgh [**5.115**], and a figure of a man holding an orb on an adjacent panel [**5.116**] is said to be her father, King Anna.
2 On the capitals of the piers of the lantern of Ely Cathedral are carved incidents from her life. (*English Medieval Sculpture*, A Gardner, fig 374)

St Eustace

St Eustace, a Roman, was converted by the vision of a crucifix in the horns of a stag which he was hunting. He was baptised and many stories were told of the hardships which befell him, his wife and sons. Finally he and his family were martyred for refusing to sacrifice to idols.

His attribute is a stag with a crucifix in its horns.

REPRESENTATIONS

1 The Vision of St Eustace is recorded on a boss in the cloisters of Norwich Cathedral [**5.117**]. The saint is kneeling before a stag carrying a crucifix in its horns; with him are huntsmen and dogs.
2 On the front of Wells Cathedral is a figure of St Eustace carrying a son in each arm. This refers to one of his hardships. One day reaching a river he found he could not cross with both his children. He left one on the bank and carried one across to the other side. When he returned he found a wolf had made off with the one he had left behind and on crossing the river a second time he found a lion had carried off the one he had taken across.

St Faith

St Faith was a thirteenth-century martyr who suffered by fire. She is said to have been stretched on an iron bedstead and roasted. Her attributes are a gridiron and a saw.

5.118 *St Faith holding fire in her hand* Horsham, St Faith

5.119 *St Francis as a deacon, holding a book with crucifix on cover* Torbryan

5.120 *St Francis* (right) *standing before a crucifix* Bradninch

REPRESENTATIONS

1 On a mural painting in Westminster Abbey and on a brass in Norwich, St Lawrence, she is depicted holding a gridiron.

2 In glass at Norwich, St Peter Mancroft, on the painted screen panel at Marsham, and on the painted pulpit panel at Horsham, St Faith, she holds a saw.

3 A second figure on the screen at Horsham [5.118] of a female saint holding fire in her hand could be St Faith, the fire being a reference to her form of martyrdom.

ST FRANCIS

So much has been written about St Francis, and so great is his popularity, that probably more is known about him by people today than any other medieval saint.

REPRESENTATIONS

1 On the painted screen at Hempstead is a figure of St Francis in a grey habit with his pierced hands uplifted; a cross staff rests against his shoulder. On the screen at Alphington he displays the stigmata in his hands and the wound in his side.

A figure of a deacon holding a book with a crucifix on

the cover on the screen at Torbryan [5.119] is a doubtful representation of St Francis.

2 **Preaching to the birds** A wall painting at Wiston shows St Francis, tonsured, in a habit and holding a cross, preaching to six birds of different kinds lodged in a tree. A companion sits reading near at hand.

In a splay of a window at Little Kimble is a similar wall painting but most of the saint has disappeared.

3 **Receiving the stigmata** A wall painting at Slapton shows the saint kneeling with hands raised before a crucifix from which emanates streams of blood.

An armless figure of St Francis and part of an angel's wing are all that remain of a wall painting at Doddington. On the painted screen at Bradninch [5.120] the saint with upraised hands stands before a crucifix to receive the stigmata. Two companions are with him. At Kenn he displays the wounds with the crucifix behind him.

At Norwich, St Peter Mancroft, is a much restored panel of glass in which little of the original subject remains.

ST FRIDESWIDE

St Frideswide refused to marry Algar of Mercia and retired to Binsey. Later she became abbess of a nunnery at Oxford.

5.121 *St George, St Agnes, St Hubert and St Genesius dressed as a clown(?)* Combeinteignhead

5.122 *St Genevieve holding a book and taper being lit by an angel* Kenn

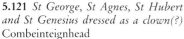
5.123 *St George in conflict with a dragon* Boston

5.124 *St George and the dragon* Beverley, St Mary

After her death her shrine in the abbey church became a place of pilgrimage. Because of her association with Oxford her attribute became an ox.

She is represented in glass in the Latin Chapel of Christ Church Cathedral, Oxford, as an abbess with crozier and book.

ST GENESIUS

St Genesius was an actor who was converted whilst clowning at a baptism service. He was subsequently martyred by beheading.

On a bench end in Combeinteignhead [5.121] are four figures: St George, St Agnes, St Hubert, and a man in the traditional garb of a clown which may be intended to represent St Genesius.

ST GENEVIEVE

St Genevieve is the patron saint of Paris. Under the influence of St German she lead a life of poverty and austerity, devoting her time to charitable works. She was believed to have been a shepherdess. Many miracles are associated with her name and she is reputed to have, by her prayers, lighted a candle and to have kept it burning in a wind.

On a painted screen panel at Kenn [5.122] she holds a

book and a taper which is being lighted by an angel, having been blown out by a hovering devil.

At Horsham St Faith is a much defaced screen panel of a saint whose attributes are difficult to see. It has been suggested that this represents St Genevieve.

ST GEORGE

According to legend, St George was a knight who was born in Cappadocia. The story of his rescue of a princess from a dragon is well known. She was about to be sacrificed to the dragon in order to save the city when St George arrived. Seeing her plight he said: 'I will help thee in the name of Jesu Christ.' He mounted his horse, made the sign of the cross, and pierced the dragon with his spear. Then he took the maid's girdle and bound it round the neck of the subdued beast which was led away and slain. The king and his people were baptised. During the Diocletian persecution St George was beheaded. He became patron saint of England as a result of his successful invocation during the wars against the French.

He is usually depicted in conflict with a dragon but as other saints are depicted in this way, his identification is not always certain.

5.125 *St George slaying the dragon with princess in background* Stratford-upon-Avon

5.126 *St George flourishing his sword* Ranworth

REPRESENTATIONS

1 He is in conflict with a dragon on misericords at Boston [**5.123**], Beverley, St Mary [**5.124**], and at Stratford-upon-Avon [**5.125**], where St George is slaying the dragon in the traditional way and the princess is praying in the background. On a painted screen panel at Ranworth [**5.126**] he is flourishing his sword. On the grille in the Chapel of Henry VII, Westminster Abbey, is a figure of him in plate armour trampling on a dragon.

2 St Mercurius of the legend of St Basil and the Emperor Julian became St George in English iconography. (See 'St Mary the Virgin: Legends of the Virgin'; see also 'St James the Greater')

St Gertrude

St Gertrude was the daughter of Pepin, an official in the court of Dagobert, a Frankish king. She refused to marry and retired to a double monastery at Nivelles, which her mother had founded. Eventually she became abbess and earned a reputation for piety and learning. She was a patron saint of travellers and was invoked against the pestilence of rats and mice.

Her attribute became mice.

She is depicted as an abbess on a painted panel on the screen at Hennock [**5.127**] where three mice are seen climbing up her crozier.

St Giles

St Giles, who became the first abbot of the Benedictine abbey at St Gilles (Provence), formerly lived a solitary life in a forest with a hind as companion. One day the hind was pursued by the king and his hunting party 'when she was sore constrained she fled for succour to the feet of Saint Giles, whom she nourished'. St Giles was wounded by an arrow intended for the hind. He was lamed and as a result he became the patron saint of cripples. The hind became his attribute.

REPRESENTATIONS

1 On a misericord in Ely Cathedral [**5.128**] St Giles, in the forest, has been hit by an arrow. He is protecting his hind from the huntsmen who are shown with their bows in the supporters.

2 In a niche in the Chapel of Henry VII, Westminster Abbey, is a figure of him mitred and holding a crozier, with the hind leaping up at him.

3 The story is told on two bosses in the cloisters of Norwich Cathedral. On the first [**5.129**] St Giles gives protection to the hind from the king, crowned and mounted on a horse, and his followers. On the second, the king surrounded by his followers prostrates himself before the saint.

5.127 *St Gertrude with three mice climbing her crozier* (right); *Sir John Schorn* (left) Hennock

5.128 *St Giles in a forest, hit by an arrow* Ely

5.129 *St Giles gives protection from the king to the hind* Norwich Cathedral

5.130 *St Govan suffering from sea sickness* St David's Cathedral

5.131 *St Gregory as a pope wearing a triple crown* St Neot

St Govan

'At St David's a misericord [5.130] is said to represent the sea-sickness of St Govan, uncle of St David, who was sent with two disciples to Rome by St Elfynt to obtain a correct form of the mass.' (*Misericords*, Francis Bond)

St Gregory

St Gregory was a pope known for his administrative ability and for his scholarship. 'He made and compiled many fair books, of which the church is greatly illumined.' He is one of the four Doctors of the Western Church. His encounter with the slave boys in the market place at Rome, and his sending of St Augustine to England are well known. Representations of the Gregory Mass recall the story that he withdrew the sacrament from a doubting woman and that, when he said mass, the Crucified Christ appeared as a witness of faith.

5.132 *St Gregory – the Mass* Paignton

5.133 *The Gregory Mass – note the Emblems of the Passion* Exeter Cathedral

REPRESENTATIONS

1 He is depicted in glass as a pope, wearing a triple crown in the chapel of All Souls College, Oxford, at Fairford and at St Neot [5.131].

2 **The Gregory Mass** An early example in stone is at Stoke Charity. A half-length figure of Christ, displaying the wound in His side, appears above the altar at which St Gregory stands, the Host in his hand.

At Paignton [5.132] is a later type; the Emblems of the Passion are prominent. The figure of Christ (now much broken) stood on the altar. St Gregory, attended by two cardinals, kneels in adoration.

In the mutilated example in Exeter Cathedral [5.133] the emblems are again prominent. On the painted screen at Wyverstone, Suffolk the saint kneels at the altar and Christ rises from an open tomb.

(See also 'The Church: Western Doctors')

ST GUDULE

St Gudule is patron saint of Brussels to where her relics were transferred when she died in AD 712. In her lifetime she was known for her devotion and piety. It is said that when the devil blew out her lantern an angel rekindled it.

At Walpole St Peter a painted screen panel of a female saint has been interpreted as being St Gudule; but it is difficult to be certain that her attribute is a lantern.

ST GUTHLAC

St Guthlac left the monastery at Repton and lived as a hermit in the Fens of Lincolnshire at Crowland. During a life of solitude and extreme asceticism he suffered temptations and was tormented by demons. After his death in the desolate region of swamps the Abbey of Crowland was established.

A sculpture in Crowland Abbey shows St Guthlac, a whip in his hand and a serpent at his feet. (*Saints and their Emblems*, M and W Drake)

5.134 *St Helen, the finding of the true Cross*   Morley

ST HELEN

St Helen was the mother of the Emperor Constantine, who converted her to Christianity. In her old age she made a pilgrimage to the Holy Land where, according to medieval tradition, she found the true Cross. This tradition became a popular subject with medieval artists. There was also an English tradition that she was the daughter of Old King Cole. Her attribute is a cross.

REPRESENTATIONS
1 A figure of St Helen wearing a crown, and holding a book which rests on a tau cross, is in the Chapel of Henry VII, Westminster Abbey.

2 In glass at Morley [5.134] are depicted ten incidents from the story of the finding of the true Cross; although the window has been restored the whole follows medieval tradition.

The incidents depicted are:
(a) The making of the Cross.
(b) Christ is nailed to the Cross.
(c) The Cross is buried.
(d) St Helen perceives where the Cross is buried.
(e) The finding of the Cross.
(f) The power of the Cross is tested by a dead body.
(g) Chosroes, who had removed the Cross, is beheaded because he refuses to become a Christian.
(h) The son of Chosroes is baptised.
(i) Heraclius, when he wishes to re-enter Jerusalem, finds the city gate walled up.
(j) The exaltation of the Cross.

3 At Ashton-under-Lyne, in glass, in four windows are recorded episodes in the life of St Helen which can be summarised as follows:
[5.135]
(a) The birth of St Helen. The inscription gives credence to the legend that she was the daughter of Old King Cole.
(b) The education of St Helen.
(c) A visit to a prison by St Helen.
   In the three panels is depicted the conversion of St Helen [5.136].

5.135 *(a) The birth of St Helen; (b) Goes to convent school; (c) Visits prisoners* Ashton-under-Lyne

5.136 *The conversion of St Helen* Ashton-under-Lyne

5.137 *(a) The betrothal of Helen and Constantius; (b) The marriage; (c) The birth of Constantine* Ashton-under-Lyne

5.138 *(a) Finding the true Cross; (b) and (c) The revival of the corpse by the true Cross* Ashton-under-Lyne

[5.137]
(a) The betrothal of St Helen and Constantius.
(b) The marriage.
(c) The birth of Constantine.

[5.138]
(a) The finding of the true Cross.
(b,c) The revival of a corpse by the true Cross.

5.139 *(a) The battle between Constantine and Maxentius; (b) The baptism of Constantine; (c) The council of Nicea*
Ashton-under-Lyne

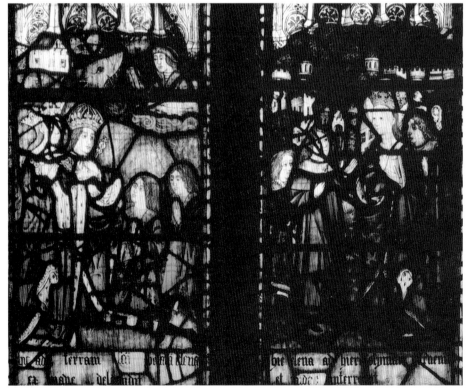

5.140 *(a) The arrival of Helen in the Holy Land; (b) The interrogation of Judas*
Ashton-under-Lyne

[5.139]
(a) The battle between Constantine and Maxentius.
(b) The baptism of Constantine.
(c) The Council of Nicea.

[5.140]
(a) The arrival of St Helen in the Holy Land.
(b) The interrogation of Judas.
The building of a church by St Helen **[5.141]**.

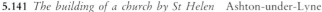

5.141 *The building of a church by St Helen*   Ashton-under-Lyne

5.142 *King Henry VI*   Barton Turf

HENRY VI

King Henry VI was never canonised as a saint although Henry VII did approach Rome with a view to obtaining formal canonisation but found it too expensive. He was venerated as a saint, and so great was the popular cult that his statue was venerated in York Minster and pilgrimages were made to his tomb at Windsor.

He is represented on several East Anglian painted screens such as at Barton Turf [**5.142**] and Eye [**5.143**].

ST HONORIUS

St Honorius was a Roman who became fifth Archbishop of Canterbury in AD 628. He supported the missionary efforts to the North and East Anglia. He was patron saint of bakers and the baker's peel became his attribute. He is represented in glass in York Minster and on the painted screen at Wolborough [**5.144**] where he holds an open book and a baker's shovel. Mr CE Keyser says of this representation: 'it is more probably intended for St Aubert, a bishop of Cambrai in the seventh century, who is thus represented with a baker's peel in a window of Ghent Cathedral, but who is not recorded elsewhere in England.'

5.143 *King Henry VI*
Eye

5.144 *St Honorius holding an open book and a baker's shovel* Wolborough

5.145 *St Hubert before a stag with a crucifix in its horns* Litcham

5.146 *St Hugh (headless figure) with a swan* Fressingfield

5.147 *St Jeron (Hieron)* Litcham

ST HUBERT

The account of St Hubert's conversion, by being confronted with a stag with a crucifix set in its horns, is so similar to that of St Eustace, and representations of the two saints are so similar, that it is not possible to differentiate between them. After his conversion he became Bishop of Liege. On a painted screen panel at Litcham [5.145] a huntsman clutching a bow kneels before a stag with a crucifix in its horns. This could be either St Hubert or St Eustace; other similar examples occur.

ST HUGH

St Hugh, a Carthusian monk, became Bishop of Lincoln in 1186. For fourteen years he worked in the diocese and was renowned for his staunch support of the Church against the Crown and his humility and devotion in his daily life. A swan is his attribute for one was said to have been his constant companion when he was at the palace at Stow.

REPRESENTATIONS

1 A headless figure with a swan on a bench end at Fressingfield [5.146] may be intended to represent St Hugh.
2 He occurs with his swan on the spire of Oxford, St Mary.
3 In glass in a north transept window of Lincoln Cathedral is depicted the 'translation of the relics of St Hugh which are carried upon the shoulders of three kings and three bishops'. (*Ancient Glass*, P Nelson)

ST IGNATIUS OF ANTIOCH

St Ignatius was Bishop of Antioch. He was identified with the child who Christ 'set in the midst of the disciples'. He clashed with the authorities and was arrested. Then began his journey to Rome during which he wrote seven letters to the churches emphasising the need for bishops in order to combat heresy. Throughout the journey he showed personal calm and courage. Few, if any, medieval representations of him are to be found but he is depicted in seventeenth-century glass in the chapel of Magdalen College, Oxford, where, with a lion at his side, he regards a crucifix.

ST JEROME

St Jerome, one of the four Western Doctors of the Church, was educated from an early age. 'He being yet a child, went to Rome and was there taught in letters of Greek, Latin and Hebrew.' After a period in the desert he devoted his life to scholarship. He is best known for his biblical translations, especially the translation of the Old Testament from Hebrew into Latin. A lion was his companion. 'A lion came halting suddenly in the monastery and when the brethren saw him, anon they fled, and Jerome came against him as he should come against his guest, and then the lion showed to him his foot being hurt.' St Jerome 'examined and healed him, and he abode ever after as a tame beast with them'.

His attributes are an inkhorn and a lion.

Although never a cardinal he is usually depicted wearing a cardinal's hat.

REPRESENTATIONS
In the chapel of Henry VII, Westminster Abbey, is a figure of him wearing a cardinal's hat and holding a book. A diminutive lion is at his side. (See also 'The Church: Western Doctors')

ST JERON (HIERON)
St Jeron worked in Holland as a missionary in the ninth century. He was martyred by the Danes.

He is depicted wearing armour covered by a robe or vestment. His attribute is a falcon. He is found on a painted screen panel in several East Anglian churches as at Trimingham and Litcham [5.147], but most are in poor condition.

ST JOANNA OF VALOIS
St Joanna was the daughter of Louis XI and the wife of Louis XII. When her marriage was declared void she accepted this and retired to a life of charity and contemplation. Later she founded an order of nuns.

At Upton, Norfolk a figure of a female saint holding a basket and large cup has been said to represent St Joanna, but this is doubtful and is more likely to be St Elizabeth of Hungary.

ST JOHN OF BEVERLEY
St John of Beverley, who ordained the Venerable Bede at Whitby Abbey, became Bishop of Hexham and Archbishop of York. He founded the monastery at Beverley where, after his death in AD 721, his shrine became a centre of pilgrimages.

REPRESENTATIONS
1 He is depicted in glass as an archbishop without any distinctive attribute as in York Minster.
2 In Beverley, St Mary, on a boss St John and King Athelstan appear side by side. (*Roof Bosses*, CJP Cave, fig 19)

ST JOHN OF DAMASCUS
St John of Damascus is represented in a mural painting in Winchester Cathedral, 'on the right John lays his head on the block, turning his face away; an executioner raises his axe, two attendants and a turbaned judge are seen. On the left the crowned Virgin and John kneeling to her.' (Walpole Society, vol. XVII, MR James and EW Tristram)

ST JOSEPH OF ARIMATHEA
To the New Testament account of St Joseph's laying the body of Christ in the sepulchre he had prepared for himself, was added the legend of his bringing the Holy Grail to Glastonbury and of his staff breaking into blossom when thrust into the ground.

At Plymtree on a defaced panel of the screen may be a representation of St Joseph holding a napkin.

At Langport in glass St Joseph is seen holding two cruets; these, legend says, contained the sweat and blood of Christ. The window at Ludlow in which St Joseph holds a blossoming thorn and a vase of ointment is probably a nineteenth-century addition.

5.148 *St Julian the Hospitaller with his oar* Wolborough

(See also 'The New Testament: The Descent from the Cross')

ST JULIAN THE HOSPITALLER
St Julian by accident became a parricide. At his wife's request, his parents, who had made a journey searching for him, occupied their bed. St Julian, thinking he had found his wife in the act of adultery, murdered them. In remorse, as an act of penance, he became a hermit and devoted the remainder of his life to ferrying travellers across a ford.

His attribute is an oar.

He is represented on the painted screen at Wolborough [5.148].

ST JULIANA OF NICOMEDIA
St Juliana was cast into prison because she refused to marry the Governor who was not a Christian. The Devil tempted her in the guise of an angel but she resisted the temptations. Finally she was tortured and beheaded. Her attribute is the Devil in chains.

REPRESENTATIONS
1 On a painted screen panel at North Elmham [5.149] Juliana holds the Devil captive by a chain.
2 At Hempstead she is threatening the Devil, whom she is leading, with an uplifted birch.

5.149 *St Juliana of Nicomedia holding the Devil captive* North Elmham

5.150 *St Lawrence in a dalmatic with a gridiron* Ranworth

5.151 *St Lawrence with a gridiron* Torbryan

St Justina of Padua

St Justina was a virgin saint who suffered under Emperor Diocletian. A Benedictine abbey is dedicated to her at Padua.

At Heavitree on a painted screen panel is depicted a female saint with a sword through both breasts. She may be either St Justina or St Agatha. (See 'St Agatha')

St Kenelm

St Kenelm was a Mercian king who was murdered by his jealous sister Quendreda, who wished to be queen. When she failed in an attempt to poison him, Askeberd, a member of the court, at her instigation enticed the king to Clent Wood where he 'smote off this holy young king's head'. His body was taken to Winchcombe Abbey. Quendreda was reading the psalter and as the body entered the town her eyes fell from their sockets.

REPRESENTATIONS

1 On the west front of Wells Cathedral is a figure of him standing on his sister.
2 He is depicted in glass at Norwich, St Peter Mancroft, wearing a blue robe and holding a sword.

St Lawrence

St Lawrence, a deacon, was in charge of the church treasure in Rome when Pope Sixtus was seized and killed by order of the Emperor Valerian. The prefect instructed St Lawrence to hand over the church treasure. When he was commanded to produce the treasure he replied that he would in three days time. After three days he showed the poor of the city to the prefect, saying they were the treasure of the Church. In his turn he was seized and put in prison. He was martyred by being roasted on a gridiron over a slow fire. He is depicted as a deacon vested in a dalmatic and has a gridiron for an attribute.

REPRESENTATIONS

1 Vested in a dalmatic holding a gridiron as on the painted screens at Somerleyton, Ranworth [5.150], and Torbryan [5.151].
2 His martyrdom is the subject of a boss in the cloisters of Norwich Cathedral [5.152]. Before a judge seated on a throne is the saint, naked and tied to a gridiron. The gridiron is suspended over a fire which two servants are attending.
3 In glass at Ludlow is recorded his death and incidents from his life. The window consists of twenty-seven panels which are described in *Ludlow Stained and Painted Glass* (EW Ganderton and J Laford).

5.153 *St Leger as a mitred bishop holding an auger* Ashton

5.154 *St Leger* Wolborough

5.152 *Martyrdom of St Lawrence naked and tied to a gridiron* Norwich Cathedral

St Leger

St Leger was bishop of Autun in the seventh century. He aroused the enmity of the royal officer, Ebroin, for political reasons, hence the city of Autun was beseiged. St Leger, after defending the city, ransomed the lives of the inhabitants by offering up himself. He was imprisoned, tortured, blinded by having his eyes bored out with an auger, and finally he was beheaded.

Miracles occurred at his tomb in Poitiers.

His attribute is an auger.

REPRESENTATIONS

1 He occurs on the painted screen at Ashton [5.153] and at Wolborough [5.154], where as a mitred bishop he is holding an auger.
2 He is found depicted in glass at Malvern Priory and at Wiggenhall St Mary.

St Leonard

St Leonard was a member of the court of King Clovis from whom he obtained permission to release any prisoner he visited in prison. 'This Leonard got so much grace of the king, that all the prisoners that he visited were anon delivered.' In later life he became Abbot of Noblac. He became patron saint of prisoners for it was said: 'who that was in prison and called his name in aid, anon his bonds and fetters were broken.' His attribute is fetters or a chain.

REPRESENTATIONS

1 On a bench end at Wiggenhall St Mary [5.155] he is tonsured and holds a book and fetters as he does in glass at Sandringham.
2 On the painted screen at Westhall [5.156] he holds a chain and book in the left hand and a crozier with the right hand. In glass at St Neot [5.157] he is depicted as a mitred abbot holding a crozier and has a chain on his right wrist.

St Longinus

In the Gospel accounts of the Crucifixion, neither the soldier who pierced the side of Christ, nor the centurion who proclaimed 'truly this man was the Son of God' is mentioned by name. To each was assigned the name Longinus and he is included in the list of saints but is rarely depicted as a single figure.

In glass at Norwich, St Peter Mancroft, he holds a spear in one hand and points to his closed eye with the other. This is a reference to the legend that he was blind and that his sight was restored by the blood from the side of Christ.

St Louis of France

Louis IX, King of France, was canonised because of his personal piety and support of the Church throughout his long reign. His attributes are a cross, a crown of thorns, or three nails because of his devotion to the Passion of Christ. Reputed representations of St Louis, on painted screen panels, are questionable. The one at Suffield, sometimes said to be St Louis, has also been ascribed to St

5.155 *St Leonard, tonsured, holding a book and fetters*
Wiggenhall St Mary

5.156 *St Leonard holding a book and a chain and carrying a crozier*
Westhall

5.157 *St Leonard as a mitred abbot holding a crozier with a chain on his right wrist*
St Neot

Longinus and to St Jeron. Likewise the one at Gateley, Norfolk, has also been ascribed to St Louis and to St Gregory.

St Lucy

St Lucy is one of the saints who was martyred during the Diocletian persecutions. A rejected suitor denounced her to the authorities as a Christian when she broke off her engagement to marry and devoted her life to alms-giving. When she was brought before the governor, Paschasius, she refused to offer sacrifice to idols and persisted in her faith. She was ordered to be taken away but the soldiers could not move her; she had become so heavy that, even when she was bound with ropes, a yoke of oxen could not drag her away.

It was said that one of her suitors was so bewitched by her eyes that she plucked them out. This story, and the one that her eyes were miraculously restored after being gouged out by her persecutors, may have been suggested by the similarity of her name, Lucy, to light. Another miraculous story told of her is that, after a sword was thrust through her neck, she continued to proclaim her faith and to exhort others.

She was invoked by those with eye trouble. Her attributes are a sword thrust through her neck and her eyes resting on a dish or a book.

REPRESENTATIONS

1 As a martyr as on the painted screen at Eye **[5.158]** where she holds a sword and a book on which her eyes are placed.
2 Her appearance before Paschasius is shown on a mutilated boss in the cloisters of Norwich Cathedral. Two men are pulling at a rope which is attached to the saint. On the left is Paschasius and on the right a group of soldiers.
3 The subject of another boss, situated near to the former, may be the refusal of St Lucy to sacrifice to idols. An altar on which rests an idol is flanked by a crowned figure and St Lucy(?) who rests a hand on the altar.
4 At Heavitree **[5.159]** on a painted screen panel St Lucy is depicted with a sword thrust through her neck. On an adjacent panel is St Agatha with a sword thrust through both breasts. This pair of saints are similarly depicted on adjacent panels at Ugborough. (See 'St Agatha' **[5.48]**)

5.158 *St Lucy holding a sword and a book*
Eye

5.159 *St Lucy with sword through her neck*
Heavitree

5.160 *St Luke wearing a doctor's cap*
Blythburgh

ST LUKE

St Luke was the companion of St Paul and the writer of the third Gospel which bears his name, and of the *Acts of the Apostles*. St Paul refers to him as the 'beloved physician' and the *Golden Legend* says he was 'by art of medicine'. He was said to have had recourse to St Mary for information. It was also said that he 'was certified of her many things and especially such things as appertained to her'.

The winged ox, his emblem, was sometimes used as an attribute on the rare occasions he was depicted.

REPRESENTATIONS

1 Wearing a doctor's cap and holding a book as on the desk front at Blythburgh [5.160].
2 On the painted screen panel at Bramfield he 'carries the pen with which he has written the opening words of the story of the Annunciation' (*Screenwork in the County of Suffolk*, WW Lillie). See also 'The Church: Emblems of the Evangelists'.

ST MARGARET OF ANTIOCH

Little is known of St Margaret but she was frequently depicted in medieval art and many churches are dedicated to her. She was invited by Olybrius, the governor, to become his wife but when he discovered she was a Christian and she refused to renounce her faith, she was committed to prison. During her imprisonment she was confronted by a dragon which disappeared when she made the sign of the Cross. A variation of the story was that she was first swallowed by the dragon, which later was the cause of her being invoked by women in childbirth.

She is usually depicted holding a long cross which sometimes she is thrusting into the mouth of a dragon.

REPRESENTATIONS

1 Crowned and holding a long cross which she thrusts at a dragon, as on the painted screen at Westhall, Suffolk and in a niche in the Chapel of Henry VII, Westminster Abbey.
2 In a spandrel in the east aisle of the north transept of Westminster Abbey is a carving of her, in which, with hands clasped, she appears to be issuing out of a dragon. She is similarly represented in a wall painting in Eton College Chapel.
3 In glass at North Tuddenham, Norfolk, are depicted two episodes from her life. In one panel she is seen spinning as she watches her father's sheep. The servant of Olybrius

5.161 *St Mark* (left) *holding a scroll* Bramfield

5.162 *St Martin dividing his cloak and giving half to a beggar* Fornham St Martin

is commanding her to accompany him to his master. In a second panel she is seen confronting the governor in his palace.

4 Several incidents from her story are recorded in glass at Combs, Suffolk.

   (a) St Margaret is tending her sheep.

   (b) She is brought before Olybrius.

   (c) She is thrown into prison through a portcullised gateway.

   (d) In prison she is swallowed by a dragon, but emerges safely and birches the beast.

   (e) She is about to step into a cauldron of oil or pitch.

St Mark

St Mark is the author of the second Gospel, which bears his name. Little is known of him apart from his journey with Paul and Barnabas to Cyprus, where he left them, and his companionship with St Peter in Rome. 'When St Peter preached there the gospel, the good people of Rome prayed St Mark that he would put the gospel in writing, like as St Peter had preached.' It is said that he became Bishop of Alexandria where he was persecuted; he was led through the city with a rope about his neck as a result of which cruelty he died.

He is depicted in glass and on painted screen panels together with the other evangelists when each may have his emblem as an attribute. On the screen at Bramfield [5.161] he holds a scroll.

St Martha

St Martha, the sister of Mary and Lazarus, rarely occurs as a single figure in English medieval art and the story of her journey to, and work in, Marseilles did not become a subject of the artist.

REPRESENTATIONS

1 St Martha occurs in glass in the chapel of New College, Oxford, where she has no distinctive attribute.

2 She is depicted in a wall painting in Eton College Chapel 'with palm branch and girdle attached to the neck of a dragon which is at her feet. I suppose the dragon to be the Tarasque which St Martha banished from the neighbourhood of Tarascon. But I do not see why St Martha here carries a palm the proper attribute of martyrs. This makes the identification not quite clear.' (Walpole Society, vol XVII, MR James and EW Tristram)

St Martin

St Martin began life as a soldier. One day during a bitter winter in Amiens, whilst out riding, he met a naked beggar; moved with compassion he divided his cloak in half with his sword and gave half to the beggar. The same night in a vision he saw Christ wearing half a cloak. As a result of this experience he was baptised and later became Bishop of Tours. Many stories are told of his charity, humility, and ascetic life. His attribute is a naked beggar for whom he halves his cloak. Sometimes he is vested as a bishop, sometimes he wears mail. Occasionally three geese are seen at his feet. These refer to his scolding the geese for the mischief they did; also at his feast geese were killed and eaten.

REPRESENTATIONS

1 Dividing his cloak and giving half to a beggar as on a misericord at Fornham, St Martin [5.162].

2 In the Chapel of Henry VII, Westminster Abbey, there

5.163 *St Mary Cleopas with her four children* Ranworth

5.164 *St Mary of Egypt holding three loaves and a book* Kenn

5.165 *St Mary Magdalene holding an ointment pot* Wiggenhall St Mary

is a statue of him in armour over which he wears half a cloak and holds a mitre.

3 In glass at York, St Martin, his life is recorded. Amongst the incidents depicted are the division of his cloak, his consecration, his raising to life a young girl, and his death.

There may have been some confusion between St Martin of Tours and St Martin of Rome, a seventh-century pope with whom geese were also associated.

ST MARY CLEOPAS

St Mary Cleopas, the wife of Alphaeus, was reputed to be the daughter of St Anne and her second husband, Cleopas. (See 'St Mary the Virgin: The Holy Kindred'.) She was the mother of SS James the Less, Simon, Jude and Joseph Justus.

On the painted screen at Ranworth [5.163] she is depicted with her four children. The poor condition of the panel makes it uncertain what attributes they are holding. A

similar panel, also in poor condition, occurs on the screen at Houghton, St Giles. Here James holds a club, Simon a fish, Jude a boat and Justus a palm. In glass in the chapel of All Souls College, Oxford, where she is similarly represented, the boy Simon holds a saw and Jude a boat.

In glass at Hesset one of the children is holding three loaves, perhaps in order to replace Joseph Justus by Philip to comply with the *Pseudo Gospel of Matthew*.

ST MARY OF EGYPT

St Mary of Egypt, a prostitute in Alexandria, joined a pilgrimage to Jerusalem with unworthy motives. She was prevented by a mysterious power from entering the Church of the Holy Sepulchre and was converted. She entered the desert beyond Jordan where she lived in solitude and penitence, on three loaves that she took with her, dates, berries and wild herbs. She stayed there seventeen years until she was found by a monk, Zosimus. She received the

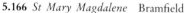

5.166 *St Mary Magdalene* Bramfield

5.167 *St Mary Salome with her sons James and John* Houghton St Giles

5.168 *St Maurus as an abbot holding an open book and a crozier* Wolborough

sacrament with great devotion and requested him to return in a year. When Zosimus returned he found her dead. He tried to bury her body but his strength failed; a lion appeared and helped to dig her grave.

St Mary of Egypt appears on a painted screen at Kenn [5.164] enveloped in her own long hair, holding three loaves and a book, and in glass without distinctive attribute in New College, Oxford.

St Mary Magdalene

According to the Gospels, St Mary Magdalene was healed by Jesus, was present at the Crucifixion, and was an early witness of the Resurrection. She was confounded with Mary of Bethany, sister of Lazarus, and with the woman 'who was a sinner'. Legend relates that she travelled with Lazarus to Marseilles. She is depicted with flowing hair and holds a pot of ointment as an attribute.

REPRESENTATIONS
1 With long hair and holding an ointment pot as in the Chapel of Henry VII, Westminster Abbey (Royal Commission, fig 124); in glass as at Oxford in the chapels of New College and All Souls College; and on a bench end at Wiggenhall St Mary [5.165].
2 This saint is depicted on several painted screens. One of the best preserved is at Bramfield [5.166].

St Mary Salome

St Mary Salome was the mother of James and John, the sons of Zebedee. She was present at the Crucifixion and was one of the women who visited the Sepulchre. Together with Mary Cleopas and Mary Magdalene she is said to have visited Spain.

St Mary Salome is represented with her two sons on the painted screen panels at Ranworth and Houghton St Giles [5.167] where James has a staff and wallet and John holds a cup.

St Maurus

St Maurus, founder of the monastery of Glanfeuil, when

5.170 *St Michael the Archangel in conflict with a dragon*   Moreton Valence

5.169 *St Meubred as a hermit holding his head*   St Neot

5.171 *St Michael the Archangel* Gloucester Cathedral

commanded by St Benedict, walked on the water and saved the life of St Placidus. He is represented as an abbot holding an open book and a crozier on the painted screen at Wolborough [5.168].

ST MEUBRED

G McN Rushforth says that a figure of a hermit, holding his head, in glass at St Neot [5.169] represents St Meubred and that he is patron saint of Cardingham church, near Bodmin.

ST MICHAEL THE ARCHANGEL

St Michael, the great archangel, leader of the spiritual forces of good against the powers of Satan and darkness, caught the imagination of men from the beginning of the Christian era. At an early date he appears in Christian art and occupies a prominent place until the end of the Middle Ages. He is represented in two roles: the winged archangel in conflict with a dragon, symbolising the power of Good contending with Satanic forces; and in the drama of the Last Judgment he holds the scales of justice in which souls are weighed.

REPRESENTATIONS
St Michael and the dragon are found from the earliest times and in most media.
1 At Moreton Valence [5.170], in the Norman tympanum of the north door, St Michael, bearded and wearing a long robe, is in conflict with a dragon.
2 He is frequently found on misericords as at Gloucester Cathedral [5.171], and winged and feathered at Carlisle Cathedral [5.172], and on painted screen panels as at Ashton and Ranworth [5.173]. He would, in all probability, have formed part of all Doom paintings and in some that survive he is still discernible with the scales weighing souls, as at South Leigh and at Wenhaston [5.174]. In the Angel Quire of Lincoln Cathedral, with outstretched wings and holding his scales, he has his place. Similarly the episode is carved in the spandrel of the wall arcading in Worcester Cathedral.

5.172 *St Michael the Archangel winged and feathered* Carlisle Cathedral

5.173 *St Michael the Archangel* Ranworth

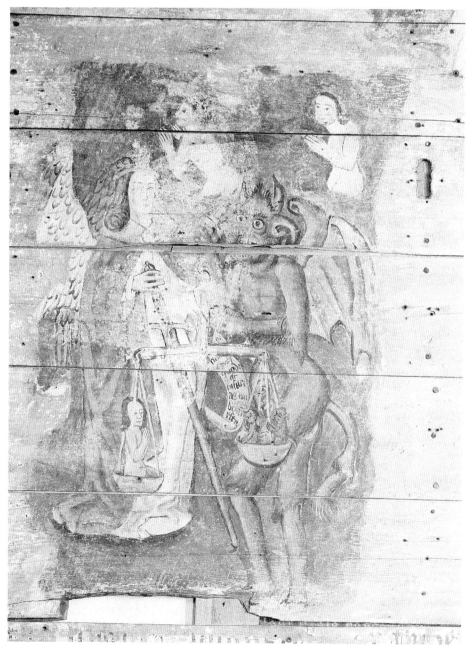

5.174 *St Michael the Archangel with scales weighing souls* Wenhaston

5.175 *St Michael the Archangel clad in armour and bearing a shield* Westhall

5.176 *St Neot, his life (together with* [5.177]) St Neot

5.177 *St Neot (see* [5.176]) St Neot

On a plaque in the Chapel of Henry VII, Westminster Abbey, St Michael holding a pair of scales tramples on a dragon.

3 On the painted screen at Westhall [5.175] the saint is clad in armour and bears a shield.

ST NEOT

G McN Rushforth considers that there were two saints called Neot. There was a Saxon prince who became a monk at Glastonbury in the time of St Dunstan and who later settled at St Neots, Cambridgeshire, where he was buried, and an earlier British or Celtic saint who lived as a hermit in Cornwall at St Neot. He considers that the incidents recorded in glass at St Neot [5.176, 5.177] are taken from

the lives of the two saints and he interprets them as follows, reading across the lights:

(a) St Neot abdicates and gives the crown to his brother.
(b) St Dunstan clothes him in Benedictine habit and he becomes a monk at Glastonbury.
(c) St Neot protects a doe.
(d) An angel shows him three fishes in a well and tells him he may eat one every day leaving the other two, and next day he will find three there.
(e) Lying in bed he tells his servant Bariusc (St Barry) to bring him one of the fish.
(f) Bariusc takes two fishes and fries one on a gridiron and boils the other.
(g) He brings the fishes to St Neot.

5.178 *St Neot as a Benedictine monk*
St Neot

5.179 *St Nicholas presenting dowries for the nobleman's three daughters*
Winchester Cathedral

5.180 *St Nicholas restoring three children in a pickling tub and saving storm-tossed sailors*
Winchester Cathedral

(h) He throws back the two cooked fishes which are restored to life.

(i) A robber steals St Neot's oxen.

(j) Stags come and offer to take the yoke. Two of his men are ploughing with them.

(k) The robber repents and returns the oxen.

(l) St Neot visits Rome and is blessed by the pope.

Incidents a, b and l relate to the Saxon saint and the remainder to his Cornish namesake. In another window at St Neot [5.178] the saint is shown as a Benedictine monk holding an abbot's crozier.

ST NICHOLAS

St Nicholas was bishop of Myra in Asia Minor. His outstanding charity was emphasised and a number of spectacular miracles were accredited to him, some of which were depicted. He became the patron saint of children, sailors and pawnbrokers because of relevant miracles. He is usually depicted as a vested bishop and his attribute is three gold balls or children in a tub.

REPRESENTATIONS

1 A figure of him mitred and holding a boy in a basket is in the Chapel of Henry VII, Westminster Abbey.

2 **Presenting three bags of gold** This story typifies his charity for he sought 'how he might distribute his riches, and not to the praising of the world but to the honour and glory of God'. He presented three bags of gold to an impoverished nobleman to buy dowries for his three daughters and save them from a life of shame. On three occasions he threw a mass of gold wrapped in a cloth into the house. This story is the origin of the pawnbroker's sign. It is illustrated on the Romanesque font in Winchester Cathedral [5.179].

3 **Restoration of three children in a tub** During a famine

5.181 *St Nicholas saving sailors*   Norwich Cathedral

5.182 *St Nicholas as a boy and a bishop*   Norwich Cathedral

an innkeeper put three children into his pickling tub. They were discovered by St Nicholas who, making the sign of the Cross over them, restored them to life. This story has been thought to have arisen through the misreading of an illustration of St Nicholas officiating at a font where he would be shown as a larger figure than the candidates for baptism. This miracle is also depicted on the Winchester font [5.180]. At Lincoln Cathedral in glass, three children are lying in bed near which are a man with an upraised axe and a woman with a candle.

4 **Saving of storm-tossed sailors**   Answering the prayers of storm-tossed sailors, the bishop appeared with them in their boat and brought them to safety. This episode is also recorded on the font at Winchester Cathedral [5.180], in glass in Malvern Priory, and on a boss in the cloisters of Norwich Cathedral [5.181].

5 **His baptism and consecration**   He appears as boy and bishop on a boss in the cloisters of Norwich Cathedral [5.182]. As a boy he emerges from a font by the side of which a woman kneels. As a mitred bishop, in a cope and holding a crozier, he is flanked by two other bishops. This may be a reference to his baptism and consecration.

6 **The destructive vase of oil**   The story is that the Devil or, according to another account, Diana goddess of Myra, in the guise of a nun, offered to the sailors of a ship, transporting pilgrims, a vase containing not holy oils but destructive oils intended to destroy the Church. St Nicholas appeared and ordered that the vase should be thrown into the sea, where it caught fire. On the font at Brighton, St

Nicholas, is a panel depicting this story. The sailors are in a boat at one end of which the nun is standing on the water and St Nicholas, a mitred bishop with crozier, appears at the other end.

St Ninian

St Ninian was a fifth-century missionary amongst the Picts. He built a stone church at Whithorn which he dedicated to St Martin of Tours. His attribute is a chain.

REPRESENTATION

In Winchester Cathedral in Prince Arthur's Chapel is a figure of St Ninian where, vested as a bishop, he holds a crozier and carries a chain over his right wrist, as he does on a painted panel of the screen at Fowlis Easter.

St Olave

St Olave, King of Norway in the second century, suppressed paganism with the sword. His latinised name was Holofius. By punning on his name, Holofius became 'whole loaf' so loaves of bread became one of his attributes and another was a battle axe.

He is presented as a crowned king, holding loaves in one hand and a battle axe in the other, on the painted screen at Barton Turf [5.183].

5.183 *St Olave holding loaves and a battle axe* Barton Turf

5.184 *St Paul holding a sword* Blythburgh

5.185 *St Paul with his sword* Ranworth

ST OSWALD

St Oswald was Christian King of Northumbria AD 634–642. He was considered a martyr because he was killed in battle against the pagan king, Penda of Mercia. He was a friend of St Aidan and was much influenced by him. One day after dining with St Aidan, when he heard of the poor outside, he ordered his silver dish to be broken and given to them. St Aidan exclaimed 'May this hand never wax old'. After St Oswald's death it was said that his hand was incorruptible and it was kept in Peterborough Cathedral.

St Oswald's head was placed in the coffin of St Cuthbert hence the latter is sometimes depicted holding the king's head. The attribute of St Oswald is a dish.

REPRESENTATIONS

1 On the west front of Wells Cathedral is a figure of him crowned and holding a dish in his left hand.

2 A crowned figure of St Oswald, holding a book and a sceptre, is on a painted screen panel at Horsham, St Faith.

An alternative St Oswald, a Benedictine monk who founded Ramsey Abbey and later became Bishop of Worcester and Archbishop of York, is depicted in glass in Malvern Priory as a bishop in the act of blessing but without a distinctive attribute.

ST OSYTH

St Osyth was a seventh-century saint of royal birth, a Mercian princess. She ran away from her husband whom she had been forced to marry. She took the veil. She was martyred by the sword when the nunnery which she had founded at Chick was sacked by the Danes.

She is depicted in glass at Long Melford holding her severed head in her hands. Her head is crowned and covered with a black veil.

ST PANCRAS

St Pancras suffered martyrdom at the instigation of the Emperor Diocletian when only fourteen years old.

He is rarely represented but at Cowfold is a brass showing him as a youth holding a palm and a book and trampling on a diminutive Saracen who holds a sword.

ST PAUL

In addition to the account of St Paul's teaching and missionary work recorded in the *Acts of the Apostles* there was the tradition of his visit to Spain and his martyrdom by beheading in Rome.

In art and in the dedication of churches he is associated with St Peter. His attribute is the sword.

5.186 *St Paul the Hermit with a raven* Wolborough

5.187 *St Peter Martyr with a sword in his skull* Hennock

5.188 *St Peter Martyr carrying a sword and a book* East Portlemouth

REPRESENTATIONS

1 Holding a sword as on the desk front at Blythburgh [5.184], and on a painted screen at Ranworth [5.185].

2 In association with St Peter as on a tympanum at Siddington and a wall painting at Clayton, where Christ gives the keys to St Peter and the Book of the Law to St Paul.

3 In the British Museum is an alabaster table depicting the beheading of St Paul. The executioner, holding a sword, stands above the body of St Paul from which his head has been severed. 'In front of the executioner is a small kneeling female figure, St Plantilla, who holds in her hands the veil she has provided for binding the eyes of the saint, whilst behind the headsman stand two guards bearing halberds. In the upper right hand corner is the crowned bearded figure of the emperor Nero ...' (*Archaeological Journal*, vol 74, P Nelson)

St Paul the Hermit

St Paul of Thebes spent his life as a hermit in the Egyptian desert, where he was said to have been fed by a raven which brought him half a loaf a day. He was visited by St Anthony, which meeting is recorded on the Ruthwell Cross.

On the painted screen at Wolborough [5.186] he is represented with a raven as his attribute.

St Peter Martyr

St Peter Martyr was a Dominican friar who worked as inquisitor in Northern Italy during the thirteenth century. Heretics contrived his death by splitting his head open with an axe and stabbing him in the heart. His attribute is a sword or axe lodged in the head.

He is depicted with a sword in his skull on a painted screen panel at Hennock [5.187], and at East Portlemouth [5.188] where he carries a sword and a book.

St Petronilla

St Petronilla is a hazy figure, her name suggested that she was the daughter of St Peter and legend grew up to support this. As a result of her supposed relationship with St Peter her attribute became a key. Representations of her and of St Sitha are difficult to distinguish, unless named, as both share the same attributes: a key or keys and a book.

St Petronilla, holding a key and a book, is depicted on a painted screen panel at Trimingham and at North Elmham.

At North Elmham, St Sitha is represented also; both are named.

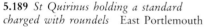

5.189 *St Quirinus holding a standard charged with roundels* East Portlemouth

5.190 *St Robert of Knaresborough, his life story (together with* [5.191]) Morley

ST QUIRINUS

St Quirinus was a tribune of Rome. He suffered martyrdom under Claudius. On a painted screen panel at East Portlemouth [5.189] he is depicted holding a standard which is charged with roundels.

ST REMEGIUS

St Remegius was Bishop of Rheims. He enjoyed the support of the queen but not of her husband, Clovis. After winning a battle, in fulfilment of a promise, King Clovis presented himself to the bishop for baptism. The cruets had not been prepared but a dove flew down carrying a vessel of holy oil.

At Dunston St Remegius is depicted in glass as a named figure. The kneeling figure before him may be King Clovis or a donor.

ST ROBERT OF KNARESBOROUGH

St Robert became a saint through popular veneration. He renounced a life of ease to live in a cell, as a hermit, on the banks of the River Nidd. He suffered damage from deer straying on his land. He shot some of them and this was

reported to the king. The king, after hearing the case, granted St Robert as much land as he could plough with the deer in a day. Episodes from this story are recorded in restored glass from Dale Abbey now at Morley [5.190, 5.191].

(a) St Robert shoots the deer. (Modern)
(b) The keepers complain to the king.
(c) St Robert appears before the king who orders 'Go whom and pin them'.
(d) St Robert catches the deer. (Modern)
(e) When the keepers complain again the king replies 'Bid hym come to me'.
(f) After St Robert's second interview the king says: 'Go ye whom and yowce them and take ye ground wt ye plode'.
(g) St Robert ploughs with the deer. (Modern)

ST ROCHE

St Roche was born in Montpellier. Charged by his father on his death bed, to work among the sick and the poor he 'clad him with the habit of a pilgrim, and covered his head with a bonnet, a scrip on his shoulder, and a pilgrim's

5.191 *St Robert of Knaresborough (see [5.190])* Morley

5.192 *St Roche as a pilgrim pointing to a plague spot on his thigh* Plymtree

staff in his right hand and so he departed'. He worked throughout Italy especially among the victims of the plague. When he caught the pestilence himself he was expelled from the city and lived in a hut, fed by a dog which brought him a loaf each day.

He is depicted as a pilgrim pointing to the plague spot on his thigh as on a painted screen panel at Plymtree [5.192], and in the Chapel of Henry VII, Westminster Abbey, where there is a figure of him in pilgrim's garb pointing to the plague spot.

ST SEBASTIAN

St Sebastian defied the Emperor Diocletian by refusing to forsake the Christian faith. He was tied to a tree and was pierced by numerous arrows. He survived but was again arrested and martyred. He is usually represented as a young man pierced by arrows.

REPRESENTATIONS

1 Pierced by arrows which protrude from his body as on the painted screen at Torbryan [5.193], and in glass at Fairford where he is tied to a tree.

2 On the painted screen at Bradninch [5.194] he is dressed as a soldier holding a long bow in one hand and arrows in the other.

3 In the Chapel of Henry VII, Westminster Abbey, almost naked, he is tied to a tree by his ankles and wrists with his hands above his head. In each flanking niche there is a figure of an archer. (*English Medieval Sculpture*, A Gardner, fig 492)

THE SEVEN SLEEPERS OF EPHESUS

The Seven Sleepers were seven Christian men who, during the persecution of Emperor Decius, went to sleep in a cave. There they remained and did not awake until the reign of Theodosius when they vindicated themselves before the emperor and the bishop.

At Westminster Abbey, in the Chapel of St Edward the Confessor, the Seven Sleepers are depicted in one of the panels on which is recorded the legendary life of the king.

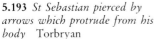

5.193 *St Sebastian pierced by arrows which protrude from his body* Torbryan

5.194 *St Sebastian with bow and arrows* Bradninch

5.195 *St Sidwell (Sativola) holding a scythe* Ashton

ST SIDWELL (SATIVOLA)

St Sidwell was martyred in the eighth century on the site of the now destroyed church in Exeter which was dedicated to her. Little is known of her and she was mainly venerated in Devonshire. She was said to have been killed by haymakers at the instigation of her stepmother who was jealous of her reputation for piety. In the place where she died a fountain sprang up. This may be another example of a legend suggested by a name.

She is usually depicted as a maiden holding a scythe, sometimes carrying her head in her hands.

REPRESENTATIONS

1 Holding a scythe as in glass in Exeter Cathedral and in the chapel of All Souls College, Oxford, and on the painted screen at Ashton [5.195], and at Kenn [5.196] where she carries her head in her hands.

2 There was a figure of her, headless and holding her head and a scythe, in her memorial church at Exeter.

ST SILVESTER

St Silvester was the pope of whom it was said that he baptised the Emperor Constantine, and in so doing cured him of leprosy. In his confrontation with the Jews he raised a bull from the dead in order to confound them.

On a painted screen panel at Houghton St Giles he is depicted wearing a papal tiara and holding a double cross, with a supplicant at his feet. He appears in glass at Wiggenhall, St Mary Magdalene, as a headless figure without distinctive attribute.

ST SITHA

St Sitha was a domestic servant known for her piety. A story told of her is that one morning she stayed longer at her prayers than usual. Remembering that it was baking day she hurried to the kitchen and found the bread ready made for the oven.

Her attributes are a bunch of keys, a rosary, and loaves of bread.

REPRESENTATIONS

1 Holding a bunch of keys as on the painted screen at Torbryan [5.197], and Barton Turf [5.198] where she is wearing an apron.

2 Holding a book and a rosary as on the painted screen at Westhall [5.199].

5.196 *St Sidwell (Sativola) carrying her head in her hands* Kenn

5.197 *St Sitha with a bunch of keys* Torbryan

5.198 *St Sitha wearing an apron and with a bunch of keys* Barton Turf

5.199 *St Sitha holding a book and a rosary* Westhall

3 Holding three loaves and a book as in glass at Mells.

4 St Sitha and St Petronilla share the same attribute, a key or keys, and are therefore not easily distinguished, but both occur on the screen at North Elmham and both are named.

St Stephen

St Stephen, one of the seven deacons, aroused the enmity of the Jews who stoned him to death.

His attribute is a stone, or a number of stones, sometimes held in a napkin. He is usually vested as a deacon in a dalmatic.

REPRESENTATIONS

1 In a dalmatic and holding stones as on the desk front at Blythburgh [**5.200**].

2 On a painted screen panel at Ranworth [**5.201**] he carries a napkin holding five stones in one hand and a book in the other. At Somerleyton he holds a book on which rests five stones and a sixth is in contact with his head.

3 Again on the painted screen at Barton Turf [**5.202**] he holds a napkin containing stones as he does at Ashton [**5.203**].

5.200 *St Stephen in a dalmatic, holding stones* Blythburgh

5.201 *St Stephen carrying a napkin holding five stones* Ranworth

5.202 *St Stephen with napkin and stones* Barton Turf

5.203 *St Stephen with napkin and stones* Ashton

5.204 *Death of St Stephen* Norwich Cathedral

5.205 *St Thomas of Canterbury, his murder* Norwich Cathedral

5.206 *The murder of St Thomas of Canterbury*
Fornham St Martin

4 His death is shown on a boss in the cloisters of Norwich Cathedral [5.204]. Before a ruler enthroned with a devil behind him, St Stephen kneels with clasped hands. Near to him is St Paul holding a coat. Two men are armed with swords, others are holding and throwing stones. In the clouds is a half-figure of God.

In the Jerusalem Chamber of Westminster Abbey is a panel of glass in which is depicted the stoning of St Stephen. Two men have lifted a large stone above their heads ready to throw at the praying saint. (Royal Commission, fig 18)

ST THEOBALD

One St Theobald, although wealthy, left home and with a companion earned a living doing manual labour in the forest of Pettingen, Luxemburg. Another St Theobald left the court of France to become a monk at Vaux de Cernay. A third St Theobald was a twelfth-century Archbishop of Canterbury.

It is not possible to say which saint is depicted in episcopal vestments, holding a crozier, on a painted screen panel at Hempstead which bears his name.

ST THOMAS AQUINAS

A Dominican friar and theologian of the thirteenth century. Born of a knightly family he was educated at the monastery of Monte Casino and later at university where he met Dominicans and joined their order. His life was devoted to study, lecturing and writing, and his most important work was the *Summa Theologica*, a comprehensive statement of his mature thought on all the Christian mysteries.

He is represented holding a monstrance jointly with St Norbert at a convent at St Leonards.

ST THOMAS OF CANTERBURY

It was not his work as statesman or archbishop, but his dramatic death which gained for St Thomas his great popularity. His shrine became a place of pilgrimage and dedications in his honour became common.

The iconography of St Thomas is fully treated in *Archaeologia*, vol 79, by G Tancred Borenius. Most of the representations are in a mutilated state, probably partly due to their destruction being especially selected by Henry VIII.

REPRESENTATIONS

1 Holding the severed crown of his head, as on the west front of Wells Cathedral and in glass in Lincoln Cathedral.
2 His murder is depicted on a boss in Exeter Cathedral and in the cloisters of Norwich Cathedral [5.205], and on a misericord at Fornham, St Martin, where it is inserted in modern woodwork [5.206].
3 At South Newington his martyrdom is depicted in a wall painting. The upper portion of the picture is missing but in the lower half St Thomas, in the presence of four armed knights, kneels before an altar on which is a chalice. His mitre is falling to the ground, his head having been struck by a sword. On an alabaster panel at Elham is depicted St Thomas calmly praying at an altar as the armed knights approach. The story is continued on other bosses in the cloisters of Norwich Cathedral.
   (a) The finding of his body by the monks.
   (b) His burial [5.207]. He is lying in the grave fully vested with the monks nearby.
   (c) The penance of Henry II [5.208]. This rare subject is also recorded in glass at Checkley.
4 In the aisle of the Trinity Chapel in Canterbury Cathedral

5.207 *The open tomb of St Thomas of Canterbury* Norwich Cathedral

5.208 *St Thomas of Canterbury, the penance of Henry II* Norwich Cathedral

are twelve windows which are composed of medallions. In these are recorded the martyrdom of St Thomas and a large number of miracles which took place through his intercession. Many of these are not found depicted elsewhere. A detailed description is given in *The Ancient Glass of Canterbury Cathedral*, Bernard Rackham.

5 At Elham [5.209] is an alabaster depicting the confrontation between King Henry with his armed soldiers and St Thomas at the Council at Northampton.

6 At Nettlestead in a small panel of mutilated glass can be seen the monks of Canterbury welcoming the Archbishop on his return from exile.

ST UNCUMBER (WILGEFORTE)

St Uncumber was reputed to be a Portuguese princess whose father tried to make her marry against her wish. She prayed that she might become unattractive and not acceptable in marriage. She grew a beard. This angered her father and resulted in her being crucified.

It has been suggested that she was not a historical figure but that the legend arose through the misunderstanding of a fully-clothed crucifix during the Middle Ages when it was no longer familiar. (*Art and the Reformation*, GG Coulton.) Her attribute is a beard.

In the Chapel of Henry VII, Westminster Abbey, is a figure of her as a bearded woman standing before a tau cross on which rests a book. On a painted screen panel at

5.209 *An alabaster depicting the confrontation between King Henry II and St Thomas of Canterbury at the Council of Northampton* Elham

5.210 St Uncumber (Wilgeforte) as a bearded woman tied to a cross Worstead

5.211 St Urith (Hieraetha) holding a scythe Hennock

5.212 St Ursula holding an arrow in each hand Kenn

Worstead [5.210] she is depicted as a bearded figure tied to a cross.

ST URITH (HIERAETHA)
It is difficult to distinguish between St Urith and her sister St Sidwell; of both it is related that they were slain by haymakers at the instigation of their jealous stepmother.

Both have a scythe as an attribute and are shown holding a decapitated head. St Urith is depicted on the painted screen at Hennock [5.211]; she is holding a scythe as is St Sidwell on an adjacent panel. She is depicted in glass at Nettlecombe.

ST URSULA
St Ursula was said to be a British princess who had eleven thousand virgins as companions. With her handmaidens she visited Rome and Cologne where she and her companions were martyred by the Huns. She herself was killed by an arrow.

St Ursula is depicted as a crowned princess with an arrow as attribute, sometimes shielding her maidens with her cloak as on the painted screen panel at Kenn [5.212] where she holds a large arrow in each hand. On the painted screen at Belstead she bears a rigged ship, crowded with her virgins, and a large arrow. She appears in glass at York, Holy Trinity, Goodramgate, and Morley [5.213] where she

5.213 St Ursula ascending into Heaven and holding eleven maidens in a sheet Morley

5.214 *St Ursula holding a large arrow and shielding her maidens under her cloak* Eye

5.215 *St Ursula holding an arrow* Ashton

5.216 *St Veronica holding a kerchief with imprint* Wolborough

5.217 *St Victor of Marseilles with sword and a windmill* Torbryan

5.218 *St Victor of Marseilles holding the sail of a windmill* Wolborough

5.219 *St Vincent holding two cruets and a book* Torbryan

5.220 *St Walstan of Bawburgh wearing royal robes and holding a sceptre* Ludham

is ascending into Heaven holding eleven of her maidens in a sheet.

On the painted screen at Eye [5.214] she is crowned and holds a large arrow and is shielding her maidens under her cloak, and at Ashton [5.215] she holds an arrow and a book.

St Veronica

St Veronica is identified with the woman who had an issue of blood, was healed by touching the hem of Jesus' garment and later followed Him to Calvary where she wiped His face. The imprint was miraculously left on her kerchief.

She is represented, holding the kerchief with imprint, on the painted screen at Wolborough [5.216] but this appears to have been repainted.

St Victor of Marseilles

St Victor was a Roman officer who helped and encouraged Christians during the persecution of the church in Marseilles by Maximian. He was tortured by being crushed by millstones and was beheaded.

On the painted screen at Torbryan [5.217] he is clothed in armour and holds a sword, the instrument of his martyrdom, and a windmill which is his particular attribute. On the painted screen at Wolborough [5.218] he is holding the sail of a windmill.

St Vincent

St Vincent, a Spanish deacon, served the Bishop of Saragossa and was imprisoned with him during the Diocletian persecution. He endured tortures inflicted by an iron hook and, like St Lawrence, he was roasted over a fire on a gridiron.

At Torbryan [5.219] on the painted screen, he is depicted as a deacon holding two cruets and a book, as he is in glass in two other Devonshire churches, Doddiscombsleigh and Payhembury. In Westminster Abbey on the grille of the tomb of Henry VII he is depicted alongside St Edward the Confessor.

St Walstan of Bawburgh

St Walstan was a royal person who became a farm worker. He refused all gifts except two calves which it had been revealed were to draw him to his burial place. He was warned by an angel that his death was near. He prayed that those farmers who visited his tomb should be granted their requests. When he died his body was carried by his own oxen from Taverham to Bawburgh where he was buried.

His attributes are a scythe and two oxen. He is depicted on the painted screen panels of several Norfolk churches. At Ludham [5.220] he wears royal robes and holds a sceptre. At Burlingham St Andrew [5.221] he is crowned and wears a royal cloak but is barefoot.

St Wenceslas

St Wenceslas was Duke of Bohemia in the tenth century. He became a Christian and avowed his intention of ruling as a Christian prince. During his reign he became known for his piety and good works. He was opposed by his

5.221 *St Walstan of Bawburgh crowned wearing a royal cloak and barefoot* Burlingham St Andrew

brother who killed him. After his death he was acclaimed as a saint. He is depicted in glass as a king without distinctive attribute in the vestibule of the chapter house of York Minster. In glass at Stoke Poges he is depicted in a plumed hat, carrying a sword with a supplicant at his feet.

St Werburga

St Werburga was a Mercian princess who took the veil and became Abbess of Ely. A popular legend about her recounts how, when a flock of wild geese devastated the crops of the villagers at Weedon, she locked up the offending birds. Next morning she found that one was missing and that it had been killed and cooked. She restored the bird to life and it flew away with its companions who never again returned to attack the villagers' crops. She has no characteristic attribute. In Chester Cathedral [5.222] where was her shrine, on a misericord is depicted the story of the geese. In the centre a servant is handing the goose to St Werburga, who holds a crozier. On the right supporter a man is confessing his theft of the goose and on the left are the confined geese.

5.222 *St Werburga with a goose* Chester Cathedral

5.223 *St William of Norwich with cross on his shoulder and holding nails in his left hand* Eye

5.224 *St William of Norwich, with a crowd of Jews mocking the boy saint, who hangs on a cross* Loddon

ST WERSTAN

St Werstan left Deerhurst Abbey, a Benedictine house, when it was sacked by the Danes and founded a small community in a chapel on the site of the present Malvern Priory. Little is known about him.

In a window in the choir clerestory of Malvern Priory are recorded four episodes from his life.

(a) He sees the site of his chapel in a vision.
(b) He sees its consecration by angels.
(c) St Edward the Confessor presents a charter to a tonsured monk.
(d) The martyrdom of him and his companions by the sword.

ST WILLIAM OF NORWICH

St William of Norwich was eleven years old when he was martyred by the Jews.

He was crucified during Holy Week and his body was hidden in a wood but its presence was revealed by a heavenly light which surrounded it.

REPRESENTATIONS

1 On the painted screen at Eye [5.223] he bears a cross on his shoulder and holds nails in his left hand.
2 On the painted screen at Loddon [5.224] his martyrdom is depicted. A crowd of Jews are mocking the boy saint, who hangs on a cross.

ST WILLIAM OF YORK

St William was consecrated Archbishop of York in AD 1142 but after only five years he was exiled. When he returned in AD 1153 the bridge over the Ouse collapsed without injury to St William or to those gathered on the bridge to greet him. This escape was attributed to his prayers. After his death many miracles were wrought at his tomb. He has no distinctive attribute.

REPRESENTATIONS

1 St William is represented in glass as a vested bishop in York Minster, York All Saints (North Street), and at Morley where John of Bridlington is his companion.
2 In York Minster is a large window known as the St William Window because it is divided into a hundred and five panels in most of which are depicted incidents from his life and miracles associated with him. We see:

(a) His enthronement as archbishop.
(b) The dispute with his rival Henry Murdoc and his consequent exile.
(c) His return and the breaking of the Ouse Bridge.
(d) His illness, death, burial and the opening of his tomb.
(e) Miracles associated with him.
    (A full description of the window is given in *Painted Glass of York*, F Harrison)

In 1957 some alabaster panels were dug up in York and are now housed in the Yorkshire Museum. Four of these depict scenes connected with St William.

(a) 'Probably represents the birth of St. William with his uncle King Stephen beside the bed ...

5.225 *St Winwalloe as an old man holding a church* East Portlemouth

(b) 'St. William's entry into York and the collapse of the Ouse Bridge.
(c) 'King Edward I falling from a mountain and saved from injury by the assistance of St. William, and the recovery of a fisherboy drowned in the Ouse.
(d) 'The translation of the body of St. William.'
    (*The Museums Journal*, vol 57, No. 2, May 1957)

ST WINIFRED

St Winifred refused the advances of an ignoble prince called Caradoc. In anger and rage he cut off her head. Where it fell, at Holywell, a spring of water with healing properties burst forth. Afterwards her head was miraculously rejoined to her body. Later she became an abbess. In the Chapel of Henry VII, Westminster Abbey, is a figure of her holding a book and a palm. Her head is on a block near her feet.

ST WINWALLOE

St Winwalloe was a Breton monk who built the monastery at Landevennec. His family had fled in the fifth century from Wales to Brittany to escape from the Saxon invaders.

On a painted screen panel at East Portlemouth [5.225], of which he is patron saint, he is depicted as an old man holding a church.

5.226 *St Withburga with a deer and a church* Burlingham St Andrew

5.227 *St Withburga, with a deer, holding a church* Barnham Broom

5.228 *Female saints on an alabaster panel* Norwich, St Peter Mancroft

St Withburga

St Withburga was one of the three saintly daughters of King Anna. Her sisters were SS Etheldreda and Sexburga. She was abbess of the nunnery at East Dereham which she founded. Here, when food was scarce, the nuns were miraculously fed by the milk of two does. Her attributes are deer and a church.

On a painted screen panel at Burlingham St Andrew [5.226] and at Barnham Broom [5.227], she is depicted as an abbess with deer and holding a church.

St Wulfstan

St Wulfstan was Bishop of Worcester when Malvern Priory was founded. As a Saxon bishop he came into conflict with Archbishop Lanfranc, who wished to deprive him of his see. He placed his crozier on the tomb of St Edward the Confessor where it became affixed and no one could take it up until St Wulfstan prayed that it should be liberated. He was allowed to remain bishop.

He is depicted in glass as a mitred bishop without a distinctive attribute in the choir clerestory of Malvern Priory.

In another window are recorded four scenes relating to the foundation of the priory. In one, St Wulfstan is presenting a charter to a monk. (*Medieval Christian Imagery*, G McN Rushforth, figs 50 and 55)

St Zosimus

St Zosimus was the companion of St Mary of Egypt. At Windsor, St George's Chapel, a misericord shows a man and a woman sitting on a bench; the woman is naked and the man is trying to place his cloak around her. This has been interpreted as being St Zosimus and St Mary.

Saints (Various)

In Norwich, St Peter Mancroft [5.228], is an alabaster panel which may have formed part of an altar reredos, on which is depicted a number of female saints amongst whom are readily recognised St Margaret with her dragon, St Barbara with her tower, St Helen with her cross, and St Catherine with a sword.

5.229 *Sir John Schorn with devil appearing out of a boot* Wolborough

5.230 *Sibyl Samia holding a cradle* Bradninch

5.231 *Sibyl Erythraea holding a rose* Bradninch

SIR JOHN SCHORN

Sir John Schorn was never canonised but he acquired great popularity and was depicted amongst the saints. He was rector of North Marston. What was remembered most about him was that he was said to have conjured the Devil into a boot. With his boot, out of which pokes a devil, he is seen on several painted screens such as Cawston, Gateley, Alphington and Wolborough [**5.229**].

SIBYLS

In the belief that all prophecy was controlled by God for His own purposes, the Early Church seized upon the words of classical writers which could be interpreted as foretelling the Christian Revelation.

The wise women, the sibyls of classical antiquity, were enlisted for this purpose and medieval writers made frequent reference to them and to their sayings.

A Dominican friar, Fileppo Barbieri, writing of the sibyls in the fifteenth century, drew up a list of twelve which he paralleled with Hebrew prophets, putting words in their mouths which could be interpreted as foretelling the coming of Christ. His work was widely read and quoted.

Apart from the painted screens of Devonshire, representations of the sibyls are rarely found in English churches. The best examples are found at Ugborough and Bradninch. The series at Bradninch is typical of English examples.

(a) Samia [**5.230**]: Samia holds a cradle because she was thought to have foretold the Nativity.

(b) Erythraea [**5.231**]: Erythraea holds a rose because she was thought to have foretold the Annunciation.

(c) Persica [**5.232**]: Persica holds a lantern because she was thought to have foretold the overpowering of evil and the coming of a Saviour.

(d) Europa [**5.233**]: Europa holds a sword because her words were thought to refer to the Flight into Egypt and the Massacre of the Innocents.

(e) Libyca [**5.234**]: Libyca holds a ewer and a basin instead of the usual candle which referred to her words of God shining in the darkness.

(f) Hellespontica [**5.235**]: Hellespontica holds a cross because her words were thought to refer to the Crucifixion.

5.232 *Sibyl Persica holding a lantern* Bradninch

5.233 *Sibyl Europa holding a sword*
Bradninch

5.234 *Sibyl Libyca with ewer and a basin*
Bradninch

5.235 *Sibyl Hellespontica holding a cross*   Bradninch

5.236 *Sibyl Agrippa holding a scourge*   Bradninch

(g) Agrippa [5.236]: Agrippa holds a scourge because her words were thought to refer to the Scourging.

(h) Tiburtina [5.237]: Tiburtina holds a hand because she was thought to have foretold the Buffeting of Christ.

(i) Cumana [5.238]: Cumana holds a sponge because her words were thought to refer to the sponge filled with vinegar.

(j) Cimmeria [5.239]: Cimmeria holds a feeding bottle in the form of a horn because her words were applied to the feeding of Christ by the Virgin.

(k) Delphica [5.240]: Delphica holds pincers and nails instead of the usual crown of thorns because of her reference to the crowning with thorns.

(l) Phrygia [5.241]: Phrygia holds a cross and banner because her words were thought to foretell the Resurrection.

5.237 *Sibyl Tiburtina holding a hand* Bradninch

5.238 *Sibyl Cumana carrying a spear and a sponge* Bradninch

5.239 *Sibyl Cimmeria holding a feeding bottle in the form of a horn* Bradninch

5.240 *Sibyl Delphica with pincers and three nails* Bradninch

5.241 *Sibyl Phrygia with cross and banner* Bradninch

5.242 *Sibyls with emblems: a pillar and a scourge* Ugborough

5.243 *Sibyls with emblems: a crown of thorns and a cross* Ugborough

5.244 *Sibyls with emblems: a jug, basin and taper*   Ugborough

5.245 *Sibyls with emblems: a cradle, a spear and a sponge* Ugborough

5.246 *Sibyls with emblems: hammer, pincers and a sword* Ugborough

Elsewhere, as at Heavitree, the series is incomplete. Just as when comparing different series of apostles we find a variation in the attribute of some of the apostles, we find an inconsistency in the attributes given to the sibyls. At Ugborough the following attributes are used:

(a,b) Pillar, scourge [5.242]
(c,d) Crown of thorns, cross [5.243]
(e,f) Jug and basin, taper [5.244]
(g,h) Cradle, spear and sponge on a reed [5.245]
(i,j) Hammer and pincers, sword [5.246]
(k,l) Three nails, lantern [5.247]

5.247 *Sibyls with emblems: a lantern and three nails* Ugborough

6

The Church

IN THE MIDDLE AGES the Church dominated men's lives in a way it does not today. Not only was the church one of the main buildings in a village or town, often, in the absence of manor house or castle, it was the largest. What took place in it affected the life of each member of the community. What was said or done coloured the thoughts, formed the attitudes and finally governed the actions, of all concerned. In spite of the destruction wrought by the iconoclasts and by natural decay, iconography enables us to see how much was done and to learn something of the teaching then current.

The administration of the sacraments is wonderfully recorded on the Seven Sacraments fonts found in East Anglia and to a lesser extent in surviving panels of glass.

The teaching concentrated upon good and evil, sin and redemption, and Heaven and Hell. The battle between good and evil was vividly conceived and was translated into imagery. The virtues and the vices were personified, and allegorical representations made use of known and readily recognised idioms. The battle was a continuing conflict with dire results for the defeated. The consequences of sin were demonstrated in pictures of stark realism. Most wall paintings have perished and much of what remains is fragmentary and faded but enough has survived to illustrate that the walls of the churches echoed a constant warning.

In contrast the presence of the Heavenly Host of Angels and the Emblems of the Passion was a reminder that man did not struggle alone against the forces of evil.

AGNUS DEI
The Agnus Dei, the figure of a lamb bearing a cross-shafted banner, was one of the earliest symbols of Our Lord as the Lamb of God. It remained in constant and frequent use.

REPRESENTATIONS
1 In a simple and somewhat crude form it occurs on a bench end at Brent Knoll [6.1].
2 In Canterbury Cathedral on a boss is a more elaborate form. 'In the centre is a lamb with a cross. The lamb has a cross-bearing nimbus showing that it is intended for the Lamb of God. In one of its forefeet is held the base

6.1 *Agnus Dei*   Brent Knoll

6.2 *Angels carrying musical instruments* Blythburgh   6.3 *Seraphim* Barton Turf   6.4 *Cherubim* Barton Turf

of the cross, the stem passes behind the body to the top of the boss, where it ends in a small plain cross, below which is a broad three-pennoned banner. Around the boss in the angles are demifigures of angels, with their wings extended and their hands holding the sides of the boss.' (*Archaeologia*, vol 84, CJP Cave)

3 The Lamb with banner and chalice is seen on the font at Kirkburn. (See 'New Testament: Ascension' [2.84])

4 On the painted ceiling in Peterborough Cathedral is 'the Agnus Dei, a lamb supporting in one of its forefeet the cross with the banner of the Resurrection; in front is a chalice into which blood is pouring from a wound in the lamb's breast.' (*Archaeologia*, vol 87, CJP Cave and Professor Tancred Borenius)

ANGELS

The representation of angels in medieval art falls into four main categories:

1 The angel as an agent in an episode such as the angel in the Annunciation and the angels ministering to Christ in paintings of the Doom.

2 Angels carrying musical instruments signifying praise and rejoicing or with outstretched wings as ministers of God witnessing to His glory as on many roofs such as Blythburgh [6.2].

3 Angels holding across the chest a shield which carries either the Emblems of the Passion or heraldic charges. The latter are particularly common on tombs.

4 The *Golden Legend* records the Nine Orders of Angels divided into three hierarchies with a description of the function of each member. To the supernatural beings mentioned by St Paul were added the other supernatural beings to whom reference is made in Scripture. The nine members were placed in three hierarchies. In the first were Seraphim, Cherubim and Thrones; in the second Dominions, Virtues and Powers; in the third Principalities, Archangels and Angels. This classification was popularised especially by writings attributed to Dionysius the Areopagite. The Nine Orders are represented in glass, as at Malvern Priory and York, St Michael, Spurriergate, and on painted screens as at Southwold and Barton Turf. There is no conformity of representation but the series at Barton Turf, which is one of the finest in execution and best preserved, follows the general pattern and is typical of the medieval representation.

6.5 *Thrones* Barton Turf

6.6 *Dominions* Barton Turf

6.7 *Virtues* Barton Turf

6.8 *Powers* Barton Turf

In one of his homilies St Gregory attributes a symbolical precious stone to each of the angels. This is reflected in the Malvern series which was originally in the main lights. Each angel has a brooch with a stone but not always the one assigned to him by St Gregory.

The pair of flying angels, carved in stone with veils in their arms, at Bradford on Avon about AD 950 are well known because of their early date and because of their power.

SERAPHIM
1 At Barton Turf [6.3] Seraphim is six winged and his body and limbs are covered with feathers. He swings a censer.
2 At Malvern, feathered and winged, he stands on a fire of red flames. He wears a yellow topaz.

CHERUBIM
1 At Barton Turf [6.4] Cherubim has six wings and a feathered body. The wings are covered with eyes. His hands are lifted in adoration.
2 At Southwold he stands with hands raised on the Wheel of Eternity. In glass at New College, Oxford, his attribute

is the Book of Knowledge. The Malvern figure has been lost.

THRONES
1 At Barton Turf [6.5] Thrones is winged and feathered as are the other two members of the first hierarchy. He wears a cloak and holds a pair of scales representing divine justice.
2 At Southwold he carries a ciborium.
3 At Malvern he holds scales and wears a red sardius and not the green jasper.

DOMINIONS
1 At Barton Turf [6.6] Dominions has four wings and is wearing a chasuble and a triple crown. He holds a sceptre.
2 At Southwold he stands above a church and in addition to a sceptre he holds a chalice and host.
3 At Malvern he is clothed in royal robes and holds a sceptre. He wears a green chrysolite.

VIRTUES
1 At Barton Turf [6.7] Virtues is four-winged and feathered. He wears a short cape and holds a sceptre.

6.9 *Principalities* Barton Turf   **6.10** *Archangels* Barton Turf   **6.11** *Angels with naked souls at his feet* Barton Turf

2 At Southwold he holds a vessel of fire and a crown.
3 At Malvern he holds an open chrismatory and is completely feathered and wears a white stone.

POWERS
1 At Barton Turf **[6.8]** Powers is clad in armour and holds a scourge. He is leading a devil by a chain.
2 At Southwold a chained dragon is under his feet.
3 At Malvern he is clad in plate armour and carries a sword and shield. At his feet is a demon. He wears a dark-pink stone.

PRINCIPALITIES
1 At Barton Turf **[6.9]** Principalities is richly clad and holds a palm in one hand and a vessel in the other.
2 At Southwold he holds a sceptre and stands upon a fortress.
3 At Malvern he holds a sword.

ARCHANGELS
1 At Barton Turf **[6.10]** Archangels has two wings. Clad in armour and carrying a sword he stands above a fortress.

2 At Southwold he carries a sword and holds a pair of scales. (The Malvern figure is lost.)

ANGELS
1 At Barton Turf **[6.11]** Angels, clad in a long robe with an alms box on his girdle, holds a long spear. At his feet two naked souls kneel with hands raised in supplication.
2 At Southwold, more fully vested, he looks down on souls held in a cloth.
3 At Malvern he wears a green emerald.

APOSTLES
The twelve apostles had a superior place in the reverence and the iconography of the Middle Ages. An early collective representation is in the porch of Malmesbury Abbey **[6.12, 6.13]**. There are many examples where the Twelve were prominent, each occupying a panel, on painted screens. These are considered as individual saints. The association of each of the apostles with a text of the Creed is dealt with under 'Saints: Apostles and the Creed'.

6.12 *Apostles (1)* Malmesbury

6.13 *Apostles (2)* Malmesbury

6.14 *Burial of the dead* Feltwell

6.15 *The Church* Rochester Cathedral

6.16 *The Church Militant* Norwich Cathedral

BURIAL OF THE DEAD

On a bench end at Feltwell **[6.14]** the burial of the dead is depicted. Three mourners are present at a funeral; one carries a thurible. The body has been wrapped in a shroud tied at each end and marked with a cross. (See 'Corporal Acts of Mercy')

THE CHURCH

The usual representation of the Church is a crowned woman holding a book. It is associated with the parallel representation of the Synagogue. They are usually found flanking a doorway as at the cathedrals at Lincoln and Rochester **[6.15]**.

In Norwich Cathedral **[6.16]** is a misericord showing a pilgrim rising from a shell. He is hooded and holds a dagger in one hand and a pack saddle in the other. This is said to represent the Church Militant. (*Report of the Friends of Norwich Cathedral*, 1948)

6.17 *Cross bearer* Trull   **6.18** *In procession* Trull   **6.19** *In procession* Trull

CHURCH PROCESSION

The cross bearer and other figures from a church procession are represented on bench ends at Trull [**6.17, 6.18, 6.19**].

At Milverton [**6.20**], on a bench end is a carving of an aspergillum in a holy water vessel which was carried in procession.

CORPORAL ACTS OF MERCY

To the six acts of mercy specifically mentioned in *Matthew* 25 vv 35 and 36 was added a seventh, Burying the Dead, from *Tobit* 1 vv 17 and 18.

Isolated single representations in glass have survived in several churches but the most complete series that remains is in glass at York, All Saints, North Street [**6.21**], where there are six panels in the window, each containing a representation of an act of mercy. Burying the Dead is omitted. Reading from left to right beginning on the top tier there is:

   (a) Feeding the hungry. A benefactor, with a servant, is distributing loaves of bread from a basket to six men.

   (b) Giving drink to the thirsty. The same six men are holding bowls which are being filled with drink from jugs.

   (c) Receiving the stranger. The benefactor stands in the doorway of his house to receive four visitors.

   (d) Clothing the naked. Master and servant, each holding a garment, stand facing five poorly clad men.

6.20 *Aspergillum in Holy Water vessel* Milverton

6.21 *Corporal Acts of Mercy (see text)* York, All Saints North Street

(e) Visiting the sick. The benefactor and a lady stand by the bed of a sick man to whom they appear to be talking.

(f) Visiting those in prison. With their feet in the stocks, three prisoners in a row face their visitor.

This theme probably had an influence on some of the subjects considered under 'Virtues and Vices'.

DEATH AND THE GALLANT

Death personified and as an agent of God was a familiar literary theme. The Gallant and Death was an expression of this conception. A young gallant and Death come face to face. This confrontation is depicted on two painted panels at Newark on Trent [6.22] where Death is a macabre creature but the Gallant is gaily dressed in doublet and plumed hat.

THE DANCE OF DEATH

The Dance of Death was an allegory in which Death suddenly calls men from various walks of life.

On a misericord at Windsor, St George's Chapel, Death

calls a man from his richly laden table. On one supporter a woman is called from her digging and on the other the call comes to a man threshing with a flail.

THE THREE LIVING AND THE THREE DEAD

This is an allegory with a literary origin; the theme was familiar in French medieval poetry.

Three courtiers are confronted with Death in three forms; each reacts in a different way but each is reminded, as the onlooker was meant to be reminded, of the inevitability of death.

The allegory is the subject of wall paintings at Charlwood and Widford. At Raunds in a wall painting the Three Living are shown as three kings and the Three Dead as three skeletons.

THE EMBLEMS OF THE FOUR EVANGELISTS

The four beasts of the Apocalypse were used to symbolise the four evangelists: the lion of St Mark, the calf or ox of St Luke, the man or (as was more usual) the angel of St Matthew, and the eagle of St John. Another explanation

6.22 *Death and the Gallant* Newark on Trent

6.23 *Angel of St Matthew* Brent Knoll

6.24 *Ox of St Luke* Brent Knoll

6.25 *Eagle of St John* Brent Knoll

for the use of the emblems was made by reference to the commencement of the individual Gospels. St Mark begins his Gospel with an account of John the Baptist, the one crying in the wilderness being the lion; St Luke begins with the sacrifice of Zacharias, the calf being the animal of sacrifice; St Matthew first gives a list of the ancestors of Christ; and St John seeks to reveal His divinity like an eagle flying into the sun. Examples of the emblems in medieval art are very common. The angel of St Matthew [6.23], the ox of St Luke [6.24] and the eagle of St John [6.25] occur on bench ends at Brent Knoll. A misericord at Stowlangtoft [6.26] shows a winged ox; other misericords at Cockington, Christchurch Priory and Norwich, St Gregory also show the emblems.

At Kenn [6.27], in four painted panels of the screen is each of the evangelists with his respective emblem as an attribute.

6.26 *Winged ox* Stowlangtoft

6.27 *The evangelists* Kenn

THE EMBLEMS OF THE PASSION

The Passion narrative was told and retold by means of symbolism. Each episode in the story was reduced to symbolic form and to each incident was attributed an emblem. The Emblems of the Passion became one of the commonest features of medieval iconography. A common form of presentation was on a shield after the manner of an armorial charge. Sometimes the shield was held by an angel.

It is impossible to mention all examples but some idea of their popularity and the extent of this form of expression is indicated by the following list of Passion emblems:

(a) The Cross
(b) The crown of thorns
(c) The three nails
(d) The spear
(e) The sponge on a fork, spear or reed
(f) The smiting hand
(g) The jug of vinegar
(h) The cock
(i) The title of the Cross
(j) The ladder
(k) The hammer
(l) The pincers
(m) The pillar of flagellation
(n) The cord
(o) The scourges
(p) The dice
(q) Drawing lots by straws in a hand
(r) The seamless coat
(s) The lantern
(t) St Veronica's handkerchief
(u) The hand of Judas holding a bag of silver
(v) The five wounds
(w) The cup of agony in the garden
(x) Malchus with severed ear
(y) The spitting Jew
(z) The ewer and basin of Pilate
(aa) A torch and brazier
(bb) The kiss of betrayal
(cc) Pilate and his wife
(dd) The High Priest
(ee) A pestle and mortar
(ff) Pots of ointment
(gg) The hand holding hair
(hh) The loin cloth
(ii) The mace and axe

At Fressingfield [**6.28** to **6.35**], in a series of eight panels on the back of the bench, the Passion narrative is related in symbolic form by means of the emblems. Passion emblems also appear on bench ends at Kirklington [**6.36**, **6.37**] and St Mawgan [**6.38**, **6.39**].

6.28 *Title of the Cross* Fressingfield

6.29 *Ladder, pincers and nail* Fressingfield

6.30 *Cross, crown of thorns, and three nails* Fressingfield

6.31 *The cock* Fressingfield

6.32 *Smiting hand and jug of vinegar* Fressingfield

6.33 *Spear and sponge* Fressingfield

6.34 *The pillar of flagellation* Fressingfield   **6.35** *Seamless coat and dice* Fressingfield

6.36 *The seamless robe; hand holding straws* Kirklington   **6.37** *Mace, axe and lantern* Kirklington

6.38 *Cord and pillar of flagellation*
St Mawgan

6.39 *Title of the Cross; pincers, ladder and lantern* St Mawgan

6.40 *Prick of conscience window (see text)* York, All Saints North Street

THE END OF THE WORLD

The signs of the end of the world are recounted by Richard Rolle de Hampole in a poem, *The Prick of Conscience*. In glass at York, All Saints, North Street [6.40], are recorded the signs of the last fifteen days based on this poem. Starting at the bottom left-hand corner and reading from left to right they are:

    (a) The rising of the sea
    (b) Subsiding of the sea
    (c) The waters return to their former level
    (d) Fishes and sea monsters come to the earth
    (e) The sea on fire
    (f) The trees on fire and fruit dropping off

6.41 *Doom slab* York Cathedral

6.42 *Hell's mouth* Southwold

(g) Earthquakes
(h) Rocks and stones consumed
(i) Men hiding in holes in the earth
(j) Only the sky and earth visible
(k) Men coming out of holes and praying
(l) Coffins with dead men's bones
(m) The stars fall from Heaven
(n) Death and mourning
(o) The end of all things
(Taken from *All Hallows in North Street*, PJ Shaw)

HELL

Hell was occupied by demons who inflicted all manner of tortures on the damned. On the 'Doom Slab' in the crypt of York Minster **[6.41]** devils are attending a fire on which is a large cauldron in which the damned are suffering torment. From the mouth of one corpse, devils are extracting a soul.

Hell's Mouth is usually represented as the mouth of a Leviathan creature such as on an arm rest at Southwold **[6.42]**, and on the Doom painting at Wenhaston **[6.43]**.

A worn misericord at Gresford shows a devil wheeling a woman to Hell's mouth in a barrow **[6.44]**, and a misericord at Ludlow **[6.45]** shows an alewife being carried off by a devil to Hell, the mouth of which is shown in the left supporter. The right supporter is a devil holding a scroll on which, presumably, is written a list of her sins.

6.43 *Doom* Wenhaston

6.44 *Woman wheeled to Hell in a barrow*
Gresford

6.45 *Alewife carried off by a devil*   Ludlow

6.46 *Paradise*   Wenhaston

6.47 (left to right) *Joel, Zephaniah, Amos, Hosea* Fairford

6.48 (left to right) *Zechariah, Isaiah, David, Jeremiah* Fairford

6.49 (left to right) *Obadiah, Daniel, Malachi, Micah*   Fairford

PARADISE

In Byzantine art Abraham, Isaac and Jacob receive souls in the garden of Paradise. In English art Paradise is rarely represented but in the Doom painting at Wenhaston [6.46] the naked redeemed are entering the gate of Paradise, which is surrounded by a wall similar to that of a fortified city.

PRAYER

In churches can be found many invocations to prayer and scenes which include individuals in an attitude of prayer but prayer itself did not assume a recognizable or symbolic form.

At Shrewsbury, on an alabaster, the prayers of a monk are seen ascending to the Trinity and the Blessed Virgin.

THE PROPHETS

The prophets were seen as Old Testament figures who foretold the events of the New Testament. They were rarely depicted with an attribute but usually they carry a scroll bearing a messianic text, a form of representation which may have derived from dramatic presentations. When there is no scroll and no name, identification is almost impossible. Even when a name has survived in a window this can be misleading owing to the transposition of glass and rearrangement.

Twelve prophets were chosen to correspond to the Creed apostles. At Fairford the scheme is complete. In three windows in the south side wall of the nave are the twelve apostles with scrolls each bearing a sentence of the Creed. On the north side, in three windows, are twelve prophets each with a scroll bearing a prophetic quotation confirming the sentence of the Creed borne by the corresponding apostle. Prophet and apostle were paralleled as follows: Jeremiah – St Peter, David – St Andrew, Isaiah – St James the Greater, Zechariah – St John, Hosea – St Thomas, Amos – St James the Lesser, Zephaniah – St Philip, Joel – St Bartholomew, Micah – St Matthew, Malachi – St Simon, Daniel – St Jude, Obadiah – St Mathias [6.47, 6.48, 6.49]. These prophets were not always the ones who were chosen and their text was not always the same.

On painted screen panels for the most part representation of prophets was restricted to isolated figures. The representations at Thornham are unusual. Of the sixteen screen panels only four are of saints and twelve are of prophets, bearing scrolls.

At Chudleigh a number of prophets are included with the saints and at Kenton prophet and apostle are depicted in an alternate series.

6.50 *Man with flowers* Malvern Priory

6.51 *Man with basket and flowers or fruit* Malvern Priory

6.52 *Seated woman with flowers* Ripple

6.53 *Seven sacraments font* Cley-next-the-Sea

ROGATIONTIDE

Representations of men holding flowers may have a reference to Rogationtide when the parishioners went in procession carrying flowers.

In Malvern Priory are two misericords: on one [6.50] is a man with a bunch of flowers in each hand, and on the other [6.51] a man with a basket on his right arm and a bunch of flowers or a cluster of grapes in his left hand. Similar misericords occur elsewhere.

At Ripple [6.52] a seated woman with a bunch of flowers in each hand is flanked by additional bunches. In this series this represents the month of May.

SACRAMENTS

In the medieval Church there were seven recognised sacraments. Little attempt was made to depict them but for two exceptions, the seven sacraments fonts and the seven sacraments windows.

The fonts, of which about fifty exist, are mostly fifteenth century and with only two exceptions are found in Norfolk

6.54 *Seven sacraments window* Doddiscombsleigh

and Suffolk. They are of pedestal type with an octagonal bowl. On each of seven sides is depicted one of the sacraments, the subject of the remaining side was usually the Crucifixion or the baptism of Christ. Most of the fonts are much mutilated but, by a survey of the whole, a general form for each sacrament can be seen. The best preserved fonts are Gresham, Walsingham and Cley-next-the-Sea [6.53].

The seven sacraments windows are less in number and are either restored or exist in part. The best examples are at Crudwell and Doddiscombsleigh [6.54]. Panels of glass, each containing a representation of a sacrament, surround the figure of Christ on the Cross or a figure of Him displaying His wounds. The panels are associated with the wounds by crimson lines.

At Buckland, in the east window, are three panels of glass depicting confirmation, marriage and extreme unction.

On the font at Salle each representation has been reduced to the simplest form and an emblem takes the place of the traditional representation.

Confirmation is symbolised by a mitre, the mass by an altar mensa, penance by a rod, extreme unction by a soul issuing from a shroud, ordination by a chalice and baptism by cruets of oil. Marriage is missing.

BAPTISM

The priest is usually shown about to immerse a naked child into the font, as at Westhall [6.55] and Gresham [6.56]. Acolytes may hold the service book and chrismatory, as at Walsingham, where a woman holds a chrism cloth.

6.55 *Baptism* Westhall

6.56 *Baptism* Gresham

6.57 *Confirmation of infants* Westhall

6.58 *Confirmation* Gresham

CONFIRMATION

The children presented to the bishop are small and in some
cases are infants, as appears to be the case on the fonts at
Westhall [**6.57**] and at Gresham [**6.58**].

6.59 *Priest anointing man in bed*   Gresham

6.60 *Priest elevating chalice for mass*   Walsingham

6.61 *Mass*   Westhall

6.62 *Mass*   Gresham

6.63 *Matrimony* Westhall

6.64 *Matrimony* Gresham

EXTREME UNCTION

A good representation of this sacrament is at Gresham [6.59] where a priest is anointing a man in bed, propped up with pillows. An acolyte holds a service book. A woman kneels at the foot of the bed and two men and a woman stand behind. On the bed is a circular dish on which are placed four whisps of wool in the form of a cross. A similar example is at Westhall but it is too defaced to see much detail.

In glass at Doddiscombsleigh communion of the sick takes the place of extreme unction. The priest holds a paten and his acolyte holds a candle.

MASS

Generally the priest, vested, stands before the altar, elevating either the chalice or the host, as on fonts at Walsingham [6.60] and at Westhall [6.61].

At Great Glemham and at Woodbridge the priest is communicating a man and a woman who hold the houseling cloth.

At Gresham [6.62] the priest is elevating the host in front of an altar on which are two candles and a missal. The sanctus bell with its dangling rope can be seen on the right.

MATRIMONY

The priest is usually shown joining the hands of the bride and bridegroom which appears to be the case at Westhall [6.63] and at Gresham [6.64].

ORDINATION

The bishop is usually shown laying his hands on the candidate's head. At Nettlecombe a candidate is having his head tonsured. At Gresham [6.65] is an acolyte with a thurible.

6.65 *Ordination* Gresham

6.66 *Sacred monogram* Nantwich

6.67 *Signs of the Zodiac* Alne

PENANCE

The confessor sits in a chair by a kneeling penitent. Sometimes the presence of good and evil is indicated by an angel and a devil. At Westhall the devil is leaving the scene. At Gresham the penitent is being scourged.

SACRED MONOGRAM

The sacred monogram adopted by Emperor Constantine and placed upon his standard instead of the Roman eagle, was formed by taking the first two letters of the Greek work for Christ, ΧΡΙΣΤΟΣ. When the P is placed in the centre of the X, the monogram assumes an added symbolism because of the resemblance to the Cross.

A second monogram was formed by abbreviating the Greek word for Jesus, ΙΗΣΟΥΣ, to *IHC*, which was sometimes written *IHS*. A later interpretation was added when the letters were taken to be an abbreviation for *Jesus Hominum Salvator*.

The first monogram was used mainly in the early Church and the second was used through the whole period of medieval art.

The monogram is found on a misericord at Nantwich [6.66].

SIGNS OF THE ZODIAC

The signs of the Zodiac had a place in the scheme of medieval iconography, and with each sign was associated a month and a labour.

They are carved together with bestiary subjects on the Norman arch over the south door at Alne [6.67].

On each of eight bosses in the vaulting of the gateway of Merton College, Oxford, is a single sign of the Zodiac.

SIX AGES OF THE WORLD/SIX AGES OF MAN

In Canterbury Cathedral with the representation in glass of the Miracle at Cana is associated the Six Ages of the World and of Man. The Six Ages of the World are typified by the figures of five Old Testament patriarchs and of Christ:
(a) Adam with a hoe
(b) Noah with his ark
(c) Abraham with a bowl containing fire
(d) David crowned and holding a harp
(e) Jechoniah crowned and holding a sceptre
(f) Christ with the Book of the Gospels.
The Six Ages of Man are represented by a figure of a man at six stages of his life, each with an appropriate label:
(a) *Infantia*, a babe
(b) *Pueritia*, a boy with a stick and ball
(c) *Adolescentia*, a youth with a sceptre
(d) *Juventus*, a bearded young man with a sword
(e) *Virilitas*, a man
(f) *Senectus*, an old man with a crutch.

SYNAGOGUE

As a parallel to the representation of Church, the Synagogue was symbolised by a female figure with bandaged eyes, holding a broken spear or staff. Sometimes she lets slip the

6.68 *Representation of the Synagogue* Rochester Cathedral

Tablets of the Law from her hand and a crown falls from her head.

With the representation of the Church, the representation of the Synagogue is found flanking doorways at the cathedrals at Lincoln and Rochester [6.68].

TREE OF JESSE

The Tree of Jesse was based on the prophecy of *Isaiah* 11 vv 1&2. 'There shall come forth a rod out of the stem of Jesse, and a branch shall grow out of his roots: and the Spirit of the Lord shall rest upon him.' It was used to show

6.69 *Tree of Jesse*   Chester Cathedral

6.70 *Wheel of fortune*
Rochester Cathedral

the earthly ancestors of Christ. The usual form was a vine growing from the loins of a recumbent figure of Jesse; amongst the branches were placed figures of kings and prophets frequently holding messianic texts. The whole formed a conventional tree at the apex of which was placed a figure of the Virgin holding the Child.

REPRESENTATIONS
1 In glass the Tree of Jesse is often found, frequently in the east window. Examples are at Thornhill, Shrewsbury, and Llanrhaeadr.
2 It is found on a boss in Worcester Cathedral.
3 The reredos at Christchurch Priory is an outstanding example.

4 It is found on a bench end in Chester Cathedral [6.69].

VICES AND VIRTUES
In addition to the individual vices and virtues, which are considered separately each under its own heading, the conflict between vice and virtue and man's battle against sin and its consequences were seen and illustrated in allegorical form.

THE CARDINAL VIRTUES
In glass in Canterbury Cathedral the four cardinal virtues are typified by crowned female figures holding scrolls and attributes.

6.72 *Miser counting coins*   Beverley Minster

6.71 *Anger*   Norwich Cathedral

(a) *Prudence* holds a serpent in one hand and two doves in the other.
(b) *Justice* holds a pair of scales.
(c) *Temperance* holds a torch in one hand and a bowl in the other.
(d) *Fortitude* carries a sword in one hand and a length of twisted rope in the other.

THE BLAMELESS STATES OF LIFE
In glass in Canterbury Cathedral the three blameless states of life, Virginity, Continence and Marriage, are typified by male figures holding inscribed scrolls.

THE WHEEL OF FORTUNE
Here a wheel is used as the motif to depict the struggle against sin. Dame Fortune is depicted turning her wheel against which struggle all manner of men. This is seen in a wall painting in Rochester Cathedral [**6.70**].

THE WHEEL OF PRIDE
The pattern of a wheel was used to group representations of a number of vices. Here again the only known examples are wall paintings.

THE PURGING OF PRIDE
Pride is represented as a woman confronted with Death who pierces her side with a spear. Associated with her are dragons and devils which typify Man's sins.
  This is the theme of a now faded wall painting at Raunds, where Pride, in the shape of a gaily dressed woman flanked by devils, faces Death. Death is a cadaver armed with a long spear with which he pierces Pride.

6.73 *Avarice sitting on his money*   Blythburgh

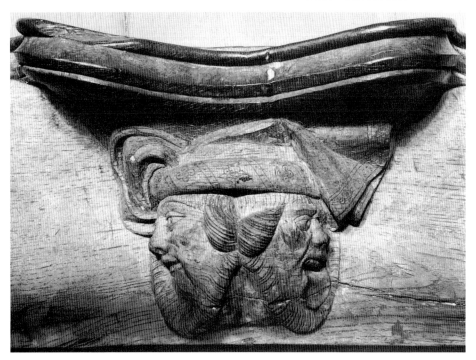

6.74 *Deceit*   Norwich Cathedral

6.75 *Hypocrisy*   Blythburgh

6.76 *Gluttony*   Norwich Cathedral

ANGER

On a misericord in Norwich Cathedral [6.71] Anger is personified: a man, astride a boar, half draws his sword and clenches his teeth.

AVARICE

In its moral teaching, avarice was greatly condemned by the Church. Art, often of the cruder kind, was used to warn the faithful against the evil of this particular sin and its consequences. Avarice is represented as follows:

1 A supporter of a misericord in Beverley Minster [6.72]

shows a miser counting coins in a chest around which appears the head of a devil complete with horns.

2 The avaricious monk is depicted on two misericords in Westminster Abbey. On one, a monk drops coins from a bag as he is being seized by a devil, and on another he is being seized to the accompaniment of a drum.

3 In Beverley, St Mary, is a misericord on which an ape (the symbol of avarice) is offering a bag to an ecclesiastic who holds a coin. See 'Creatures Natural and Mythical: Ape/Monkey' [7.13]

4 The poppy head of a bench end at Blythburgh [6.73], it

6.77 *Gluttony*   Blythburgh

6.78 *Medieval drinker*   St Winnow

6.79 *Medieval drinker*   Milverton

6.80 *Drinking bout*   Ludlow

has been suggested, shows Avarice sitting on his money.

DECEIT AND HYPOCRISY
1 In Norwich Cathedral **[6.74]** on a misericord Deceit is personified as a two-faced man under an elaborate turban. One face presents a smiling countenance, the other a snarl and protruding tongue.
2 At Blythburgh **[6.75]** a poppy head depicts Hypocrisy as a woman pretending to pray. (The face is now much worn.)

DRUNKENNESS AND GLUTTONY
1 On a misericord in Norwich Cathedral **[6.76]**, Gluttony is illustrated by a man with extended belly, precariously riding a sleepy pig. He uses both hands to steady his tankard, disregarding the fact that his hat is falling from his head.
2 A poppy head at Blythburgh **[6.77]** shows Gluttony, who by his shape and posture has obviously fed well.
3 The medieval drinker can be seen on bench ends at St Winnow **[6.78]** and Milverton **[6.79]**.
4 A misericord at Ludlow may show a drinking bout in an alehouse **[6.80]**. On a misericord at Wellingborough **[6.81]** a

6.81 *Drunkenness* Wellingborough

6.82 *Gambling* Ely Cathedral

6.83 *Devil as tempter*
Oxford, New College

6.85 *Devil's intervention*   Enville

6.84 *Distraction by the devil*   Ely Cathedral

6.86 *Devil astride couple at prayer:
Irreverent behaviour*   Gayton

man and a woman stand on either side of a table. The man's hand is missing; he probably held a drinking vessel. He is scratching his head with his left hand. The woman is holding a cup in one hand and a jug in the other.

GAMBLING
On a misericord in Ely Cathedral [6.82], two men are shown casting dice on a board. On the left supporter is shown a man with a goblet and a large jug and on the right supporter is seen 'the wife with a hive of honey upset; emblematic of the fact that all her savings have gone in drink and gambling'. (*Misericords*, F Bond)

IRREVERENT BEHAVIOUR
On a misericord in the chapel of New College, Oxford [6.83], the Devil as tempter hovers over a man and a woman. They are seated in a pew and the presence of the Devil appears to have distracted their attention from their devotions, as in Ely Cathedral [6.84] where the man holds a book and the woman a rosary. Again, at Enville [6.85] the intervention of the Devil is a distraction.

Chattering in church was strongly condemned. The Devil was present also as eavesdropper and recorder of this particular vice.

Similarly on a misericord at Gayton [6.86], an angelic-

6.87 *Man with hare riding a goat* Gloucester Cathedral

6.88 *Woman half naked, riding a goat*
Worcester Cathedral

6.89 *Man clothed in net riding a hart*
Norwich Cathedral

looking devil is astride a man and a woman. The man is clutching a large rosary.

LECHERY

The goat and the hare were each associated with lechery and sensuality and probably those representations of men and women riding a goat and carrying a hare had a moral force which is now lost. An additional feature found in such representations is that the rider is sometimes clothed in a net. This may show the influence of, and my incorporate aspects of, the story of the Clever Daughter. The Clever Daughter when commanded to appear neither riding nor walking, neither clothed nor unclothed, and bearing a gift which was not a gift, appeared before the king on a goat enveloped in a net bearing a hare which escaped when offered.

Lechery is depicted on several misericords:
1 At Gloucester Cathedral [6.87] a man with a hare attached to his belt rides a goat.
2 At Worcester Cathedral [6.88] a woman enveloped in a net is holding a hare to her bosom and riding a goat.
3 At Norwich Cathedral [6.89] a man clothed in a net and holding a hare is astride a hart. At Stratford-upon-Avon [6.90] a naked woman, holding a bunch of flowers, is astride a stag.
4 At Beverley, St Mary, [6.91] is a curious composite misericord on which a man, naked with a netlike pattern on his body, holds a hare and rides a goat. He flanks a king with a large sceptre on the other side of whom is a man astride a lion.

6.90 *Naked woman on a stag*
Stratford-upon-Avon

6.91 *Composite portrayal of lechery*   Beverley, St Mary

6.92 *Vanity*   Norwich Cathedral

PRIDE AND VANITY

1 A misericord in Norwich Cathedral [**6.92**] shows an overdressed man beating about the bushes with his scamping dogs. This is said to represent Vanity. (*Report of the Friends of Norwich Cathedral*, 1948)

2 In Blythburgh [**6.93**] is a poppy head, one of a series depicting the vices, of a woman showing Pride by her elaborate apparel.

SLOTH

1 In the *Report of the Friends of Norwich Cathedral* (1948) a misericord in the cathedral [**6.94**] is described as Sloth,

illustrated by Chaucer's *Nun's Priest's Tale*. Dame Malkin, distaff in her hand and the dog, Coll, barking at her feet, chases the fox whilst a pig eats the broth. Pans and pots are littered about and two little birds are seen on a shelf.

2 At Blythburgh a poppy head [**6.95**] shows Sloth as a man in bed.

THE PSYCHOMACHIA

Tertullian describes the virtues and vices as living creatures in concrete form struggling against each other in the arena, but it was the poet Prudentius who made the idea popular. In his poem *The Psychomachia*, he describes the battle

6.93 *Pride*   Blythburgh

6.94 *Sloth*   Norwich Cathedral

6.95 *Sloth as a man in bed*   Blythburgh

6.96 *Psychomachia*   Stanton Fitzwarren

6.97 *Psychomachia*   Southrop

6.98 *Pietas; Misericordia*   Stanton Fitzwarren

of the Christian virtues as armed virgins against the pagan vices. Each virtue carried an appropriate weapon and engaged in single combat with the opposing vice.

In England the best representations are on a font at Stanton Fitzwarren [**6.96**], and on a similar font at Southrop [**6.97**], which could be a copy of the former.

On the doorway of the chapter house of Salisbury Cathedral, where the poem is illustrated, the virtues have lost their dignity.

The font at Stanton Fitzwarren is divided into ten arched panels. In each is an armed virtue trampling on the crouched figure of a vanquished vice. The name of each virtue is on the arch above and the name of the opposing vice is at the side.

Pietas, armed with sword and shield, tramples on *Discordia* [**6.98**].

Misericordia, armed with sword and round shield, tramples on *Invidia* [**6.98**].

Modestia, armed with sword and shield, tramples on *Ebrietas* [**6.99**].

6.99 *Modestia; Temperancia*   Stanton Fitzwarren

6.100 *Pudicicia; Eclesia*   Stanton Fitzwarren

6.102 *Largitas*   Southrop

Temperancia, armed with sword and shield and carrying a banner, tramples on *Luxuria* [**6.99**].

Paciencia, armed with sword and round shield, tramples on *Ira*.

Pudicicia, armed with sword (broken) and round shield, tramples on *Libido* [**6.100**].

Eclesia, a crowned figure holding a chalice, pierces with a tall cross a dragon, *Serpen Occiditur* [**6.100**].

Cherubin is an angel with six wings holding a sword [**6.101**].

Largitas, armed with a sword, tramples on *Avaricia* [**6.101**].

Humilitas, armed with a club and shield, tramples on *Superbia*.

The font at Southrop follows a similar pattern but the name of each vice is written in reverse suggesting that the

6.101 *Cherubim; Largitas*   Stanton Fitzwarren

6.103 *Paciencia* Southrop

6.105 *Western Doctors of the Church: St Gregory and St Jerome* Trull

carver was not fully aware of what he was doing:

    Largitas, carrying a shield, whips *Avaricia* [6.102].

    Paciencia, armed with a knotted whip and round shield, tramples on *Ira* [6.103].

    The other panels follow the Stanton Fitzwarren pattern.

WESTERN DOCTORS OF THE CHURCH

The Western Doctors of the Church are:

(a) *St Gregory*, who showed his administrative ability as pope and his learning in his scriptural commentaries. He is usually depicted as pope with a papal tiara and sometimes with a dove as an attribute, a reference to the inspiration of the Holy Spirit.

(b) *St Jerome*, who translated the Old Testament from Hebrew into the Latin Vulgate. He is depicted as a

6.104 *Western Doctors of the Church: St Ambrose and St Augustine of Hippo* Trull

6.106 *St Augustine and St Gregory* Methley

6.107 *St Jerome and St Ambrose* Methley

cardinal and is sometimes accompanied by a lion, a reference to the story of his having removed a thorn from a lion's paw and the resulting companionship.

(c) *St Ambrose*, who was Archbishop of Milan and a renowned scholar.

(d) *St Augustine*, who was Bishop of Hippo and a learned theological writer. They are represented on the pulpit at Trull [**6.104, 6.105**]. As painted figures on the pulpit at Castle Acre each carries a lettered scroll. At Methley [**6.106, 6.107**] they are depicted in glass in the traditional way.

7
Creatures Natural and Mythical

EVEN THE INFREQUENT visitor to cathedrals and churches must be familiar with carvings, some strange and unrecognisable, which relate in some way to the natural world. A more frequent visitor knows how such carvings abound. They are to be found inside and outside the buildings, in the roof on the bosses and under the seats on the misericord carvings; they are to be found almost everywhere except on the altar. Some are readily recognised but some appear strange and fanciful. They can be divided into two categories: those that are natural creatures, both bird and beast, and those which present a more curious appearance belonging to the world of fancy and myth. A few of the natural creatures owe much to the observation of the carver and are true to life. Some at first sight appear to be the work of an unskilled man but the same man may have shown considerable skill in other parts of the carving. Again, some appear distorted or display an unusual characteristic which could be attributed to ignorance. Ignorance there must have been, but this is not the full explanation. The medieval carver, and those who employed him, knew and used the Bestiary.

The Bestiary assumed its medieval form in the twelfth century, having developed from the *Physiologus*, a natural history book of the earlier period. In the Bestiary were described the life style and habits of both real and mythical creatures. In some cases the description of both bird and beast owed little to scientific observation. Credulity and imagination, stimulated by travellers' tales and previous writers, gave birth to mythical creatures. Into each description was incorporated biblical references and from this account, whether true or fanciful, were drawn moral and religious lessons. Many of the Bestiaries were illustrated, so not only were carvers influenced by the written word but scholars have demonstrated how some work is based on such illustrations. The identification of, and significance of, a particular carving is often dependent on a knowledge of what is contained in the Bestiary. The preaching friars in their sermons to the common people drew upon the world around them and upon the familiar folklore. References to the deceitful fox, the obnoxious cockatrice, the curious sciapod or the powerful dragon, would help to establish belief in this world of familiar and strange creatures.

In many cases, after examination, identification of carvings of creatures can be certain but there are others where there is doubt and differing interpretations are acceptable. This is particularly the case with some composite creatures. Even allowing for poor execution on the part of the carver, and ignorance on the part of the present-day observer, here it would appear that the carver has indulged in a degree of freedom of the imagination and has produced something which does not conform with any known creature or with any known written description.

7.1 *Amphisbaena fighting*   Ripon Cathedral

7.2 *Amphisbaena in conflict*   Halsall

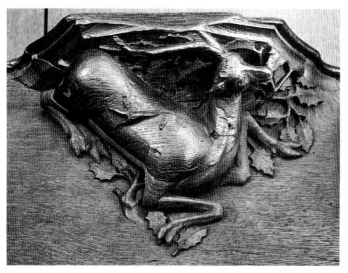

7.3 *Antelope*   Boston

7.4 *Two antelopes*   Ripon Cathedral

AMPHISBAENA

The amphisbaena, a strange creature described by classical writers, is drawn in the Bestiaries as a winged dragon with a second head in the tail. As medieval carvers were prone to putting a second head on any fabulous creature there can be some confusion in identification. As its name suggests it was reputed to possess the ability to move backwards and forwards and was regarded as a deadly serpent, the symbol of deceit.

REPRESENTATIONS

1 Either alone or in conflict with another amphisbaena as on a misericord in Ripon Cathedral [7.1], and at Halsall [7.2].

2 In conflict with a centaur as on a boss in the Muniment Room, Westminster Abbey, where the centaur has thrust a spear into the amphisbaena which is attacking it with both heads. (*Roof Bosses*, CJP Cave, fig 230)

7.5 *Chained antelope*   Ripon Cathedral

7.6 *Lion and deer in conflict*   Beverley Minster

ANTELOPE/HART

The antelope and the hart had a literary distinction which is not always seen in medieval representations. Early writers emphasised the enmity between the hart and the serpent. The hart was said to renew its horns each year by eating serpents. The antelope had two serrated horns by which it could saw through trees. The two horns symbolised the Old and the New Testament by which man armed himself. Its horns became entangled in foliage as man by sin became entangled in the snares of the world. Chained and collared it became a common heraldic device.

REPRESENTATIONS

1 Entangled in foliage by its horns as on a misericord in Boston [7.3].
2 With characteristic serrated horns as on a misericord in Ripon Cathedral [7.4].
3 Chained and collared as on a misericord in Ripon Cathedral [7.5].
4 In association with a lion as on a misericord in Beverley Minster [7.6]
5 Eating a serpent as on a misericord supporter in Ely Cathedral.
   See also: 'Everyday Scenes: Hunting' [8.40, 8.45, 8.46]; 'Saints: St Hubert' [5.145], 'St Giles' [5.128, 5.129].

APE/MONKEY

Medieval carvers made no clear distinction between ape and monkey. The monkey was a great favourite in the Middle Ages as is witnessed by the many representations. In the literature several types of apes and monkeys are described. Satyrus was a great ape like the orang-utan. It is depicted with bearded face and human hands and arms. The Callitriches were smooth-haired apes and the Cynocephalus were a dog-headed race of apes or baboons. Literary distinctions are not always maintained in carvings. We find the monkey used in the satire of music and medicine and in circus-like activities such as riding other animals. The ape was associated with avarice and deceit. The monkey was reputed to be particularly fond of its offspring.

7.7 *Natural monkey*   Salle

7.9 *Ape with urine bottle*   Boston

7.8 *Callitriche and cynocephalus*   Ufford

7.10 *Ape with monkey as a bagpipe*   Norwich Cathedral

REPRESENTATIONS

1 A natural monkey as on an elbow rest at Salle [7.7].

2 Satyrus, the great ape, as on misericords in Chichester Cathedral and Chichester, St Mary.

3 Callitriches and Cynocephalus are seen on a bench end at Ufford [7.8].

4 Monkey with swaddled child is found as a supporter on misericords in Beverley Minster (see 'Dragon' [7.56]) and in Manchester Cathedral (see 'Stories and Proverbial Sayings: Reynard Stories' [9.35]).

5 The monkey and the ape both appear in scenes where doctors and medicine are satirised. On a misericord at Boston [7.9] an ape, holding a large urine bottle, faces a fox carrying a bucket. On a misericord at Beverley, St Mary, a wodehouse has pierced a fox with an oversize arrow. The injured fox appears to be proffering something to a monkey, perhaps trying to purchase a medicament. (See 'Wodehouse' [7.148])

The supporter of another misericord in Beverley Minster is a monkey nursing a bedridden fox. (See 'Everyday Scenes: Hunting' [8.44])

6 The monkey is sometimes found in a comic role, as on a misericord in Norwich Cathedral [7.10], where an ape uses a monkey as a bagpipe to the amusement of a laughing dog, and where a monkey, armed with a birch, is being taken for a ride by another monkey [7.11]. In the same category are the supporters of misericords in Beverley Minster (see 'Bear' [7.24, 7.27] and 'Dragon' [7.56]) and Manchester Cathedral. (See 'Stories and Proverbial Sayings: Reynard Stories' [9.35])

7 Monkey riding other animals. In Beverley Minster a monkey rides a horse and leads three bears (see 'Bear' [7.24]) and a monkey astride a dog is the supporter of another misericord in the same church.

8 On a misericord in Lincoln Cathedral two monkeys carry a dead monkey on a bier.

7.11 *Monkey riding on a wheel barrow*   Norwich Cathedral

7.12 *Lion with snarling ape*   Ripon Cathedral

7.13 *Ape offers money to ecclesiastic*
Beverley, St Mary

9 In Winchester Cathedral on a misericord an ape leads a sleepy owl.

10 In New College Chapel, Oxford on a misericord a hooded ape is rising from a shell. The significance of this is obscure.

11 On a misericord in Ripon Cathedral [7.12] a lion and a snarling ape face each other.

12 In Beverley, St Mary [7.13], is a curious misericord where an ape offers a bag of money to an ecclesiastic. Perhaps this has some reference to the ape's association with avarice.

13 On a misericord in Windsor, St George's Chapel, an ape is in conflict with a wyvern.

(See also 'Stories and Proverbial Sayings: Leading Apes into Hell' [9.18])

ASP

The asp is described as a kind of venomous snake. When an attempt is made to enchant it out of its hole, it puts one ear to the ground and puts its tail in the other to shut out the sound.

The Bestiaries differentiate between several kinds of asps but the carvers made no attempt to make a distinction and it is not found in English churches in a characteristic posture.

An asp-like creature is found on a misericord in Exeter Cathedral. (See 'Basilisk' [7.15].) On the Ruthwell Cross is an early figure of Christ who is said to be treading on an asp.

BASILISK/COCKATRICE

The basilisk was hatched from the seven-year-old egg of a cock, on a dung heap. This creature with the body of a serpent and the head, wings and feet of a cock could slay by a glance, or by poison emitted from its eyes, those who looked upon it. The danger could be avoided by using a mirror when the basilisk became the recipient of its own venom. This remedy was suggested to Alexander by the

7.14 *Cockatrice* Malvern Priory

7.15 *Asp and basilisk* Exeter Cathedral

7.16 *Bat with outstretched wings*
Dunblane Cathedral

7.17 *Bat with outstretched wings* Edlesborough

philosophers when a basilisk, causing death, was found in his camp.

Representations are found on misericords in Malvern Priory [7.14], and in Exeter Cathedral [7.15] where an asp and a basilisk, with foliated tails, face each other.

The weasel was immune if it first ate rue. Reference to this is made on a misericord in Worcester Cathedral where a basilisk is the central subject and a weasel with a sprig of rue in its mouth is one of the supporters.

BAT

No particular symbolism was attached to the bat except that its habit of hibernating in groups was taken as a mark of unusual affection.

On a misericord in Dunblane Cathedral [7.16] the bat is depicted with outstretched wings. It is found, with some imperfections, on several other misericords such as at Edlesborough [7.17], and Wells Cathedral.

BEAR

The bear was a familiar animal in the Middle Ages and bear baiting was a common pastime. As would be expected, the

7.18 *Dog attacks chained bear*   Gloucester Cathedral

7.19 *Bear baiting*   Boston

7.20 *Dogs attacking bear*   Manchester Cathedral

7.21 *Lion and bear in conflict*   Norwich Cathedral

bear in various forms is frequently found in medieval carving. Heraldically it occurs as the Warwick Badge, the bear and ragged staff.

REPRESENTATIONS

1 Bear baiting is well depicted as on a misericord in Gloucester Cathedral [7.18] where a dog attacks a collared and chained bear. The bear master is seen in the background and his large hat lies on the ground. A similar scene is on a misericord at Boston [7.19], and at Manchester Cathedral [7.20] five dogs are attacking a collared bear.

2 On a misericord in Norwich Cathedral [7.21] a lion and collared bear are in conflict.

3 In Bristol Cathedral [7.22] is a misericord where two naked men with diminutive wheelbarrows flank a roped and muzzled bear.

4 At Sherborne [7.23] on a misericord a hairy chained bear is eating acorns.

5 At Beverley Minster is a series of misericords on which the bear features.

   (a) A monkey on horseback leads by a chain three muzzled bears. On the left a bear eats a bone, and on the right

7.22 *Bear and men with barrows*
Bristol Cathedral

7.23 *Bear eating acorns*
Sherborne

7.24 *Monkey leads three chained bears*
Beverley Minster

7.25 *Men with bears*   Beverley Minster

7.26 *Men attempting to put bear into barrow*   Beverley Minster

7.27 *Bear hunt*   Beverley Minster

a monkey uses a dog as bagpipes [**7.24**].

(b) Three men pull a bear in a large basket. On the left a man is muzzling a bear and on the right a man is dancing with a bear [**7.25**].

(c) Three men are pulling a bear with a rope seemingly hoping to put it into a small wheelbarrow. On the left a man holds a dog by the collar and on the right a bear licks its paw [**7.26**].

(d) The bear hunt. Three dogs attack a bear and two men run to the scene, one of them blowing a horn. On the left a man raises a whip to a monkey and on the right a monkey plays the bagpipes to a dancing bear [**7.27**].

6 At Stratford-upon-Avon [**7.28**] is a misericord on which two muzzled bears flank a ragged staff, the Warwick Badge.

The bear occurs also in the Reynard Cycle. (See 'Stories and Proverbial Sayings: Reynard Stories')

7.28 *Bears and staff – the Warwick badge*   Stratford-upon-Avon

BIRDS DRINKING OR EATING

The peacock was the emblem of immortality and in Byzantine art we find peacocks drinking from a chalice. This was an association of sacramental significance which was continued in Western art either in the form of birds drinking from a chalice, or eating in the branches of a vine, or in a form derived from the former with the same significance. There are numerous carvings of birds: pecking at foliage, feeding on corn or drinking. If any sacramental significance were intended it is very tenuous.

7.29 *Birds eating from a sack*
Carlisle Cathedral

7.30 *Doves pecking at a leaf*
Exeter Cathedral

REPRESENTATIONS

On a tomb slab at Bishopsthorpe two doves peck at a vase. On a misericord in Carlisle Cathedral [7.29] two birds eat from a sack and in Exeter Cathedral [7.30] two doves peck at a leaf. The supporting subjects of two peacocks on a misericord in Lincoln Cathedral are two long-legged birds drinking from a fountain.

BLEMYA

The blemya, perhaps the product of travellers' tales, is an abnormal human being, headless but with eyes and mouth in the stomach.

Blemyae are the supporting subjects of misericords in Norwich Cathedral and Ripon Cathedral, in each case the central subject is the Grapes of Eschol. (See 'Old Testament: Grapes of Eschol' [1.37])

In the Victoria and Albert Museum is a misericord on which blemyae are the supporting subjects of two men threshing corn. (See 'Everyday Scenes: Threshing' [8.95])

BULL/COW

Apart from several carvings of the head of an ox and a recumbent bull on a misericord at Passenham the bull and the cow usually appear in association with, or as part of, another subject. The milkmaid, a man riding an ox, a cow chewing its cud, and other subjects are dealt with separately. The winged ox is the emblem of St Luke.

The Bestiaries say of oxen that they are noted for their friendly disposition towards, and affection for, each other brought about by being yoked together. (See also 'The Church: Emblems of the Four Evangelists')

CALADRIUS

The caladrius was a white bird without any dark spot. It inhabited royal palaces and possessed peculiar properties. A sick man, when faced with a caladrius, instantly knew his fate for if the bird turned away from him he was doomed to die. On the other hand if the illness was not fatal the bird faced the patient and itself took the illness, which was

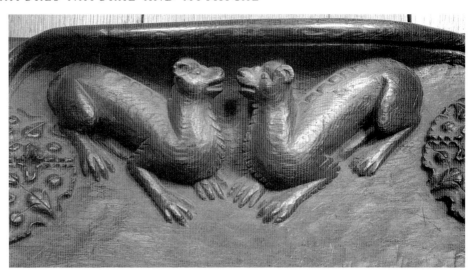

7.32 *Animals with camel-shaped heads*
Hereford, All Saints

7.31 *Camel* Boston

7.33 *Camel – recognised by its humps* Stratford-upon-Avon

destroyed when it flew through the air into the sun. The caladrius was compared with Christ who was without spot and who turned His face against the Jews.

A representation of the caladrius is found on the Norman doorway at Alne. 'In the sculpture the main part of the couch is not visible, and the man's head appears to rest upon a stool. The folds of the coverlet are well indicated. The bird is very large out of proportion to the other details.' (*Archaeological Journal*, vol 69, GC Druce)

CAMEL

The camel was an animal whose true anatomy was little known to medieval carvers. The examples we find are fanciful representations. The camel's ability to go long periods without water led to its being associated with temperance and its kneeling habit invoked the idea of humility.

One of the best representations is a supporting subject on a misericord at Boston [**7.31**]. Two squatting animals with camel-shaped heads are on a misericord in Hereford, All Saints [**7.32**].

7.34 *Camel in conflict with unicorn* Manchester Cathedral

On a misericord at Stratford-upon-Avon [**7.33**] the camel can be recognised by its humps and at Manchester Cathedral [**7.34**] it has a rider who appears to be in conflict with another rider mounted on a unicorn.

7.35 *Cat chasing mouse*   Royston

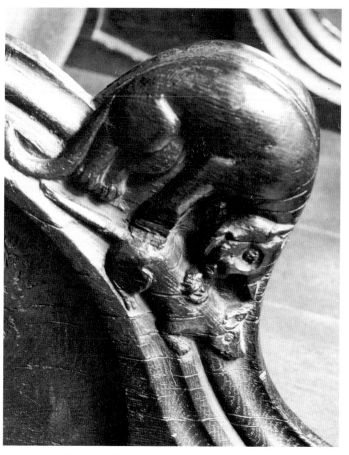

7.36 *Cat and mouse*   Boston

7.37 *Cat with goat playing citoles*   Hereford Cathedral

CAT

The cat appears as a natural animal and, in a satyrical way, in a topsy-turvy world where the usual roles are reversed.

REPRESENTATIONS

1 Chasing a mouse, as on a boss at Royston [**7.35**], and on an elbow rest at Boston [**7.36**].
2 Playing the fiddle, as on misericords in Beverley Minster and Hereford Cathedral [**7.37**] where it has the goat playing the citole for a companion.
3 Satyrically in a hanging scene on a misericord in Malvern Priory [**7.38**] where three mice are hanging a cat.

CENTAUR

Known to the classical world and one of the signs of the Zodiac, the centaur at an early date found a place in Christian iconography. Three names were used to describe the centaur: the *onocentaur*, an ass in which the head is replaced by the upper half of a man; *hippocentaur*, a horse in which the head is replaced by the upper half of a man; and *sagittarius*, the centaur armed with bow and arrow, so frequently found in Romanesque work. The significance of the centaur in art is rarely seen clearly; it was used to symbolise human passions and to typify Our Lord.

7.38 *Mice hanging cat* Malvern Priory

7.39 *Centaur* Exeter Cathedral

7.40 *Centaur shoots arrow into supporting subject* Exeter Cathedral

REPRESENTATIONS

1 Centaur with bow and arrow as on a misericord in Exeter Cathedral [7.39], where we find a female centaur; on another misericord [7.40] a male centaur has shot an arrow into a supporting subject.

2 Centaur with a musical instrument as on a misericord in New College Chapel, Oxford [7.41], where a centaur plays a pipe and drum and the supporters, also centaurs, play a horn and a trumpet.

3 Centaur in conflict with an amphisbaena. (See 'Amphisbaena')

7.41 Centaurs playing instruments Oxford, New College

7.42 Crowing cock Beverley Minster

7.43 Crab Durham Cathedral

7.44 Crane with stone in its claw Denston

COCK/HEN

The cock and the hen appear without any intended symbolism as creatures of the farmyard. The hen with her brood appears on a misericord in Beverley Minster and another misericord in the same church shows the crowing cock [7.42].
(See also 'Pig' [7.115]; 'Stories and Proverbial Sayings: Reynard Stories' [9.25])

CRAB

The crab cunningly attacks the oyster, its favourite food. When the oyster opens its shell the crab inserts a pebble to prevent it closing, so that it can safely extract the oyster with its claws.

In Durham Cathedral [7.43] are two similar misericords on each of which is depicted a crab.

CRANE

The crane cannot be distinguished easily from other long-necked birds except when the carver incorporates one of its characteristics mentioned in the Bestiaries. Here it is said that the crane eats sand and picks up stones to give it ballast and to prevent its being blown off course when in flight.

Also when on guard duty during the night it holds a stone in its claw. If drowsiness should overtake it the falling stone arouses it.

REPRESENTATIONS

1 At Denston [7.44] is a misericord on which is a crane with a round stone in its claw.
2 Cranes are the subject of the poppy head of the desk end of the precentors' stall in Lincoln Cathedral. One of the birds holds a round stone in its claw.

CROCODILE

The crocodile was mentioned in the Bestiaries where its hard tough skin and its dung, which was reputed to have medicinal properties, were noted as two of its characteristics. Its enemy was the Hydrus, a water snake, which having rolled itself in the mud, was swallowed by the crocodile and then either destroyed its bowels to be emitted in the usual way, or gnawed a way out through the crocodile's side.

The crocodile is represented on a corbel at Kilpeck, where it is swallowing a Hydrus.

7.45 *Dog gnawing at a bone*   Christchurch Priory

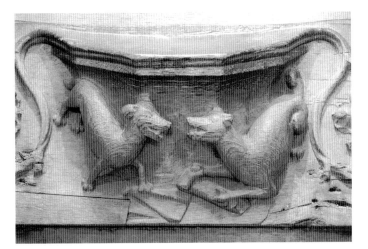

7.46 *Dogs quarrel over a bone*   St David's Cathedral

7.47 *Hunter with dogs sharpens a knife*   Boston

DOG

The dog is often seen as part of a scene such as hunting, bear baiting, or homelife. Mythology and symbolism are not associated with it.

In Christchurch Priory [**7.45**] is a misericord on which an emaciated dog gnaws at a bone, and in St David's Cathedral [**7.46**] two dogs face each other quarrelling over a bone.

On a misericord at Boston [**7.47**] a hunter flanked by his two dogs is sharpening his knife.

DOLPHIN

The dolphin had a reputation as a powerful swimmer and was thought to be musical and to respond to the human voice. A special species in the Nile was the enemy of the crocodile which it cut with its swordlike dorsal fin. Dolphins are the supporting subjects on a misericord depicting a mermaid at Ludlow and in Norwich Cathedral (see 'Siren'). At Norwich the dolphin is swallowing its young.

At Salle [**7.48**] two dolphins are leaping from the water in a playful way.

7.48 *Dolphins leaping from water*   Salle

7.49 *Traditional dragon* Weston-in-Gordano

7.50 *Dragon* Carlisle Cathedral

7.51 *Dragon supported by birds and leaves* Ripon Cathedral

7.52 *Two wyverns attack man in armour* Worcester Cathedral

DOVE

Although the dove is mentioned in the Bestiaries where its attributes are such that it is compared to preachers, it only appears in medieval art as a natural bird.

It occurs in representations of the Flood and as the emblem of the Holy Spirit in such subjects as the Baptism of Christ and the Trinity. Two doves are depicted on a misericord in Exeter Cathedral. (See 'Birds' [7.30])

DRAGON/SERPENT/WYVERN

Carvings of dragons, in varying forms, abound. Some assume a ferocious appearance. The only serpentine creature which can be distinguished readily from the traditional quadruped dragon is the wyvern which is a biped. Its role is interchangeable with that of the dragon and it is best considered as a type of dragon. In whatever guise it appeared, the dragon symbolised the Devil and Satanic power and forces.

7.53 *Knight stabbing a dragon*
Exeter Cathedral

7.54 *Two creatures with tail round victim*   Beverley Minster

7.55 *Dragon swallowing man*   Carlisle Cathedral

REPRESENTATIONS

1 Traditional dragon, as on a misericord in Weston-in-Gordano [7.49], a crude serpent-like wyvern with forked tongue, Carlisle Cathedral [7.50], and Ripon Cathedral [7.51] where it is supported by small birds on leaves.

2 Dragon in conflict with a man. On a misericord in Worcester Cathedral [7.52] two wyverns attack a man in armour carrying a sword and shield. In Exeter Cathedral [7.53] a knight is stabbing a dragon and in Beverley Minster [7.54] two wyvern-like creatures have wound their tails round their victim.

There is a misericord in Carlisle Cathedral [7.55] on which a dragon has half swallowed a man. This may represent Judas in the jaws of Satan. A similar representation is found on misericords in Worcester and St David's Cathedrals.

3 Dragon and lion in conflict as on a misericord in Beverley Minster [7.56], and in Chester Cathedral [7.57] where the supporters are a wyvern and a wodehouse in conflict.

7.56 *Lion and dragon in conflict – monkey with child on supporter*   Beverley Minster

7.57 *Wyvern and wodehouse in conflict*   Chester Cathedral

7.58 *Wodehouse faces dragon*   Beverley Minster

7.60 *Chained wyverns face each other*   Nantwich

7.59 *Wodehouse and wyvern*   Manchester Cathedral

7.61 *Apocalyptic dragon*   Oxford, New College

7.62 *Wyvern with a woman's head*   Ludlow

7.63 *Dragon with human arms and hands*
Canterbury Cathedral

4 Dragon and wodehouse in conflict as on a misericord in Beverley Minster [7.58] where a wodehouse clothed in skins and armed with a club and shield faces an angry dragon. There is a similar misericord in Manchester Cathedral [7.59].
5 Dragon and griffin in conflict are seen on a misericord at Boston.
6 Chained wyverns face each other on a misericord at Nantwich [7.60].

7 Dragons fighting, a frequently found subject, can be seen on misericords in Gloucester and Ripon Cathedrals.
8 The Apocalyptic Dragon or Hydra representing the Seven Deadly Sins is seen on a misericord in the chapel of New College, Oxford [7.61].
9 The wyvern on a misericord in Ludlow [7.62] has lost its ferocious appearance and has been given a woman's head with an attractive headdress.

7.64 *Dragon facing figure emerging from a shell* Nantwich

7.65 *Dragon with figure coming out of shell* Chester Cathedral

7.66 *Double-headed eagle* Boston

10 At Canterbury Cathedral [**7.63**], in the crypt, is a Romanesque capital on which is carved a dragon or wyvern which has been given a pair of human arms and hands. With one hand it holds its tail and with the other a spear with which it has pierced a terrified dog.

11 On a misericord at Nantwich [**7.64**] a dragon faces a human figure emerging from a shell. A similar subject occurs in Lincoln Cathedral and Chester Cathedral [**7.65**]. The significance is not clear.

DUCK

The duck occurs as prey in hawking and similar scenes. At Herne are two misericords where it is represented alone: on one it is shown alighting on the water and on the other preening itself.

(See also 'Everyday Scenes: Hunting and Hawking' [**8.42**])

EAGLE

Of the eagle it was said that, to rejuvenate its plumage and its youth, it soared to the sun and then plunged into the water. 'So that thy youth is renewed like the eagles' (*Psalms* 103 v 5). Thus it became the symbol of the Resurrection and the Christian life strengthened by baptismal grace. 'But they that wait upon the Lord shall renew their strength, they shall mount up with wings as eagles.' (*Isaiah* 40 v 31)

Emile Mâle has suggested that the double-headed eagle was introduced into the art of Western Christendom by fabrics brought back by soldiers from the crusades.

The eagle in several forms became common in heraldry.

REPRESENTATIONS

1 Double-headed eagle as on a misericord at Boston [**7.66**], and at Wantage.

7.67 *Eagle used as heraldic charge*   Whalley

7.68 *Eagle pouncing on a lamb and a bird*   Norwich Cathedral

7.69 *Elephant and castle*   Gloucester Cathedral

7.70 *Elephant and castle*   Beverley, St Mary

2 It was used as a heraldic charge, as at Whalley [7.67].
3 On a misericord in Norwich Cathedral [7.68] an eagle is pouncing on a lamb and a small bird at the same time. On a misericord in the Victoria and Albert Museum it is alighting on a rabbit.

(See also 'Stories and Proverbial Sayings: The Lathom Legend' [9.16, 9.17]; 'The Church: Emblems of the Four Evangelists' [6.25])

ELEPHANT

An elephant appeared in London as early as 1255. Much was written about it but most of the carvings are quaintly inaccurate. The Persians and Indians, it was said, fought from castles erected on its back. Although the largest of

animals it was thought to be afraid of mice. The elephant is usually shown complete with castle, as on a misericord in Gloucester Cathedral [7.69], and Beverley, St Mary [7.70], and on a poppy head in Ripon Cathedral [7.71]. An elephant and a dragon in conflict appear on a misericord in Carlisle Cathedral.

FOX

The fox, a familiar animal, was popular because of the literature about it and because of the appeal of its crafty, cheeky ways. Its craft is recognised in the Bestiary story: when unable to find a prey it rolls in red clay to assume the appearance of blood, holds its breath to give a swollen appearance, and lying on its back it shams death. This

7.72 *Fox shams death* Nantwich

7.71 *Elephant and castle on poppy head*
Ripon Cathedral

7.73 *Fox shams death* Chester Cathedral

attracts the birds which quickly discover the fraud when the cunning fox springs to life and finds them easy victims.

This episode is depicted on misericords in Whalley, Nantwich [**7.72**], and Chester Cathedral [**7.73**].

Other stories of his deceitful life are considered under 'Reynard Stories'.

There are many examples on misericords of the fox as the farmyard thief; its favourite quarry is the traditional goose. (See also 'Stories and Proverbial Sayings: Reynard Stories')

FROG

The frog was known for the croaking noise it makes. This was aligned with the voice of heretics. Also is recorded the curious belief that if a dog swallows a live frog it loses the power to bark.

A fat frog is the supporter of a misericord in Edlesborough [**7.74**]. At Windsor, St George's Chapel, a man is being forcibly fed with a frog.

7.74 *Frog on supporter of a misericord* Edlesborough

7.75 *Goats browsing on vegetation*
Winchester College Chapel

7.76 *Male griffin* Cartmel Priory

GOAT

More than one type of goat is mentioned in the Bestiaries. Hyrcus, the He-Goat, was a lascivious and butting animal. Because of this vice he was associated with, and appears in, representations of Lechery. (See 'The Church: Vices – Lechery' [6.87, 6.88])

The goat is sometimes depicted browsing on vegetation as on a misericord in Winchester College Chapel [7.75], and on a boss in the cathedral at Norwich.

GOOSE

The goose appears incidentally as part of composite scenes usually in association with Reynard the Fox.

A goose is a supporting subject on a misericord at Stratford-upon-Avon.

7.77 *Griffin attacking rabbit*
Ripon Cathedral

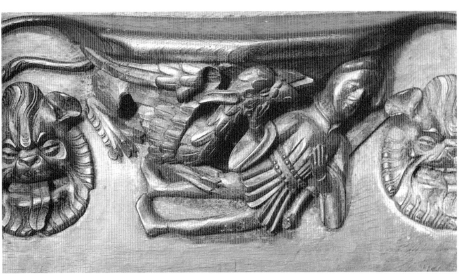

7.78 *Griffin attacks a man*
Carlisle Cathedral

7.79 *Griffin attacked by a man* Norwich Cathedral

GRIFFIN

The griffin was a fabulous creature compounded of the forepart of an eagle and the hindquarters of a lion. It was reputed to be a creature of great strength and pre-Christian writers cast it in the role of guardian of treasures.

According to F. Bond, the male griffin can be distinguished by two straight horns and a beard.

REPRESENTATIONS

1 The male griffin as on a misericord in Cartmel Priory **[7.76]**.

2 Griffin attacking an animal such as a rabbit as on a misericord in Ripon Cathedral **[7.77]**. In Wells Cathedral on one misericord a griffin is eating a lamb and on another a griffin and a lion are in conflict. At Boston a griffin opposes a dragon.

3 In conflict with a man as on a misericord in Carlisle Cathedral **[7.78]** where it attacks a prostrate man, and in Norwich Cathedral **[7.79]** where it is attacked by a man,

7.80 *Hare* Wensley

7.81 *Heraldic falcon with fetterlock* Ludlow

7.82 *Hedgehog* Cartmel Priory

armed with spear and shield, to prevent its preying on a lamb. At Chester Cathedral and Nantwich the griffin appears to have the best of the conflict.

4 Guarding the Tree of Life as on a misericord in Beverley, St Mary.

HARE
According to Pliny, the hare combined both sexes in itself. It was the symbol of lust and fecundity.

The hare is carved in a naturalistic way on a bench end at Wensley [7.80].

On a misericord at Godmanchester a hare is crouched on a bunch of radiating leaves.

HAWK
The hawk is common in hawking scenes but occasionally it is found alone, usually with its prey in its talons, as on a misericord in Wells Cathedral where it has seized a rabbit. The heraldic falcon with fetterlock is also found as on a misericord at Ludlow [7.81].

HEDGEHOG
The hedgehog was also known as the *urchin*. It was said to roll on fallen fruit and to carry it away impaled on its spines to feed its young. Isidore claims that it could climb trees to cast down the fruit.

It is found as a supporter on a misericord in Cartmel Priory [7.82], and in Oxford, New College Chapel.

7.83 *Two herons(?)*
Chester Cathedral

HERON
There are many representations of long-legged birds most of which are difficult to identify. The central subject of a misericord in Chester Cathedral [7.83] may be two herons.

HIPPOPOTAMUS
At Eynesbury [7.84] two heads rise from the top of a poppy head. These have been seen as hippopotamuses, but as no other example is known, and as this poppy head is one of a series on which are carved unidentifiable creatures, such an identification is doubtful.

HOOPOE
In the Bestiaries the hoopoe, with a crest similar to a peacock, was described as a foul bird which frequented graves. One account relates that: 'when the young of these birds see their parents grown old and unable to fly or see through blindness then these their children pluck off the very old feathers from their parents and lick their eyes and cherish their parents under their wings, until their feathers grow again and their eyes become bright so that they are made quite young again in body as before and can see and fly and show their gratitude to their children, because they have fulfilled their duty towards their parents with such love.' (*Antiquary*, vol 50, GC Druce)

The hoopoe is seen with clearly defined crests on a misericord at Windsor, St George's Chapel.

HORSE
The horse appears as part of other subjects, usually bearing a rider as in hunting and fighting scenes.
(See also 'Stories and Proverbial Sayings: Cart before the Horse' [9.7])

7.84 *Hippopotamus* Eynesbury

7.85 *Hyena attacking a corpse*
Carlisle Cathedral

7.86 *Ibex* King's Lynn, St Nicholas

HYENA

The Bestiaries emphasise the foul nature of the hyena, the inhabitant of graveyards and despoiler of bodies, symbolising vice battening on corruption. On a misericord in Carlisle Cathedral [7.85] a hyena is attacking a corpse, on a boss at Queen Camel it is dragging a corpse from its grave and on the doorway at Alne it holds a large bone.

IBEX

The ibex had two powerful horns which preserved it from harm no matter from what height it fell. It symbolised learned men who used the Old and the New Testament to combat adversity.

A figure on a bench end at King's Lynn, St Nicholas [7.86], may be intended for an ibex but there are so many carvings of antelopes, deer, etc, without distinguishing traits that this is uncertain.

IBIS

'In the Bestiaries the ibis is usually bringing serpents' eggs to its young ones on a nest. As it feeds on carrion, a corpse, dead dog, dead fish, rats or eels are introduced into the picture.' (*Antiquary*, vol 50, GC Druce)

On a misericord at Lavenham [7.87] it is seen pecking a human head. It is feeding on a serpent on a misericord at Windsor, St George's Chapel.

JACULUS

The jaculus was a form of dragon or flying serpent 'so named from *jaculum* a dart or javelin, because it was supposed to dart with exceeding swiftness from a tree on to its prey' (*Archaeological Journal*, vol 67, GC Druce). A possible representation is on the Norman doorway at York, St Margaret Walmgate.

7.87 *Ibis pecking a human head*   Lavenham

7.88 *Leopard*   Dunblane Cathedral

LEOPARD

A crudely carved figure of a leopard with clearly marked spots and a geometrically curled tail occurs on a misericord at Dunblane Cathedral [7.88].

LION

The artist was faced with a difficulty in depicting the lion because of its reputed dual nature. It was said to sleep with its eyes open; this was associated with Christ's resting in the tomb for three days. Also the lioness was said to give birth to dead cubs which came to life when their sire breathed upon them three days after their birth; this was in turn associated with the Resurrection. So it followed that the lion was a good beast symbolising Christ, the Lion of Judah, and the Resurrection. Yet it was written in scripture that the Devil 'goeth about like a roaring lion, seeking whom he may devour' which suggested that, paradoxically, the lion also symbolised the Devil and thus had a dual nature.

Its reputation for sleeping with its eyes open may be the reason for its being the guardian of church doors, and why on the font at Eardsley one eye is open and one is closed.

7.89 *Natural lion*   Exeter Cathedral

7.90 *Natural lion*   Manchester Cathedral

7.91 *Man and a lion in conflict*   Norwich Cathedral

7.92 *Wodehouse flanked by lions*   Beverley, St Mary

REPRESENTATIONS

1 The natural lion as on a misericord in Exeter Cathedral [**7.89**], and Manchester Cathedral [**7.90**].

2 A lion breathing on its cubs is shown on a boss in Canterbury Cathedral. ·

3 Lion and bear. (See 'Bear' [**7.21**])

4 Lion and deer. (See 'Antelope' [**7.6**])

5 Lion and dragon. (See 'Dragon' [**7.56**])

6 Lion and griffin. (See 'Griffin')

7 Lion and man.

   On a misericord in Beverley Minster, a lion places its paw on the head of a prostrate man, and at Norwich Cathedral [**7.91**] a man and a lion are in conflict.

8 Lion and mermaid. (See 'Siren' [**7.130, 7.131**])

9 Lion and monkey.

'On a misericord in St George's Chapel, Windsor, the lion is shown eating a dead monkey, which the Bestiary

7.93 *Wodehouse and lion in conflict* Hereford Cathedral

7.94 *Wodehouse and lion in conflict* Norton

7.95 *Lion with human face* Winthorpe

tells us it does when sick and so cures itself.' (*Animal Carvings*, MD Anderson)

10 Lion and wodehouse.

On a misericord in Beverley, St Mary [**7.92**] a wodehouse is flanked by two amiable lions. In Norwich Cathedral a wodehouse leads two lion cubs by a chain and in Hereford Cathedral [**7.93**], and at Norton [**7.94**] a wodehouse and a lion are in conflict.

11 The lion is found with a human face as on an elbow rest at Winthorpe [**7.95**].

LIZARD

The true lizard cannot be distinguished from the many forms of serpent and dragon which resemble it.

The best-known representation is on a corbel in the north transept of Wells Cathedral where, surrounded by vine leaves, it is stealing the fruit. (See *Sculpture in Britain*, Lawrence Stone, plate 76B)

7.96 *Mantichora*   North Cerney

7.97 *Osprey*   Ribbesford

MANTICHORA

The mantichora was another fabulous creature of uncertain composition. The body of a lion with a serpent's tail and a human face with three rows of teeth seem to be its distinctive features.

It may occur at Kilpeck, North Cerney [7.96], and on a misericord in Windsor, St George's Chapel.

OSPREY

On the Norman capital of the doorway at Ribbesford [7.97] is a carving incorporating two birds. Below is a bird with a large fish. Above is a bird with a large wing span and a pointed beak with a smaller fish. This has been identified as an osprey but identification is uncertain and it could be any fish-eating bird.

OSTRICH

According to the Bestiaries the ostrich enjoyed a remarkable digestion and was able to eat iron. That is why on a supporter of a misericord at Stratford-upon-Avon [7.98] the ostrich is depicted with a horseshoe in its mouth.

OTTER

As a supporting subject on a misericord in Windsor, St George's Chapel, the otter is depicted carrying a fish in its mouth.

OWL

Medieval writers differentiated between the various kinds of owl but representations are based on two observed facts,

7.98 *Ostrich eating iron*
Stratford-upon-Avon

7.100 *Owl being mobbed* Norwich Cathedral

7.99 *Owl mobbed by small birds* Norwich Cathedral

7.101 *Owl with other birds*
Gloucester Cathedral

the first of these being that it was a bird of prey and the second that when it ventured out during the daytime it could be subject to mobbing by the small birds. The owl's nocturnal habits and avoidance of bright light led to its symbolising darkness and ignorance and finally the Jew in his blindness.

REPRESENTATIONS

1 Mobbing of the owl by small birds as on misericords in Norwich Cathedral [7.99, 7.100], and in Gloucester Cathedral [7.101].

2 The owl, with or without its prey, usually a mouse, as on a misericord in Ely Cathedral [7.102], or at Old Malton.

7.102 *Owl with mouse* Ely Cathedral

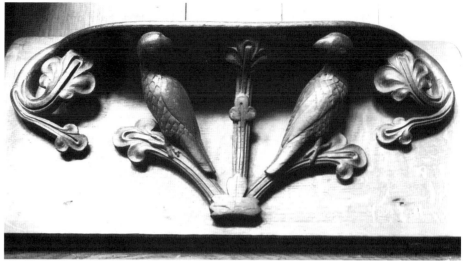

7.103 *Birds with heads like parrots* Exeter Cathedral

7.104 *Peacock* Oxford, New College

7.105 *Peacock* Cartmel Priory

PANTHER

Of the panther it was said that when it had eaten well it hid in its den and slept. After three days it roused itself and gave out a roar and out of its mouth came a sweet smell. Hearing the roar all the animals, except the dragon, followed the panther because of its perfumed breath. The dragon was afraid and hid from the panther.

At Alne on the Norman doorway a dragon and a panther are face to face. On a boss in Tewkesbury Abbey 'is a representation of a panther surrounded by nine other beasts who all have their snouts close up to the panther; they include an ape, a ram, a goat and a horse; there is also a wild man, that is a man with shaggy hair over his body.' (*Roof Bosses*, CJP Cave, fig 219)

PARROT

The parrot, it was said, has a broader tongue than other birds and is thus able to produce articulate words; its beak and head are very hard. It can be taught by striking the head with an iron bar.

The parrot is rarely depicted in a readily recognisable form but it occurs on a misericord in Wells Cathedral and in New College Chapel, Oxford, and two birds with parrot-like heads are depicted on a misericord in Exeter Cathedral [7.103].

PEACOCK

The peacock was the associate of Roman empresses. It was the symbol of immortality and its flesh was reputed to be

7.106 *Pelican in her piety* Norton

incorruptible. These two ideas were carried into Christian symbolism, to which were added the two notions that its crying out in the night at the thought of losing its beauty typified Man lost in a sinful world, and that the loss of its tail when moulting signified the loss of foresight, for the tail is that which is to come. Its strutting and displaying were seen as a show of pride and vanity.

REPRESENTATIONS
With tail spread and crest erect as on a misericord at Oxford, New College Chapel [7.104], and at Cartmel Priory [7.105]. At Lincoln Cathedral on a misericord two peacocks with sweeping tails cross each other.

PELICAN
The pelican was regarded as an emblem of self-sacrifice and parental devotion. It was said that it killed its young because, as they developed, they irritated the parents by flapping their wings. After three days the parent pierced its breast and the blood flowed on the dead young; this restored them to life.

In the Bestiaries the nest is illustrated as being made of basket work and this is reproduced in medieval carvings.

REPRESENTATIONS
1 At South Brent on a bench end a pelican is depicted in a tree.
2 The Pelican-in-her-Piety is depicted on a misericord at Norton [7.106] where she is alighting on a nest in which are three young birds. Below is the text '*In omni opere memento finis*'.
3 On a misericord in Lincoln Cathedral the pelican is shown in the traditional way, but on one of the supporters the parent is attacking one of its young.

PHOENIX
There are many variations of the story of the phoenix voluntarily perishing in flames on its nest and a young bird arising from the ashes.

At St Just-in-Roseland is a painted boss and at Queen Camel a wooden boss on which is depicted a phoenix. (*Roof Bosses*, CJP Cave)

The phoenix surrounded by flames is shown on a misericord in Westminster Abbey.

7.107 Sow suckles piglets
Worcester Cathedral

7.108 Sow and litter amongst oak foliage with acorns
Chester Cathedral

PIG

The pig was a common animal in the Middle Ages and the swineherd a familiar figure. The swineherd taking his pigs under the oak trees in the autumn was part of the yearly round. The killing of the pig when the acorns had gone was an economic necessity. The pig, because of its noisy habits, was used to satirise music, especially the bagpipes, so we find the pig playing the bagpipes to its dancing litter.

REPRESENTATIONS

1 **Pig with its litter**   On a misericord in Worcester Cathedral [7.107] a sow suckles five piglets and again at Chester Cathedral [7.108] the sow and litter are amongst oak foliage with acorns and the swineherd looks on.

2 **Pig feeding on acorns**   On a misericord in Worcester Cathedral [7.109] a swineherd, with a long pole, is knocking down acorns for two pigs, feeding at the foot of the tree.

Similarly at Malvern Priory [7.110] where a pig forms each of the supporters.

7.109 Swineherd knocking down acorns for pigs Worcester Cathedral

At Gloucester Cathedral [7.111] two pigs feed under a tree in which a squirrel is eating acorns.

The fattening of the pig is the labour associated with October.

3 **Pig in a satyrical role**
(a) On a misericord in Ripon Cathedral [7.112] a sow is playing the bagpipes to two dancing piglets. The same subject occurs in Beverley Minster [7.113] and Manchester Cathedral [7.114] where in each case a saddled pig is one supporter and a pig playing the harp is the other.

7.110 *Swineherd and pigs* Malvern Priory

7.111 *Pigs eating acorns, squirrel in tree* Gloucester Cathedral

7.112 *Sow playing bagpipes* Ripon Cathedral

7.113 *Sow playing bagpipes; pigs saddled and playing harp on the supporters* Beverley Minster

7.114 *Pig in satyrical role* Manchester Cathedral

7.115 *Pig in pulpit* Christchurch Priory

7.116 *Killing the pig* Bristol Cathedral

7.117 *Pig killing, November* Ripple

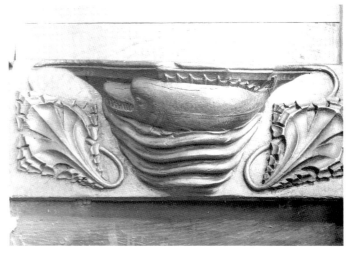

7.119 *Serra* Bishop's Stortford

7.118 *Sciapod* Dennington

(b) At Christchurch Priory [**7.115**], on the support for an elbow rest, is a pig in a pulpit; by the side of the pulpit is a cock on a form. This is probably part of a satyrical picture.

4 **Killing the pig**   In the yearly cycle, after the corn harvest came the killing of the pig.

This is depicted on a misericord in Bristol Cathedral [**7.116**] and at Ripple [**7.117**].

This is often the representation of the month of November. (See also 'Saints: St Anthony' [**5.56**]; 'The Church: Vices – Gluttony' [**6.76**])

RAM

The ram's head appears on several misericords. In Winchester and Ely Cathedrals a reclining ram is the central subject, and in Beverley Minster a ram is a supporting subject. (See 'Everyday Scenes: Sheep Shearing' [**8.83**])

RAVEN

When the raven is depicted it is usually because of its association with the Flood. (See 'The Old Testament: Noah' [**1.57**])

At Beverley Minster, a raven perched on a branch and a dove perched on foliage are the supporting subjects on a misericord.

SALAMANDER

The salamander was a lizard with a knotted or a branched tail. It was so cold by nature that it lived in fire thus symbolising the man who could resist the temptations of the world.

The salamander is found carved on the fonts at Salehurst and Youlgreave.

SCIAPOD

The sciapod was a man with a single leg and a greatly enlarged foot. He lay on the ground and used his foot as an umbrella to shade him from the sun. With him were associated the brachmani.

On a bench end at Dennington [**7.118**] the carver has given him two legs. Under his arm are three defaced brachmani.

SERRA

The serra had wings like a griffin with which it entered into competition with sailing ships, according to one story, but another story emphasises the sharp crest along its back with which it could cut the hulls of ships. On a misericord at Bishop's Stortford [**7.119**] it rides on the sea and it is distinguished by a mouth with savage teeth and a prominent ridge along its back.

SHEEP

Representations of sheep, when they occur, are devoid of symbolic significance and are usually incidental to other subjects such as shepherds with their sheep in Nativity scenes, and pictures of country activities such as sheepshearing. (See 'Everyday Scenes: Sheepshearing' [**8.83**])

An incomplete misericord in Wells Cathedral has for its main subject a sheep suckling her lamb.

The Agnus Dei is a subject by itself. (See 'The Church')

7.120 *Siren beguiling sailors*   Boston

7.121 *Mermaid with feet of a bird*   Carlisle Cathedral

7.122 *Mermaids with bird-like feet*
Hereford, All Saints

7.123 *Mermaid with mirror and brush*
(probably replacing a comb)
Ripon Cathedral

7.124 *Mermaid with mirror and comb*
Ludlow

7.125 *Mermaid supported by dolphins*   Gloucester Cathedral

SIREN

The siren, or mermaid as it became, is one of the commonest mythological creatures in medieval art. The siren of Greek mythology was repeated in the Bestiary with embellishments. GC Druce refers to two traditions: the bird siren in the form of a woman to the waist with the feet of a falcon and the tail of a fish; and the fish siren in the form of a woman with a fish's tail from the waist. Both forms occur and the intended symbolism was the same in each case. The siren was the temptress, the seducer charming sailors by song and music until they became drowsy and then attacking them in

their sleep. The symbolism is carried to the extreme when we find the mermaid suckling the lion.

REPRESENTATIONS

1 Beguiling sailors as on a misericord at Boston [7.120] where a mermaid plays a recorder to two sailors in a boat.
2 The mermaid with the feet of a bird, suggesting the bird siren tradition, as on a misericord in Carlisle Cathedral [7.121], and Hereford, All Saints [7.122].
3 The traditional medieval mermaid, holding a comb and a mirror as on a misericord in Ripon Cathedral [7.123] (the

7.126 Mermaid flanked by wyvern and winged man Bristol Cathedral

7.127 Mermaids with tabors beating mask-like head Exeter Cathedral

7.128 *Mermaid and merman*
Stratford-upon-Avon

7.129 *Mermaid holding a fish*
Exeter Cathedral

7.130 *Mermaid suckling a lion*   Hereford Cathedral

7.131 *Mermaid suckling a lion*   Norwich Cathedral

brush is not original and probably replaces a comb), Ludlow [**7.124**], and Gloucester Cathedral [**7.125**], where she is supported by dolphins.

On a misericord in Bristol Cathedral [**7.126**] there is an unusual presentation of a mermaid with upraised hands, flanked by a wyvern and a winged man who holds her tail.
4 Mermaids with a tabor on a misericord in Exeter Cathedral [**7.127**] about which GC Druce says: 'a pair of them symmetrically arranged are beating a tabor over a masklike head below. The latter may be intended for the head of a sailor, but if it should be regarded as a mask perhaps it denotes the comedies and tragedies mentioned in the bestiaries'.
5 Mermaid and merman as on a misericord in Chichester Cathedral, and Stratford-upon-Avon [**7.128**].
6 Mermaid holding a fish on a misericord in Exeter Cathedral [**7.129**].
7 Mermaid suckling a lion as on a misericord in Hereford Cathedral [**7.130**], Wells Cathedral, Norwich Cathedral [**7.131**], and Edlesborough.
8 Mermaid in conflict with a naked man on a boss in Lincoln Cathedral.

SMALL CREATURES

Small creatures, such as the mole, did not have a place in the Bestiaries and are without symbolism. They are not frequently found in medieval art, but at Hereford, All Saints there are a number of misericords [**7.132, 7.133**] on which mole-like and fanciful small creatures appear.

SNAIL

The snail occurs as a natural creature. On a misericord in Beverley Minster (See 'Dragon' [**7.54**]) a man is poking it with a stick and on another misericord at Boston a bird is pecking at it.

When it is found on tombs, such as at Lincoln and Winchester Cathedrals, there is a suggested connection with death and decomposition.

7.132 *Mole-like creatures*   Hereford, All Saints

7.133 *Small creatures*   Hereford, All Saints

7.134 *Sphinx carrying a rider* Stratford-upon-Avon

7.135 *Squirrel* Salle

7.136 *Swan* Oxford, New College

'Combat between birds and snakes is common to both Persian and Hindu mythology and it was through the medium of oriental textiles, ivories or metalwork that the subject found its way to Canterbury.' (*English Romanesque Sculpture 1066–1140*, G Zarnecki)

SPHINX

The Assyrian Sphinx was a winged quadruped with a human head either male or female. In the transition to Christian art it has undergone such modification that it is difficult to recognise it with certainty and to separate it from the many monsters with human heads.

At Stratford-upon-Avon **[7.134]** on a misericord the sphinx carries a rider.

SQUIRREL

The squirrel is usually shown eating a nut as on an elbow rest at Salle **[7.135]**, and in the Gloucester Cathedral misericord depicting swine feeding on acorns. (See 'Pig' **[7.111]**)

SNAKE

It is difficult to distinguish the snake from the serpent and similar creatures but there are isolated cases where it is possible to recognise it.

On a capital in the crypt of Durham Castle is a coiled snake.

On a capital in the crypt of Canterbury Cathedral a bird is devouring a snake.

7.137 *Swan on elbow rest* Salle

7.138 *Swan* Ludlow

7.139 *Tiger hunting with mirrors*
Chester Cathedral

7.140 *Tiger with mirror* Lakenheath

SWAN

The swan, common in the Middle Ages, appears collared as the heraldic bird and as the graceful inhabitant of still lakes. It can be seen on a misericord in the chapel of New College, Oxford [**7.136**], and on an elbow rest at Salle [**7.137**], and on a misericord in Ludlow [**7.138**].

TERROBULI

The terrobuli were male and female firestones. When apart they did not blaze but, when the female approached the male, they burst into flames. Here was an obvious moral and a warning.

At Alne on the Norman doorway they are represented as in the Bestiaries as half-length human figures surrounded by flames.

TIGER

The Bestiary contains the curious story of the capture of the tiger cub. The hunter having stolen the cub, the tigress

7.141 *Unicorn* Beverley Minster

7.142 *Unicorn captured by a seated virgin* Boston

7.143 *Unicorn captured by a virgin* Chester Cathedral

7.144 *Unicorn captured by huntsman hiding behind a tree* Cartmel Priory

7.145 *Unicorn trampling on a serpent* Durham Castle Chapel

finding her lair empty would set off in pursuit. In order to escape, the hunter would throw down small mirrors in which the tigress would see her reflection. Mistaking the image of herself for her cub she would stay by the mirror, thus enabling the hunter to escape with the stolen cub.

The story is represented on a misericord in Chester Cathedral [**7.139**], on a boss at Queen Camel, and on an elbow rest at Lakenheath [**7.140**].

UNICORN

The unicorn according to legend was a small, fierce, swift, kid-like creature with a single sharp horn in the centre of its forehead. The Bestiaries differentiated it from the monoceros but it is doubtful if the distinction is maintained with any accuracy in medieval representations. The unicorn could only be captured by guile, being susceptible to the purity of a virgin; a maiden was seated in its usual haunts when it would place its head in her lap and go to sleep. The concealed huntsman could then make an easy capture of the sleeping animal. Another method was for the huntsman to retreat behind a tree when the pursuing unicorn would fasten its horn in the tree. It is easy to see how the unicorn became a symbol of purity and the legend of its capture an

7.146 *Unicorn supporting the Royal Arms* Wells, St Cuthbert

7.147 *Two wyverns turning away from two wodehouses* Beverley, St Mary

allegory of the Incarnation. The allegory is carried further when the unicorn is shown trampling on a human-headed serpent in accordance with the psalmist's words: 'Thou shall tread upon the lion and the adder: the young lion and dragon shall thou trample under foot.' (*Psalms* 91 v 13)

After the union of England and Scotland the unicorn became the sinister supporter of the Royal Arms.

REPRESENTATIONS

1 Alone as a beast with an enormous long horn (Monoceros) as at Beverley Minster [7.141].
2 Captured by a seated virgin as on misericords at Boston [7.142], Chester Cathedral [7.143], and Lincoln Cathedral.
3 Captured by a huntsman retreating behind a tree as on a misericord in Cartmel Priory [7.144].
4 Trampling on a dragon or serpent as on a misericord in Durham Castle Chapel [7.145] and Windsor, St George's Chapel.
5 Supporter of the Royal Arms as in the Carolean Arms at Wells, St Cuthbert [7.146].

WEASEL

In the Bestiaries the weasel is given characteristics more easily ascribed to the ferret or mongoose. The only characteristic which caught the attention of the medieval carver was its immunity from the basilisk after it had eaten rue. (See 'Basilisk')

WHALE/SEA TORTOISE

The medieval carver did not distinguish between the whale (Balena) and the sea tortoise (Aspido chelone) both of which appear in the Bestiaries. Two stories were told about the sea tortoise which were transferred to the whale. Sailors mistook a sleeping sea tortoise for an island and discovered their mistake by lighting a fire which awakened it and led to their destruction when it submerged. It was also said that

when the creature was hungry it opened its mouth and emitted a sweet odour so that fishes streamed into its mouth and its jaws closed when it was full.

The first story is illustrated on the Norman doorway at Alne and on a boss at Queen Camel.

WODEHOUSE

The wodehouse or wild man of the woods had mythological origins but men who had taken to the woods and were forced to dress in skins and live by hunting and foraging must have been common figures in medieval life. No doubt the description of such men would be enriched by local fancy and by travellers' tales.

'Sometimes the wild man is not wild by nature but by ascetic devotion, and there are many versions of the legend of the Hairy Anchorite including some which identify him with St John Chrysostom.' (*The Imagery of British Churches*, MD Anderson)

REPRESENTATIONS

1 Wodehouse and wyvern. At Beverley, St Mary [7.147], a misericord shows two wyverns turning away from two wodehouses armed with a club. A wodehouse mounted on a wyvern forms the supporters of a misericord in Chester Cathedral. (See 'Dragon' [7.57])
2 Wodehouse and fox. In Beverley, St Mary [7.148], is a curious misericord: a wodehouse has pierced with an arrow a fox who is appealing to a monkey for medical aid.
3 Wodehouse as a Hairy Anchorite is the subject of a wall painting at Idsworth. The legend 'is curiously combined with scenes from the life of St John the Baptist. The painting shows an old man, covered with hair all over his body, but with a halo, emerging on all fours from some bushes. Huntsmen and dogs, in attendance on a crowned bowman, complete the scene which evidently represents the discovery of the anchorite by the king whose daughter he had murdered

7.148 *Wodehouse and fox* Beverley, St Mary

7.149 *Wolf licking its paw* Faversham

7.150 *Yale* Oxford, All Souls College

seven years before, a crime which he still sought to expiate in crawling nakedness.' (*The Imagery of British Churches*, MD Anderson)
4 Wodehouse and lion. (See 'Lion' [7.94])
5 Wodehouse and dragon. (See 'Dragon' [7.58])

WOLF

The Bestiaries give many details about wolves but they do not appear to have caught the imagination and interest of the medieval carver.

The wolf appears mainly as the attribute of St Edmund. (See 'Saints: St Edmund' [5.104])

At Faversham [7.149] on a misericord a wolf with a heavy mane along the length of its back is licking its paw, a possible reference to the belief that it was in the habit of biting its feet to make it tread more softly. At Boston on a misericord a man grasping a sword is being attacked by a pack of wolves.

YALE

The yale is known mostly as a heraldic creature such as a dexter supporter on the Hudson monument in Westminster Abbey and as the supporters of the arms of Christ's College, Cambridge. It may occur on a misericord in All Souls College Chapel, Oxford [7.150]. (*City of Oxford*, Royal Commission on Historical Monuments)

8

Everyday Scenes

TODAY THROUGH THE medium of press and television we are being presented constantly with pictures of contemporary life. We are indebted to the medieval artist, especially the wood carver when working on a misericord or bench end, for pictures of medieval life. These carvings speak for themselves. Through them we are enabled to see men at work and at play, men in the fields and by the fireside. The population was mainly rural, following, for the most part, agricultural occupations. Not surprisingly such occupations figure largely in those representations which remain and we have a record of the yearly round which was vital to medieval man's survival. These, with scenes of homelife, of various trades and crafts, and of leisure pursuits, present a comprehensive picture of medieval man, his work, his play and his environment.

ALEWIFE

The alewife or her male equivalent was one of the most familiar characters in the Middle Ages. Her conduct was governed by law and by custom. On a misericord at Ludlow [8.1] a man is drawing ale into a jug from a diminutive barrel. A stock of drinking vessels is by his foot.

In the chapel of All Souls College, Oxford, on a misericord [8.2], an alewife is drawing ale and we notice her dirty habit of putting the bung into her mouth.

On another misericord at Ludlow she is being carried off to Hell by devils, perhaps for selling bad beer or giving short measure. On the right, as supporter, another devil reads her crimes from a scroll and on the left the mouth of Hell is shown. (See 'The Church: Hell' [6.45])

THE VILLAGE BAKERY

It has been suggested that a misericord at Ripple [8.3] shows a picture of the communal bakehouse when a guard had been set on it at Lammastide, to prevent disputes. Between the two guards are seen a loaf and the mouth of the oven.

At Ripple this occupation is associated with July.

8.1 *Alehouse wife* Ludlow

8.2 *Drawing ale*   Oxford, All Souls College

8.3 *Bakery*   Ripple

8.4 *Ball game*   Gloucester Cathedral

8.5 *Recumbent beggar*   Christchurch

BALL GAMES

On a misericord in Gloucester Cathedral **[8.4]** two players show elegance and poise as they participate in a ball game.

BEGGAR

During times of depression and famine many poor people must have had to resort to begging, but representations of

8.7 *Binding corn*   Worcester Cathedral

8.6 *Bellringer*   Stoke Dry   **8.8** *Stooking corn*   Victoria and Albert Museum

beggars are rare. At Boston a blind beggar is being led by his dog through a town gate.

On a misericord at Christchurch Priory **[8.5]** a recumbent beggar holds a begging bowl.

BELLRINGER
The bellringer was depicted as early as the twelfth century. He can be seen, tolling a bell, on the column of the Norman chancel arch at Stoke Dry **[8.6]**.

BINDING AND STOOKING THE CORN
When the corn was cut it was bound into sheaves and put into stooks. On a misericord in Worcester Cathedral **[8.7]** corn is being cut with a sickle to make bands for binding the corn into sheaves.

On a misericord in the Victoria and Albert Museum, which it is thought came from King's Lynn, St Nicholas **[8.8]**, a man is stooking. He is helped by a woman who is carrying two sheaves to him.

8.9 *Stooking corn*
Thorpe Salvin

8.10 *Bird scaring* Ripple

8.11 *Blacksmith* Greystoke

8.12 *Blacksmith* Ugborough

8.13 *Butcher* Worcester Cathedral

In one of the panels of the Norman font at Thorpe Salvin [8.9] a man is tying corn and in the background is a stook of three sheaves.

BIRD SCARING

On a misericord at Ripple [8.10] two men are waving their hands to frighten off the birds. One of them has what appears to be a small flag and the other carries a stick over his shoulder.

In the Ripple series this is the occupation assigned to April.

BLACKSMITH

Each village would have its blacksmith. His work was essential in an agricultural community but this has not assured him a prominent place in the representations of everyday life.

In Ely Cathedral on a misericord a blacksmith is depicted shoeing a horse which is held by two men, and at Greystoke [8.11] three men are shoeing or grooming a horse.

On a boss at Ugborough [8.12] he is hammering a shoe at a forge.

BUTCHER

On a misericord in Worcester Cathedral [8.13] is seen a butcher in the act of killing a beast. At Malvern Priory [8.14] is a similar scene. Here the pole axe has disappeared. The ox, in a comical position, has a quizzical expression.

8.14 *Killing ox*   Malvern Priory

8.15 *Children at play*   Sherborne Abbey

(See also the killing of the pig under 'Creatures Natural and Mythical: Pig' [**7.116, 7.117**])

CHILDREN AT PLAY

In Sherborne Abbey is a misericord [**8.15**] which shows children armed with bows and arrows playing with a rocking horse. On another misericord in Westminster Abbey we see a boy astride a rocking horse.

COCK-FIGHTING

At Westminster Abbey, a misericord depicting children's activities has as a central subject two boys with cocks, suggesting cock-fighting.

8.16 *Cook*   Minster

8.17 *Jesters*   Boston

8.18 *Jesters*   Beverley Minster

8.19 *Acrobats*   Oxford, New College

COOK

Cooking is featured in scenes of 'Homelife' but on misericords at Minster and Maidstone the cook is depicted in isolation.

At Minster [8.16] he is stirring a pot and holding a ladle and other cooking utensils. At Maidstone he is holding a ladle and a meat hook.

ENTERTAINERS

There are, especially on misericords, representations of entertainment made by the people themselves and by professional entertainers. Often bands of men and women, jesters, acrobats, contortionists and musicians, travelled from village to village, from fair to fair and from monastery to monastery offering entertainment.

REPRESENTATIONS

1 **Jester**   The jester in traditional fool's hood and scalloped tunic is shown on misericords at Boston [8.17], where two jesters are each using a cat as bagpipes, and at Beverley Minster where three jesters dance hand in hand, the right supporter being a jester with pipe and drum and the left a jester with bladder and stick [8.18].

2 **Acrobat**   Two acrobats are balancing on a man's head, on a misericord in the chapel of New College, Oxford [8.19].

3 **Contortionist and Grimacer**   The man in the uncomfortable and ungentlemanly posture on a misericord in the chapel of All Souls, College, Oxford [8.20], may be a contortionist as also may be the two men who have assumed curious positions on two misericords in Ely Cathedral.

The grinning and distorted faces found on misericords and elsewhere may relate to a coarse form of entertainment.

4 **Juggler**   A misericord in the chapel of All Souls College, Oxford [8.21], shows a man sitting on a stool who may be juggling with a ball which he is kicking.

8.20 *Contortionist*   Oxford, All Souls College

8.21 *Juggler*   Oxford, All Souls College

8.23 *Man and woman grinding corn*   Ely Cathedral

8.22 *Fuller/Cloth worker*   Spaxton

8.24 *Hedging* Ripple

8.25 *Couple with cooking pot over fire*
Boston

5 Dancer On a misericord in Chichester Cathedral, a woman dances to the music of a man playing a viol.

FULLER/CLOTH WORKER
On a bench end at Spaxton [8.22] is depicted a fuller, with the implements used in his craft.

On a supporter of a misericord at Brampton (see 'Mowing and Reaping' [8.70]) a cloth worker is cutting his material on a table with a large pair of shears.

On a misericord at Norton a woman is carding wool.

GOLDSMITH AND SILVERSMITH
On the supporters of a misericord in Windsor, St George's Chapel, a goldsmith or a silversmith is working on a chalice. Although such craftsmen must have been highly skilled and have had influential patrons this appears to be the only representation found in English churches.

GRINDING CORN
The grinding of corn was a routine occupation in the medieval household. On a misericord in Ely Cathedral [8.23] a man and a woman are employed grinding corn in a quern.

The supporter of a misericord in Beverley Minster shows a woman similarly employed. (See 'Homelife' [8.30])

HEDGING AND DITCHING
At Ripple [8.24] a misericord·represents hedging and ditching. One man is digging and another is splitting a stake. Between them is a stack of stakes. This is the occupation of February.

8.26 *Kitchen scenes* Ludlow

8.27 *Man with cooking pot* Worcester Cathedral

8.28 *Couple by fire, woman spinning* Ripple

8.29 *Woman serving calf's head*
St David's Cathedral

HOMELIFE

Homelife centred round the hearth and the cooking of food; the medieval carvers have left us many such domestic scenes. Some of these scenes may be from a months series, the sequence of which time and change have obliterated.

REPRESENTATIONS

1 **The domestic hearth** Pictures of the fireside are seen on misericords. At Boston [8.25] a man and his wife sit on either side of a fire over which is suspended a cooking vessel from a pot hook. The man holds a pair of bellows

8.30 *Woman seizing man by hair, dog in pot; Supporters: woman grinding corn, man chopping* Beverley Minster

8.31 *Lovers* Hereford Cathedral

8.32 *Couple quarrelling* Hereford Cathedral

8.33 *Scold* Stratford-upon-Avon

8.34 *Gagged scold* Ludlow

and the woman a ladle and dish. At Ludlow [8.26] a man sits warming himself in front of a blazing fire, a three-legged pot forms the right supporter and two flitches of bacon the left. At Worcester Cathedral [8.27] a man, still wearing his outdoor clothes but for his boots, sits in a semicircular chair before a fireplace stirring the contents of a pot and warming his feet. The right supporter is a dog, its eye on the pot, and the left two flitches of bacon. At Ripple [8.28] a man and his wife sit on either side of a fire on which is a cooking vessel. He is still wearing his outdoor clothes including thick mittens. She, with her cat by her side, is spinning. At St David's Cathedral [8.29] a woman is serving a calf's head.

2 **Dog and pot** On a misericord in Beverley Minster [8.30]

a dog has buried its head in a pot and a woman is pulling her husband's hair. This may be a reference to a dirty domestic habit and a slatternly wife or a medieval version of Alfred and the Cakes. On the left a woman is grinding corn and on the right a man is chopping firewood.

3 **Domestic harmony and discord** Two misericords in Hereford Cathedral [8.31, 8.32] give both sides of the domestic picture. On the first a man and his wife are happily playing a game and on the second a quarrel is in progress and pots are flying. A misericord at Stratford-upon-Avon [8.33] shows a similar domestic conflict.

4 **The nagging wife** The scold was either gagged and bridled or wheeled to the ducking pond. On a misericord at Ludlow [8.34] a head with a distorted mouth may represent

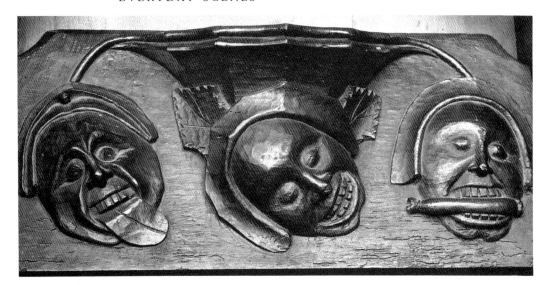

8.35 *Gagged woman* Stratford-upon-Avon

8.36 *Wife on way to ducking pond* Beverley Minster

8.37 *Woman in garden* Gloucester Cathedral

8.38 *Huntsman*
Gloucester Cathedral

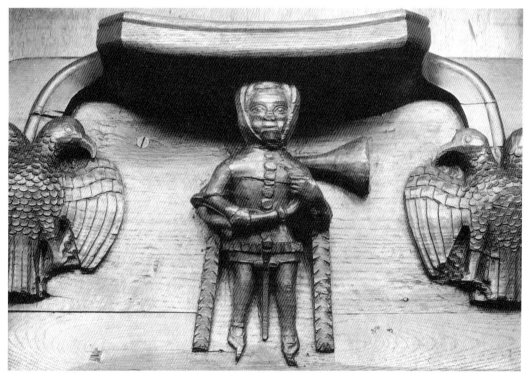

8.39 *Man with horn*
Worcester Cathedral

a scold who has been gagged. At Stratford-upon-Avon [8.35] is a more obvious example. A misericord in Beverley Minster [8.36] may depict a wife, who refused to take her punishment quietly, en route for the ducking pond.
5 On a misericord at Gloucester Cathedral [8.37] a lady accompanied by her dog is walking in a garden.

HUNTING AND HAWKING
At a time when the country was well forested and a large part of the population were country folk, hunting and hawking were not only favourite pastimes but a means of providing food and controlling pests.

REPRESENTATIONS
1 The huntsman blowing his horn as on misericords in Gloucester Cathedral [8.38] where he is accompanied by his dog; in Worcester Cathedral [8.39] where he has wrapped his horn round his body and in Norwich Cathedral [8.40] where the huntsman carries a bow and arrows and the dogs hold a stag at bay.
2 Hawking as on a misericord at Ripple [8.41], where the hawksman is followed by his doleful dog. The hawk has been lost due to damage. On a misericord, which is probably a reproduction, in Gloucester Cathedral [8.42] is depicted a lively hawking scene. A hawk is alighting on a duck in

8.41 *Hawking* Ripple

8.40 *Huntsman* Norwich Cathedral

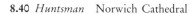

8.42 *Man hunting*
Gloucester Cathedral

front and a beater takes up the rear.
3 Fox hunting as on misericords in Gloucester Cathedral
[8.43] where the fox has found refuge in a tree, and in
Beverley Minster **[8.44]** where the fox has gone to earth.
4 Stag hunting as on misericords in Beverley Minster **[8.45]**
where dogs protected by spiked collars are pulling a stag
down, and in Gloucester Cathedral **[8.46]** where a huntsman
is pursuing a wounded stag.
5 Boar hunting is depicted on a misericord in Beverley
Minster **[8.47]** where a huntsman is spearing one boar whilst
his dog attacks another. On a misericord in Beverley, St
Mary **[8.48]**, a knight is attacking a boar with a spear in his

8.43 *Hunting – fox finds refuge in tree* Gloucester Cathedral

8.44 *Fox hunting* Beverley Minster

8.45 *Stag hunting* Beverley Minster

8.46 *Stalking deer* Gloucester Cathedral

8.47 *Boar hunt* Beverley Minster

8.48 *Knight and boar*
Beverley, St Mary

8.49 *Hare hunt*   Ely Cathedral

8.50 *Empty-handed hunter*   Boston

right hand and is grasping his dagger with his left hand.

6 Hare hunting is represented on a misericord in Ely Cathedral [8.49] where a man holds two dogs on a leash and carries a hare over his shoulder.

7 Ferreting is shown on the supporter of a misericord in Worcester Cathedral where a man working with two ferrets has a rabbit slung over his shoulder. (See 'Scribe' [8.81])

8 The empty-handed hunter is seen on a misericord at Boston [8.50], where he is being harangued by his wife because there is nothing for the pot.

Another unsuccessful hunter, falling from his horse, is depicted on a misericord at Ely Cathedral.

Hunting and hawking at Ripple are attributed to June.

THE JOUST AND THE TOURNAMENT

Medieval representations of the joust and the tournament

8.51 *Man tilting at a sack* Bristol Cathedral

8.53 *Labours of the month with signs of the Zodiac* Brookland

8.52 *Jousting*
Worcester Cathedral

which have survived are mostly in a satirical vein. Other comical conflicts may be examples of a satirical approach to a pastime which had ceased to have any practical value.

REPRESENTATIONS

1 The satirical approach is seen on a misericord in Bristol Cathedral [8.51] where a man mounted on a pig rides to tilt a sack.

2 At Worcester Cathedral [8.52] the combatants are more fittingly armed and are better mounted on chargers. They are shown at the point of contact and one has almost unseated his opponent. The supporters of the misericord are men with musical instruments. The one on the left with drums has a look of horror on his face as he contemplates being crushed by the falling horse.

LABOURS OF THE MONTHS

Representations of the months and seasons found in carvings in churches have their origin in the psalters and calendars.

In these it was the practice for each month to be prefaced with the sign of the Zodiac for that month and a relevant occupation. The choice of subject for each month was not always the same and the same diversity of choice is found when the series is translated into wood or stone. Two of the best series are found on Norman fonts at Brookland [8.53], where each occupation appears in conjunction with a sign of the Zodiac, and at Burnham Deepdale. Here the series is complete and in the original order. At Ripple, on misericords, there is a complete series but they are not in the original order.

Representations on misericords amongst other subjects are found, for example, at Malvern Priory and Worcester Cathedral. The task of identification has been made difficult by their not being in the original order. It is not always certain when a representation of a month or an everyday scene was intended.

The individual examples are described under their own headings, as for example 'Hunting and Hawking' and

8.54 *Janus with two cups*   Malvern Priory

8.55 *Water carrier*   Ripple

8.56 *Loading farm cart with corn*   Victoria and Albert Museum

'Ploughing' but the representation of January was sometimes different.

The god of January was Janus. He was depicted with two heads; with one he looked to the Old Year and with the other to the New Year. A misericord at Worle shows two heads in a single hood. With January was associated feasting and drinking so, on the Brookland font, Janus with two heads is seated at table with a goblet and drinking horn.

On a misericord at Malvern Priory **[8.54]** he is seated at table and is holding up two cups; at Ripple **[8.55]** a man is emptying two jugs, a possible reference to Aquarius.

LEADING CORN

A misericord in the Victoria and Albert Museum, thought to have come from King's Lynn, St Nicholas, depicts a man loading a cart with sheaves of corn which are being passed to him on the end of a fork by a woman **[8.56]**.

8.57 *Lecturer*   Oxford, New College

LECTURER

On a misericord in the chapel of New College, Oxford **[8.57]** a doctor at his desk is receiving a book from a scholar; on either side of him are attendant figures. The left supporter is a man laden with books and the right is a man reading from a book.

8.58 *Malting* Ripple

8.59 *Masons* Beverley Minster

8.60 *Mason with tools* Christchurch Priory

8.61 *Carver* Great Doddington

MALTING

On a misericord at Ripple **[8.58]** are two men each with a long box under one arm and a sack in the other hand. Underneath are wavy bands which it has been suggested represent a pile of grain. The men are perhaps collecting corn to take for malting. Another interpretation is that they are separating corn into bins for seed and into sacks for grinding into flour.

In the series at Ripple this is the occupation of September.

MASON CARVER

1 On a misericord in Beverley Minster **[8.59]** two masons appear to be quarrelling. One has an upraised mallet and the other a chisel. In Christchurch Priory **[8.60]** on a misericord is a mason with a mallet and chisel.

2 At Great Doddington **[8.61]** on a misericord is a carver,

8.62 *Carver* Wellingborough

8.63 *Carver working at his bench* Victoria and Albert Museum

8.64 *Men fighting* Gloucester Cathedral

seated at a bench working on a rose like the supporting subjects of the misericord, and at Wellingborough **[8.62]** a carver is working on a similar rose with his tools neatly arranged on either side.

3 On a misericord in the Victoria and Albert Museum, thought to have come from King's Lynn, St Nicholas **[8.63]**, a carver is at work at his bench, under which a dog is lying. In the background is finished work and two men working at a second bench. A saw is depicted in one supporter and a chisel or gouge in the other.

MEN IN CONFLICT

In addition to representations of the joust and tournament there are scenes depicting conflicts of a violent nature between men.

REPRESENTATIONS

1 Two men on foot, one of whom has pierced the abdomen of his opponent with a sword, form the subject of a misericord at Gloucester Cathedral **[8.64]**.

8.65 *Man cutting off head* Gloucester Cathedral

8.66 *Conflict* Eardisley

8.67 *Mowing* Malvern Priory

8.69 *Mowers with sickle and crotch* Worcester Cathedral

8.68 *Three mowers with scythes*
Worcester Cathedral

8.70 *Mowing and hay gathering* Brampton

8.71 *Reaping corn* Brampton

8.72 *Reaping wheat* Ripple

2 Another misericord at Gloucester [8.65] shows a knight who has alighted from his horse severing the neck of a man who is swinging a large club.

3 An early example of men fighting is found on the Romanesque font at Eardisley [8.66].

MILKING

Milking was part of daily life. On the supporters of a misericord in Beverley Minster milking is charmingly depicted. On one side a cow is contentedly licking itself; on the other a milkmaid, seated on a stool, is milking a cow. (See 'Stories and Proverbial Sayings: Cart before the Horse' [9.7])

MOWING AND REAPING

The scythe and the sickle were used for cutting the hay and the corn. On a misericord in Malvern Priory [8.67] a mower is swinging his scythe. In Worcester Cathedral [8.68] on one misericord three mowers armed with scythes are in line of battle; on a second misericord [8.69] the same three men in similar formation using sickle and crotch are either cutting the corn, which can be seen in the background, or weeding.

At Brampton [8.70, 8.71] are two misericords the principal subject of which is an agricultural scene. On the first a man is mowing with a large scythe and a woman is gathering up the hay, using a rake with ugly-looking teeth. On the second a man is reaping corn using a sickle. At his side is a woman holding a sickle and behind a man is blowing a horn. The left supporter shows a woman gleaning and the right a row of sheaves.

At Ripple [8.72] a man and a woman are cutting the wheat with sickles. This scene represents August.

8.73 *Man riding seated backwards* Hereford Cathedral

8.74 *Riding facing horse's tail* Hereford, All Saints

8.75 *Man with pack* Ludlow

8.76 *Pedlar* Oxford, All Souls College

NAKED RIDER

In Hereford Cathedral [**8.73**], and Hereford, All Saints [**8.74**], are two similar misericords on which a naked man rides a horse facing its tail. It is difficult to say if this is an example of the medieval love of a topsy-turvy world or if it is of some significance which is now not apparent.

PEDLAR

The pedlar, who played so much larger a part in the life of the community in the Middle Ages than he does today, is depicted on misericords in very similar style in Ludlow [**8.75**], and in the chapel of All Souls College, Oxford [**8.76**]. In each case he carries his pack on his back and is adjusting his shoe.

See also 'Stories and Proverbial Sayings: Reynard Stories' [**9.33, 9.34, 9.35**].

PLOUGHING

A lively misericord in Lincoln Cathedral [**8.77**] shows a man ploughing. To the plough is yoked first a pair of oxen and then a pair of horses in the lead.

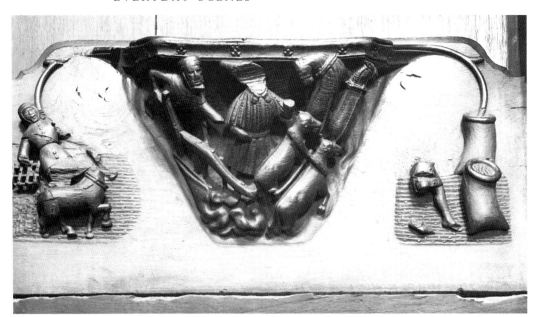

8.77 *Ploughing*
Lincoln Cathedral

8.78 *Man in stocks* Blythburgh

8.79 *Schoolmaster birching boy*
Norwich Cathedral

PUNISHMENT

The stocks are viewed romantically nowadays but they must have been viewed differently when they were the accepted form of punishment. The poppy head of a bench end at Blythburgh **[8.78]** shows a man in the stocks.

SCHOOLMASTER

When the schoolmaster is depicted he is usually shown thrashing his pupils. On a misericord in Norwich Cathedral **[8.79]**, surrounded by boys with books, he is birching one placed across his knee; at Boston **[8.80]** the boy is attempting to protect himself with a book and at Sherborne Abbey the master is being careful to remove the boy's clothing.

8.80 *Boy being whipped* Boston

8.81 *Scribe working on manuscript* Worcester Cathedral

8.82 *Sexton* Ludlow

8.83 *Sheepshearing* Beverley Minster

8.84 *Sailing vessel* Bishop's Lydeard

SHEEPSHEARING

A misericord in Beverley Minster [**8.83**] depicts the annual sheepshearing in a lively and natural way. The shepherd is astride a short-horned sheep clipping its fleece; by his side is a pot of tar. A woman appears to be dressing the hoof of another sheep. The left supporter is the shepherd patting his dog and holding his crook; the right supporter is two rams butting each other.

SHIPS AND SHIP BUILDING

On the outside of the Greenway Chantry Chapel of Tiverton church are carved a number of sailing ships. Although these are worn and weathered many details are discernible to those versed in nautical matters. Similar carvings are found on the south wall of Cullompton church.

Sailing vessels are seen on bench ends at Bishop's Lydeard [**8.84**] and St Winnow [**8.85**], where the ship appears to be at sea in a storm. At East Budleigh [**8.86**] on a bench end is seen a three-masted ship riding the waves. Two masts carry furled sails and rope ladders. The third mast carries an unfurled sail and a pennon. A sailor is in the rigging of the mizzen mast. In the foreground is anchored a small boat and ashore is a castle or the gateway of a fortified town.

On a misericord in St David's Cathedral [**8.87**] two men are seen working on the hull of a ship.

SCRIBE

At Worcester Cathedral [**8.81**] is a curious misericord which shows a scribe, sitting at a desk, working on a manuscript. The inkwell is held by an eagle. It is difficult to decide what is the significance of the snake or small animal issuing from the scribe's hood and seizing a small bird.

SEXTON

The right supporter of a misericord at Ludlow [**8.82**] consists of a tomb, shovels, bones and a hand holding a holy water bucket which suggests that the central figure could be a sexton. It is difficult to account for the barrel and the bellows at his side.

8.85 *Ship at sea in storm*   St Winnow

8.86 *Three-masted ship riding the waves*
East Budleigh

8.88 *Sowing*   Worcester Cathedral

8.87 *Boat building*   St David's Cathedral

8.89 *Sower filling seed box*   Malvern Priory

SOWING

The medieval sower, sowing broadcast, is frequently seen on misericords. At Worcester Cathedral [**8.88**], and Malvern Priory [**8.89**], he is refilling his seed box from a sack. On a misericord at Ripple [**8.90**] the man is sowing and is followed by a horse dragging a harrow. The furrows are well marked as they are on the supporter of a misericord in Lincoln Cathedral [**8.91**], where the sower appears to be placing a stone in a sling presumably prior to casting it against the bird which is stealing his corn. March is the month represented.

8.90 *Sower followed by harrow*   Ripple

8.91 *Sower placing stone in sling to scare birds (on supporter)*
Lincoln Cathedral

8.93 *Moon* Ripple

8.92 *Full sun* Ripple

SUN AND MOON

Amongst the calendar subjects chosen to indicate the months and seasons the sun and the moon have their place.

Good examples of the full sun [8.92], and the moon [8.93], are found amongst the misericords at Ripple.

THATCHING

In his book on Suffolk churches, HM Cautley says that a figure on a bench end at Ixworth Thorpe [8.94] is a thatcher with his thatching comb.

THRESHING

A misericord in the Victoria and Albert Museum, thought to have come from King's Lynn, St Nicholas [8.95], depicts two men threshing with flails.

8.94 *Thatcher* Ixworth Thorpe

8.95 *Threshing* Victoria and Albert Museum

8.96 *Devil as a dentist* Ely Cathedral

TOOTHACHE

Heads in which the mouth is held open by the hands revealing the teeth are frequently found, especially amongst bosses. These can be regarded as grimaces but some may have a reference to toothache.

In Ely Cathedral [8.96] is a misericord on which a devil is shown in the role of a dentist, inspecting a patient's mouth.

THE VINEYARD

The vine, because of its sacramental symbolism, is a recurring motif in medieval iconography. Gathering grapes as an occupation is depicted on misericords in Ely Cathedral, Westminster Abbey and Gloucester Cathedral [8.97], where a man is collecting bunches of grapes and putting them in a basket, held by another man.

8.97 *Gathering grapes* Gloucester Cathedral

8.98 *Weeding with crotch and sickle* Malvern Priory

8.100 *Man carrying sack to mill* Bristol Cathedral

8.99 *Post windmill* Bishop's Lydeard

WEEDING

Weeding was done by crotch and sickle. The weed was held down by the crotch and was cut off by the sickle leaving the root in the ground. This is shown on a misericord in Malvern Priory **[8.98]**.

8.101 *Wooding in December*   Ripple

8.102 *Collar wrestling*   Hereford Cathedral

WINDMILL

A post windmill of four sails with the miller is seen on a bench end at Bishop's Lydeard [8.99]. On a misericord in Bristol Cathedral [8.100] a man riding an ox and carrying a sack on his head is approaching a post mill with four sails.

WOODING

A misericord at Ripple [8.101] is thought to represent the collecting of dried wood from the forest 'by hook or by crook'. As the misericord is damaged it cannot be certain what the two men are holding. December is the month represented by this scene.

8.103 *Wrestling*   Gloucester Cathedral

8.104 *Wrestlers with attendants*   Norwich Cathedral

WRESTLING

Wrestling was a favourite sport and is frequently repre-sented on misericords. Two forms were in vogue, the usual holds and collar wrestling. Amongst the examples of collar wrestling are misericords at Hereford Cathedral **[8.102]**, Gloucester Cathedral **[8.103]**, and Norwich Cathedral **[8.104]**, where seconds wearing top hats appear to be in attendance.

9
Stories and Proverbial Sayings

SOME STORIES WERE told and retold so that they grew in familiarity. Some were told in the chimney corner, by mothers to their children and fathers to their sons. Others, perhaps less reputable, would be told after a village feast. These stories included medieval romances, beast epics, nursery tales and proverbial sayings, some of which were illustrated by the carver.

AESOP'S FABLES
The Fables of Aesop were known to the Middle Ages. A collection of them was made in the fourteenth century by a monk, Maximus Planudes, and some carvings were based on them.

REPRESENTATIONS
1 The sick lion and the fox on a misericord in Gloucester Cathedral [9.1].
2 The fox and the sour grapes on a misericord in Chester Cathedral [9.2].

9.1 *The sick lion and the fox*
Gloucester Cathedral

9.2 *The fox and the sour grapes*   Chester Cathedral

9.3 *The fox and the stork*   Chester Cathedral

9.4 *The fox and the stork*   Holt

3 The fox and the stork on a misericord in Chester Cathedral [**9.3**] and on a doorway at Holt [**9.4**].
4 The ass, envious of the dog which tried to disport itself with its master, on a misericord in Gloucester Cathedral [**9.5**].

ARISTOTLE

In the *Lay of Aristotle* is found the story of how Aristotle rebuked his pupil Alexander for the attention he was paying to a lady. She heard of this and decided to have her revenge. Under Aristotle's window, scantily dressed, she sang and gathered flowers. Aristotle was attracted, went into the garden and succumbed to the wiles of the lady. To please her he pretended to be a horse and she drove and rode him.

Alexander seeing the episode said: 'If love can make such a fool of an old man no wonder that a young man cannot escape.' The episode may be depicted on a misericord in Exeter Cathedral [**9.6**] where Aristotle, wearing philosopher's cap, is saddled and on all fours. A similar misericord is in Chichester Cathedral.

THE CART BEFORE THE HORSE

A misericord in Beverley Minster [**9.7**] may refer to the saying 'putting the cart before the horse'. A man on horseback appears to be pushing a cart in front of them.

9.5 *Man with ass* Gloucester Cathedral

9.6 *Aristotle* Exeter Cathedral

9.7 *The cart before the horse*
Beverley Minster

9.8 *Knight falling*
Lincoln Cathedral

9.9 *Fallen knight*
Lincoln Cathedral

FALLING KNIGHT

In Lincoln Cathedral are two misericords depicting a knight in plate armour. On one **[9.8]** an arrow has pierced his back and he is falling from his stumbling horse. On the other **[9.9]** the knight lies with his head in the lap of a woman, now headless, who is holding his horse.

The origin of these subjects is unknown and their significance not determined.

FATHER TIME

On a misericord at Great Oakley **[9.10]** is depicted Father Time, an old man holding a large scythe. By his side is an hour glass.

9.10 *Father Time*   Great Oakley

9.11 *Flight of Alexander*   Wells Cathedral

9.12 *Alexander prepares for flight*
Gloucester Cathedral

9.13 *Alexander in flight*   Gloucester Cathedral

FLIGHT OF ALEXANDER

The story is told of how Alexander having come, as he thought, to the end of the world, wished to confirm it. He had two starving birds yoked together and a basket, as a seat, fixed in the middle of the yoke. Then the birds were induced to rise into the air by his lifting a piece of liver at the end of a spear and maintaining it just in front of the birds' faces. It is recorded that Alexander suffered from the cold caused by the birds' wing movement but was able to view the earth surrounded by sea. In medieval carving the birds chosen for the experiment are usually griffins, probably because of their reputed great strength. The usual form of representation is seen on a misericord in Wells Cathedral **[9.11]**. In Gloucester Cathedral are two misericords depicting the episode. On the first **[9.12]**, Alexander between two

9.14 *Jack the Giant Killer*
Oxford, New College

9.15 *Knight and swan*   Exeter Cathedral

9.16 *Lathom legend*   Manchester Cathedral

griffins, collared and chained with folded wings, appears to be preparing for the flight. A hook at the end of each of the two spears he is holding is ready to receive the piece of liver. On the second [9.13], the griffins with outstretched wings and the upraised bait suggest that Alexander is in flight.

JACK AND THE BEANSTALK

On a misericord in the chapel of New College, Oxford [9.14], is depicted the nursery story of *Jack and the Beanstalk*. In the centre is the giant who appears to be grasping several small creatures in his large gloved hands. On the left, amongst beans, is Jack's widowed mother and on the right, also surrounded by beans, is Jack himself.

9.17 *Lathom legend*
Stratford-upon-Avon

9.18 *Spinster leading apes into hell*   Bristol Cathedral

9.19 *Red Riding Hood*   Chester Cathedral

KNIGHT AND SWAN

A story which may have come from northern mythology, the swan drawing a hero across the sea of death, is depicted on a misericord in Exeter Cathedral **[9.15]** where a knight in helmet with visor down, sits in a boat which is being pulled across the water by a swan.

THE LATHOM LEGEND

The story was told of a baby which was carried off by an eagle but which survived and finally inherited the family estates. The story is depicted on a misericord and on a bench end in Manchester Cathedral **[9.16]**. Here, in a tree, is shown a nest containing a child in swaddling clothes, over which, with uplifted wings, an eagle presides. Below a process of witnesses appear to be hurrying to a castle with the news.

A misericord at Stratford-upon-Avon **[9.17]** where an eagle grips a swaddled child in its talons may refer to the same story.

LEADING APES INTO HELL

In Bristol Cathedral **[9.18]** is a misericord which illustrates the strange medieval conception of a spinster leading apes into hell. The apes represent the souls of unmarried men.

RED RIDING HOOD

On a misericord in Chester Cathedral **[9.19]** an animal in disguise is talking, or offering something, to a human. Francis Bond, in his pioneer work on misericords, interprets this as the wolf disguised as the grandmother talking to little Red Riding Hood. Other interpretations are feasible. The wolf could be a fox in traditional disguise and the human an adult.

9.20 *Bruin*   Bristol Cathedral

9.21 *Tybert the cat*   Bristol Cathedral

9.22 *Reynard preaching*
Beverley Minster

9.23 *Reynard preaching*   Ludlow

REYNARD STORIES

Judging by the number of carvings still surviving, stories of Reynard must have been very familiar and popular in the Middle Ages. Some of these were embodied in *The Romance of Reynard*, a beast epic in which animals take names and parts fitted to their character. Cunning is emphasised in the role of Reynard. The most complete series is on misericords

in Bristol Cathedral. In the *Shifts of Reynardine*, Zani the ape encourages Reynard to turn doctor, furnished with implements taken by him and his companions from the pack of a sleeping pedlar.

Reynard's thieving habits in the farmyard, known to all, were told in Chaucer's *Nun's Priest's Tale*.

REPRESENTATIONS

1 **Bruin**, sent to fetch Reynard to King Lion's court, falls victim to his cunning. On being told there was honey in a cleft tree, he poked his head in, dislodging the wedges and becoming prisoner. His cries aroused the priest and his flock who set about him with staves. Illustrated on a misericord in Bristol Cathedral [**9.20**].

2 **Reynard and Tybert** Tybert, the cat, was enticed into a trap set for the thieving Reynard. His cries awakened the priest, stark naked, and Dame Jullock his wife, who belaboured the poor cat with staves. Illustrated on a misericord in Bristol Cathedral [**9.21**].

9.24 *Reynard preaching*   Beverley, St Mary

9.25 *Reynard preaching to birds and animals*   Brent Knoll

9.26 *Lectern, book and foxes* Beverley, St Mary

9.27 *Ecclesiastic with foxes* Beverley, St Mary

9.28 *Reynard judged by a lion* Brent Knoll

3 **Isengrin and Bruin** On a misericord in Bristol Cathedral Isengrin, the wolf, and Bruin dance on receiving news of Reynard's capture.

4 **Reynard preaching** Reynard in the guise of a priest was used to satirise preaching. On a misericord in Beverley Minster [9.22], with a rosary in his hand, he preaches from a pulpit with a monkey as his clerk; in Ludlow [9.23] he is mitred and occupies a pulpit; and in Beverley, St Mary [9.24], a cowled Reynard in a pulpit is flanked by two ecclesiastics with scrolls and two cowled monkeys.

On a bench end in Brent Knoll [9.25], mitred and holding a crozier, he preaches to birds and animals. In the same satyrical vein are two misericords in Beverley, St Mary. On one, two cowled foxes are reading from a book on a lectern or held by an eagle [9.26]. On the other, two foxes with cowls, from each of which emerges a goose, and holding croziers, flank an ecclesiastic with a scroll. They appear to be receiving instructions of some kind [9.27].

5 **Reynard on trial** On a bench end in Brent Knoll [9.28] Reynard is in shackles and a lion as judge appears to be instructing a jury of birds.

6 **Reynard is hanged** On an adjacent bench end in Brent Knoll [9.29] the jury of birds appear to have turned executioner; they are hoisting Reynard onto a scaffold. On a misericord in Beverley Minster [9.30] the geese are executioners; on the left they are pulling on the rope and on the right they hold sword and mace as sign of their office. The left supporter is Reynard espying two geese and the right a monkey removing the rope from his dead body.

9.29 *Jury of birds as executioners*
Brent Knoll

9.30 *Reynard hanged by geese*
Beverley Minster

9.31 *Reynard fleeing, chased by Dame Malkin*
Beverley Minster

9.32 *Fox with goose*   Ripon Cathedral

9.33 *Zani stealing from packman*   Bristol Cathedral

7 *The Nun's Priest's Tale*   On a misericord in Beverley Minster [9.31] Reynard flees with a goose chased by Dame Malkin. In Ripon Cathedral [9.32] Reynard with the goose is in the centre, the left supporter is Dame Malkin with her distaff and the right is her dog, Coll.

8 **The Packman**   Zani, the ape, and his companions stealing from the packman are shown on a misericord in Bristol Cathedral [9.33], Beverley Minster [9.34], and Manchester Cathedral [9.35].

9 The supporters of the misericord in Manchester Cathedral [9.36], which is similar to the Ripon misericord depicting *The Nun's Priest's Tale*, express medieval humour. On the left a fox armed with a birch is teaching two young foxes to read; on the right a fox is reading from a book held at arm's length.

9.34 *Packman with monkeys*
Beverley Minster

9.35 *Ape stealing*
Manchester Cathedral

9.36 *Dame Malkin*
Manchester Cathedral

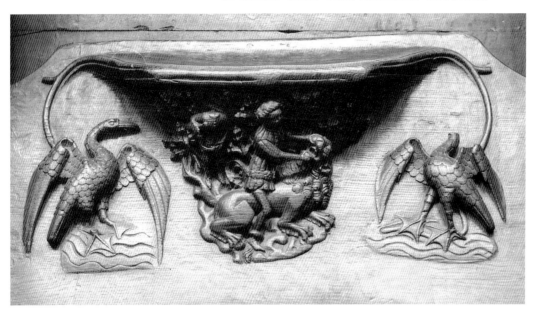

9.37 *Man astride lion*
Chester Cathedral

9.38 *Shoeing the goose* Beverley Minster

RICHARD COEUR DE LION

On a misericord in Chester Cathedral [9.37] is a man astride a lion, pulling its jaws apart. The presence of a second figure, possibly an attendant, gives support to the suggestion that this refers to the popular story of Richard, Coeur de Lion pulling out the heart of a lion.

SHOEING THE GOOSE

A man, with uplifted hammer in one hand and a shoe in the other, in the act of shoeing a goose, is seen as the supporter of a misericord in Beverley Minster [9.38]. On a misericord at Whalley [9.39], the goose is in a rack and the anvil and forge, complete with bellows, are depicted. The meaning of the scene is made plain by the wording underneath: 'Who so melles hy(m) of y al me(n) dos let hy(m) cu(m) hier + shoe ye ghos.'

SIR YVAIN

Sir Yvain pursued a knight into a castle only to have his horse impaled by the falling portcullis and to be captured. He was liberated from the castle by a lady showing him a postern.

Representation of this romance is depicted on several misericords. At Lincoln Cathedral [9.40] only the hind part of the horse is visible in front of the portcullis. Each supporting subject is a handsome head in chain armour. At Enville [9.41], part of both knight and horse are visible under the portcullis. Above, from the windows of the gatehouse, heads protrude. On each side is an armed knight in an archway.

9.39 *Goose with forge* Whalley

9.40 *Sir Yvain* Lincoln Cathedral

9.41 *Sir Yvain under portcullis*   Enville

9.42 *Tristram and Iseult*
Lincoln Cathedral

SUPPING WITH THE DEVIL

At Windsor, St George's Chapel, a misericord depicts a horned devil taking food from a dish on a table; likewise an old man takes food using a very long spoon.

This illustrates the saying 'He who sups with the devil needs a very long spoon.'

TRISTRAM AND ISEULT

Tristram, a courtly knight, visited Ireland to ask for the hand of Princess Iseult for his uncle, King Mark. On the return journey he and the princess inadvertently drank a love potion intended for King Mark. The king and his courtiers chased the lovers who had many escapades before they were caught. Tristram fled to Brittany where he married. On a misericord in Lincoln Cathedral [9.42], and Chester Cathedral [9.43], the lovers are seen hand in hand and the head of King Mark, who is hiding in a tree, emerges from

9.43 *Tristram and Iseult*   Chester Cathedral

9.44 *Valentine and Orson*   Beverley, St Mary

the foliage. In each case the supporters are a knight and a woman with a small dog.

VALENTINE AND ORSON

Valentine and Orson were twins. Orson was carried off by a bear and Valentine was stolen by King Pipin. Orson grew up in the forest and became a wildman, much feared in the neighbourhood. Valentine was brought up at court. Valentine hunts in the forest for the wildman not knowing that he is his brother; but when they meet they recognise each other and become companions. At Beverley, St Mary [9.44], on a misericord their meeting is recorded. Each carries a bow and arrows. Valentine, as befits his position, is richly dressed but Orson wears the simple clothing of a peasant.

Bibliography

A SHORT SELECTIVE list of those books which have been most useful in the preparation of this work and to which reference is sometimes made. A full bibliography would be too lengthy. My debt to those writers mentioned and to those not mentioned is equally acknowledged.

ANDERSON, MD *Animal Carvings in British Churches*, Cambridge University Press, Cambridge, 1938
The Medieval Carver, Cambridge University Press, Cambridge, 1935
History and Imagery in British Churches, John Murray, London, 1971
The Imagery of British Churches, John Murray, London, 1955
Drama and Imagery in English Medieval Churches, Cambridge University Press, Cambridge, 1963

BATSFORD, H and FRY, C *The Cathedrals of England*, Batsford, London, 1960
BONAVENTURA (Pseudo) *Meditations on the Life of Christ*, Princeton University Press, Princeton NJ, 1961
BOND, F *Fonts and Font Covers*, Oxford University Press, London, 1908
Dedications of English Churches; Ecclesiastical Symbolism; Saints and Emblems, Oxford University Press, London, 1914
Screens and Galleries in English Churches, Oxford University Press, London, 1908
The Chancel of English Churches, Oxford University Press, London, 1916
Wood Carvings in English Churches: Vol I *Misericords*, Vol II *Stalls*, Oxford University Press, London, 1910
BOND, FB and CAMM, B *Rood Screens and Rood Lofts* (2 volumes), Pitman, London, 1909
BORENIUS, T 'The Iconography of St Thomas of Canterbury' *Archaeologia*, vols 79, 81 and 83
BRIEGER, P *English Art 1216–1307*, Clarendon Press, Oxford, 1957

CAUTLEY, HM *Norfolk Churches*, Norman Adlard, Ipswich, 1949
Suffolk Churches and their Treasures, Batsford, London, 1923
CAVE, CJP *Roof Bosses in Medieval Churches*, Cambridge University Press, Cambridge, 1948
'Roof Bosses in the Nave of Tewkesbury Abbey', *Archaeologia*, vol 79
'The Roof Bosses in the Transepts of Norwich Cathedral', *Archaeologia*, vol 83
'The Roof Bosses in Canterbury Cathedral', *Archaeologia*, vol 84
'Roof Bosses of Lincoln Cathedral', *Archaeologia*, vol 85
COLGRAVE, B 'The St Cuthbert Paintings on Carlisle Cathedral Stalls', *Burlington Magazine*, LXXIII

COOK, GH *The English Medieval Parish Church*, Phoenix House, London, 1954
Medieval Chantries and Chantry Chapels, Phoenix House, London, 1947
COULTON, GC *Medieval Panorama*, Cambridge University Press, Cambridge, 1938
Art and the Reformation, Cambridge University Press, Cambridge, 1953
COX, JC *English Church Fittings, Furniture and Accessories*, Batsford, London, 1923
Benchends in English Churches, Oxford University Press, London, 1916
Pulpits, Lecterns and Organs, Oxford University Press, London, 1915
CROSSLEY, FH *English Church Monuments*, Batsford, London, 1921
English Church Craftsmanship, Batsford, London, 1941

DRAKE, M and W *Saints and their Emblems*, T Werner Laurie, London, 1916
DRUCE, GC 'Notes on the History of the Heraldic Jall or Yale', *Archaeological Journal*, vol LXVIII 271
'The Caladrius and its Legend, sculptured upon the Twelfth-Century Doorway of Alne Church', *Archaeological Journal*, vol LXIX 276
'Some Abnormal and Composite Human Forms in English Church Architecture', *Archaeological Journal*, vol LXXII 286
'The Amphasbaena and its Connexions in Ecclesiastical Art and Architecture', *Archaeological Journal*, vol LLXXII 268
'The Elephant in Medieval Legend and Art', *Archaeological Journal*, vol LXXVI, 301–4
'Notes on Birds in Medieval Church Architecture', *Antiquary*, vol 50
'Animals in English Wood Carving', *Walpole Society*, vol 3
'Queen Camel Church, Bosses on the Chancel Roof', *Somerset Archaeological and Natural History Society*, vol LXXII

EVANS, J *English Art 1307–1461*, Clarendon Press, Oxford, 1949

FARMER, OG *Fairford Church and its Stained Glass Windows*, 6th edition, Fairford Church, Fairford, 1956

FOWLER, J 'On Medieval Representations of the Months and Seasons', *Archaeologia*, vol 94

FRYER, AC 'On Fonts with Representations of the Months and Seasons', *Archaeological Journal*, vol LIX
'On Fonts with Representations of Baptism and the Holy Eucharist', *Archaeological Journal*, vol LX

GANDERTON, EW and LAFORD, J *Ludlow Stained and Painted Glass*, Friends of the Church of St Lawrence, Ludlow, 1961

GARDNER, A *English Medieval Sculpture*, Cambridge University Press, Cambridge, 1951

GOULBURN, EMG and HAILSTONE, E *The Ancient Sculptures in the Roof of Norwich Cathedral*, Autotype Fine Art, London, 1876

HARRISON, F *The Painted Glass of York*, SPCK, London, 1927

HUSENBETH, FC *Emblems of the Saints in Works of Art*, Longmans Green, London, 1860

HUTCHINSON, FE *Medieval Glass at All Souls College*, Faber and Faber, London, 1949

JAMES, MR *The Apocryphal New Testament*, Clarendon Press, Oxford, 1955
Norfolk and Suffolk, Dent, London, 1930

JAMES, MR and TRISTRAM, EW 'The Wall Paintings in Eton College Chapel and in the Lady Chapel of Winchester Cathedral', *Walpole Society*, vol XVII

JAMESON, MRS *Legends of the Madonna*, Longmans Green, London, 1891

KEYSER, CE *Norman Tympana and Lintels*, 2nd edition, Elliott Stock, London, 1927,
'Saints on Devonshire Screens', *Archaeologia*, vol 56

LE COUTEUR, JD *English Medieval Painted Glass*, SPCK, London, 1926

LILLIE, WW Screenwork in the County of Suffolk, *Suffolk Institute of Archaeological and Natural History*, vols 21 and 22

LITTLE, AG *Franciscan History and Legend in English Medieval Art*, Manchester University Press, Manchester, 1937

LONG, ET 'Church Screens of Dorset', *Archaeological Journal*, vol LXXXI

LONGHURST, MH *English Ivories*, Putnam, London, 1926

MACKLIN, HW *The Brasses of England*, Methuen, London, 1907 (republished EP Publishing, Wakefield, 1975)

MALE, E *Religious Art in France, The Twelfth Century*, Princeton University Press, Princeton, 1978
Religious Art in France, The Thirteenth Century, Princeton University Press, Princeton, 1984
Religious Art from the Twelfth to the Eighteenth Century, Routledge and Kegan Paul, London, 1949

NELSON, P *Ancient Painted Glass in England 1170–1500*, Methuen, London, 1913
'Some Examples of English Medieval Alabaster Work', *Archaeological Journal*, vol LXXI
'Earliest Type of English Alabaster Panel Carvings', *Archaeological Journal*, vol LXXVI
'Some Fifteenth Century Alabaster Panels', *Archaeological Journal*, vol LXXVI
'Some Unpublished English Medieval Alabaster Carvings', *Archaeological Journal*, vols LXXVII, LXXXII, and LXXXIII
'Some Further Examples of English Medieval Alabaster Tables', *Archaeological Journal*, vol LXXIV

'English Alabasters of the Embattled Type', *Archaeological Journal*, vol LXXV
'Some Additional Specimens of English Alabaster Carvings', *Archaeological Journal*, vol LXXXIV

NORFOLK AND NORWICH ARCHAEOLOGICAL SOCIETY, *The Sculptured Bosses in the Roof of the Bauchan Chapel of Our Lady of Pity in Norwich Cathedral*, Norwich, 1908
The Sculptured Bosses in the Cloisters of Norwich Cathedral, Norwich, 1911

RACKHAM, B *The Ancient Glass of Canterbury Cathedral*, Lund Humphries, London, 1949

READ, H *English Stained Glass*, Putnam, London, 1926

RICKERT, M *Painting in Britain: The Middle Ages*, Penguin, London, 1965

RICE, DT *English Art 871–1100*, Clarendon Press, Oxford, 1952

ROYAL COMMISSION ON HISTORICAL MONUMENTS, *Oxford, HMSO, 1939*
Westminster Abbey, HMSO, 1924

RUSHFORTH, G McN *Medieval Christian Imagery*, Clarendon Press, Oxford, 1936

SAUNDERS, OE *A History of English Art in the Middle Ages*, Clarendon Press, Oxford, 1932

SHAW, JP *All Hallows in North Street*, The Church Shop, York, 1908

STONE, L *Sculpture in England: The Middle Ages*, Penguin, London, 1972

TRISTRAM, EW *English Medieval Wall Painting. I: The Twelfth Century*, Oxford, 1944
English Medieval Wall Painting. II: The Thirteenth Century, Oxford, 1950
English Medieval Wall Painting. III: The Fourteenth Century, Oxford, 1955
The Cloister Bosses, Norwich Cathedral, Friends of the Cathedral Church of Norwich, 1938

VALLANCE, A *English Church Screens*, Batsford, London, 1936
Greater English Church Screens, Batsford, London, 1947
Old Crosses and Lych-gates, Batsford, London, 1933

VORAGINE, JACOBUS DE *The Golden Legend*, Longmans Green, 1941 (reprinted Arno Press, New York, 1956)

WHITE, TH *The Book of Beasts*, Jonathan Cape, London, 1956

WILLIAMSON, WW 'Saints on Norfolk Rood Screens and Pulpits', *Norfolk Archaeology*, vol 31

WOODFORDE, C *Stained Glass in Somerset*, Oxford University Press, 1946 (reprinted Kingsmead Reprints, Bath, 1970)
A Guide to Glass in Lincoln Cathedral, SPCK, London, 1933
The Norwich School of Glass Painting in the Fifteenth Century, Oxford University Press, Oxford, 1950
'Stained and Painted Glass in Hengrave Hall', *The Proceedings of the Suffolk Institute of Archaeology and Natural History*, vol 22, pt 1, 1934
The Stained Glass of New College Oxford, Oxford University Press, Oxford, 1951

ZARNECKI, G *English Romanesque Sculpture, 1066–1140*, Alec Tiranti, London, 1951
Later English Romanesque Sculpture, 1140–1210, Alec Tiranti, London, 1953

Index